CUSTER

The Man,
the Myth,
the Movies

D1567948

JOHN PHILLIP
LANGELLIER

Foreword by
Brian W. Dippie

STACKPOLE
BOOKS

0 11557 03201 7

Published by
STACKPOLE BOOKS
5067 Ritter Road
Mechanicsburg, PA 17055
www.stackpolebooks.com

Printed in the United States of America

10 9 8 7 6 5 4 3 2 1

Cover design by Tracy Patterson

Front cover photos courtesy of: Glen Swanson (top left and top center), Library of Congress (top right), and Richard E. Lamotte, C.D.G. (bottom).

FIRST EDITION

Library of Congress Cataloging-in-Publication Data
Langellier, J. Phillip
    Custer : the man, the myth, the movies / John Phillip Langellier ; foreword by Brian W.
Dippie.—1st ed.
      p.   cm.
    Includes bibliographical references (p.) and index.
    ISBN 0-8117-3201-1
    1. Custer, George Armstrong, 1839–1876.   2. Custer, George Armstrong,
1839–1876—Legends.   3. Little Bighorn, Battle of the, Mont., 1876—Folklore.   4. Custer,
George Armstrong, 1839–1876—In motion pictures.   5. Generals—United
States—Biography.   I. Title.

E83.876.C983 L35   2000
973.8'2'092—dc21
  [B]
                            99-089800

To
Professor Brian W. Dippie,
Rev. Vincent A. Heier,
and Kevin Mulroy, Ph.D.,
in gratitude for their generous
assistance and encouragement.

***

"When a person becomes a model
for other people's lives,
he has moved into the sphere
of being mythologized."

—Joseph Campbell,
The Power of Myth

Contents

Foreword

Custer's Last Stand began small. That is, on the scale of battles established by the Civil War, it was small potatoes. A few thousand Sioux and Cheyenne Indians defeated the 7th Cavalry—a force of 650 soldiers, scouts, and civilian employees—along the Little Bighorn River in south-central Montana Territory, completely destroying one contingent of 212 men on June 25, 1876, and killing and wounding another 116 under the command of Maj. Marcus A. Reno over two days of fighting. The total annihilation of the forces led by Lieutenant Colonel, brevet Major General, George Armstrong Custer created a sensation in 1876, of course, but like most sensations, it had every chance of blowing over. Indeed, the likelihood was that it would blow over, meriting at most a few paragraphs in standard American history texts. One that appeared in 1878, John Clark Ridpath's *A Popular History of the United States of America, from Aboriginal Times to the Present Day,* covered the entire Sioux War in two pages and the Custer battle in seven sentences:

> Generals Custer and Reno, who were sent forward with the Seventh Cavalry to discover the whereabouts of the Indians, found them encamped in a large village extending nearly three miles along the left bank of the Little Horn. On the 25th of June, General Custer, without waiting for reinforcements, charged headlong with his division into the Indian town, and was immediately surrounded by thousands of yelling warriors. Of the details of the struggle that ensued very little is known. For General Custer and every man of his command fell in the fight. The conflict equaled, if it did not surpass, in desperation and disaster any other Indian battle ever fought in America. The whole loss of the Seventh Cavalry was two hundred sixty-one killed, and fifty-two wounded. General Reno, who had been engaged with the savages at the lower end of the town, held his position on the bluffs of the Little Horn until General Gibbon arrived with reinforcements and saved the remnant from destruction.

That was it for the Custer battle in a 691-page popular history published just two years after the fight. And to rub salt into the wound for those who think Custer must have mattered more than his contemporaries, Ridpath turned away from the disaster of Little Bighorn with the bland remark: "The excitement occasioned by the outbreak of the war with the Sioux, and even the interest felt in the Centennial celebration, was soon overshadowed by the agitation of the public mind, attendant upon the twenty-third Presidential election."

So much for Custer's Last Stand . . . or so it seemed. Today probably not one American in a thousand could say anything about the presidential election of 1876—but many would have an opinion on Custer's Last Stand. For even in 1876, forces were at play that would give that brief, sanguinary encounter on the Little Bighorn an afterlife vastly exceeding any reckoning of its historical significance, elevating Custer's Last Stand into the rarefied realm of enduring national myths.

The Custer myth is, ultimately, a visual construct. What we see when we hear the words "Custer's Last Stand" is a picture whose details might vary but whose core elements do not: Custer is always visible, usually standing erect in buckskins at the center of a cluster of soldiers completely surrounded by Indians, fighting desperately against hopeless odds. This image owes nothing to history and everything to nineteenth-century artists who, in picturing Custer's finale, gave it instantly recognizable visual form. The movies simply followed their lead. Alfred Waud's *Custer's Last Fight,* which illustrated Frederick Whittaker's *A Complete Life of General George A. Custer* (1876), has a simplicity, symmetry, and strength that naturally appealed to early filmmakers whose research into the Custer story presumably consisted of little more than a quick perusal of Whittaker's florid tome. Waud's illustration can be seen directly mimicked in the Last Stand sequences of *The Scarlet West, The Flaming Frontier, The Plainsman, They Died with Their Boots On, Sitting Bull,* and even *Little Big Man,* where it is introduced for purposes of parody—the ultimate tribute to its wide familiarity.

The link between art and the Custer films' visuals is paralleled by the link between fiction and the films' plotlines. Just as Hollywood borrowed freely from the artists, it turned for inspiration to published stories and novels—*Britton of the Seventh, Bob Hampton of Placer, The Last Frontier,*

Fort Apache, Warpath, Bugles in the Afternoon, The Seventh Cavalry, Tonka, The Glory Guys, Little Big Man—and, in the days of television dramas, *The Court-Martial of George Armstrong Custer* and *The Legend of Walks Far Woman*.

The amalgamation of various elements of popular culture—art, fiction, and film—has, collectively, popularized and perpetuated the Custer saga through the twentieth century. One can only guess as to what the future holds. But Custer's fluctuating personal reputation—even as the Last Stand remains visually consistent—would seem to ensure Custer and his final battle mythic currency well into the next millennium. After all, popular myth survives by adapting to new circumstances, and Custer's Last Stand continues to express changing social values and the continuity between past and present, proving at once vitally flexible and comfortingly stable.

In *Custer: The Man, the Myth, the Movies,* John Langellier focuses on the medium most responsible for perpetuating the Custer myth in the twentieth century. His detailed examination of Custer movies builds on the pioneering work of Paul Hutton and others to provide the first book-length, in-depth look at Custer's cinematic portrayal. His discussion of the Custer films will prove of interest to everyone concerned with American popular culture and the mythic West, and students of the Custer myth will find it invaluable.

Brian W. Dippie

Acknowledgments

My decades of following Custer to the Little Bighorn took me to numerous places and allowed me to meet with many people along the way. One of my first contacts was with John D. Ryan, author of *Custer Fell First*, who, despite the several generations that divided us, kindly met with me in the mid-1960s as an equal. At the end of our interview he autographed my copy of his book and dubbed me a budding historian. With that heady accolade, I moved on.

Nearly a decade later, at the University of San Diego, I received considerable support for my work in the field, most notably from Dr. Raymond S. Brandes, then chair of the Department of History. Ultimately, he headed my thesis committee and, along with fellow professors Iris Engstrand and Carl Gilbert, laid the groundwork for this present study. I owe a debt of gratitude to these three fine mentors, most particularly to Dr. Brandes, who remains an influence on me to this day.

Years after completing my graduate work, I resurrected this project. Eventually I returned to the Margaret Herrick Library, where my original research had been conducted. Many individuals there assisted me, but no one more so than Sam Gill. At the Little Bighorn Battlefield National Monument, Kitty Deernose and Douglas McChristian also

Cast members, complete with studio ambulance, casually observe as Custer again faces his irrevocable fate, in this case with Errol Flynn fighting heroically during the prerequisite last stand scene of Warner Bros.' They Died with Their Boots On *(1941).*

facilitated this undertaking, as did the staffs of the Huntington Library, the Montana Historical Society, and the West Point Museum, as well as the research center of the Autry Museum of Western Heritage, where Dr. Kevin Mulroy responded to numerous demands on his time with grace and professionalism and saw to it that I received a number of illustrations to support this study.

Rev. Vincent Heier likewise generously supplied me with photographs and considerable information from his private collection, and he allowed me to draw heavily from his own studies on Little Bighorn fiction for chapter 2. Reverend Heier also reviewed the manuscript and made valuable suggestions. Other pictorial sources included the Motion Picture Academy of Arts and Sciences, Dan Gagliasso, Richard Lamotte, Neil Summers, and most notably, Glen Swanson.

Further, many individuals lent critical support. Robert M. Utley, one of the foremost scholars on the topic of Custer and the Little Bighorn, was candid in pointing out errors and necessary revisions to my manuscript. Dr. Paul Andrew Hutton, whose writings have shaped certain aspects of my approach, reviewed those sections of the book related to film and television and encouraged me to complete this publication. Dr. Brian Dippie served as the book's godfather in that his excellent articles and provocative *Custer: The Anatomy of an American Myth* provided invaluable roadmaps for me throughout the years. He likewise graciously made succinct comments on the draft of this work, although any errors are those of my own doing, and was kind enough to provide the foreword. So, too, do William C. Davis, Leigh Ann Berry, and other colleagues at Stackpole Books deserve my thanks.

Finally, my wife and daughter were ever patient as I attempted to put Custer to rest. Now that this project is completed, we can have our weekends and evenings together once more.

Introduction: Inventing Custer

The seed of this project was planted in the late 1950s, when my parents allowed me to stay up late one night to watch *They Died with Their Boots On*. As a young boy enthralled with cowboys and Indians, this sprawling action feature made a lasting impression.

With the passage of years, I began to study the activities of the U.S. Army in the West at the local library. Later, my interest took me to many historical societies, museums, historic sites, and repositories, where I pored over special collections. In the process, I learned that Errol Flynn's rendition of Custer, though captivating, was far from reality. Admittedly, for many years, I continued to look at the subject with an uncritical eye, but after all, *They Died with Their Boots On* was only a film meant to entertain. Or was it? Could it be true that, as an early study of the Western film genre had postulated, such movies had "a more lasting effect than the authentic traditions they copy"?[1]

Here was a proposition that begged further exploration. I was completing my undergraduate education, so I made that my topic for a term paper for a class in film history. For many weeks, I made the journey north from San Diego to Los Angeles, where the Motion Picture Academy of Arts and Sciences' Margaret Herrick Library provided a wealth of material.

That paper later led to additional visits to the Herrick Library when, as a graduate student, I undertook "Custer's Celluloid Image" as my master's thesis. In 1973, with the completion of my master's program, I thought I had put the issue to rest. This was not to be the case.

From time to time, I was asked to give lectures and write occasional articles based on my thesis, and I continued to read ever-mounting writings that appeared subsequent to my own earlier work.[2] One of the first titles consulted, Bruce A. Rosenberg's *Custer and the Epic of Defeat*, helped me appreciate that the Little Bighorn battle bore the classic stamp of earlier "last stands," where brave, outnumbered men were besieged and defeated by overwhelming numbers of the enemy.

Beyond this, when it came to the fallen central figure of the Little Bighorn, Rosenberg indicated that Custer fit a classic mold. He was a dashing young man in his prime boldly going to his fate, in the process leaving behind a devoted, loving wife. This meant that the young hero's death was more than just the conclusion of an exciting life. It was the means by which others could judge his extraordinary deeds.[3]

As I continued to revisit the subject, another influential volume came to my attention. Among other key points, Brian Dippie's *Custer's Last Stand: The Anatomy of an American Myth,* first published in 1976, set forth the proposition that Custer and his disastrous battle were unusual in that a significant incident and an uncommon personality had been melded into a myth.[4] This merger of a famous man and his bold final fight offered the very substance of adventure and romance required to join an elite circle of heroes, from King Arthur's Knights of the Round Table to British lancers at the Charge of the Light Brigade.

Custer, then, was but one of a multitude who fit Joseph Campbell's framework of the "hero with the thousand faces," wherein a particular sequence of actions is followed so that one self-sacrificing deed is done over and over again by many different people.[5] This story of the champion going forth on a quest, only to be cut to pieces, then resurrected, is universal, contends Campbell. All cultures have turned to such myths—tales that explain the cosmos and the place of the people in it.

Here was the crux of Custer's long notoriety. Despite the fact that other notable figures had come to the fore during the so-called Indian wars, Custer alone was held as the embodiment of core beliefs so closely tied to the United States' national identity.[6] He was to be vested with the mantle of mythic hero as El Cid, Roland, and a litany of others had been in previous times and diverse places, to become one of those half truths or traditions that form an integral part of the ideology of a society.

But how had Custer come to be viewed as a great man in the first place, so that his death at the Little Bighorn would make such an immediate impact? For one thing, the charismatic Custer had made good copy for the press of his day, thereby turning him into a celebrity during the Civil War and immediate postwar years.[7] Much of his rise to glory came from his exposure in popular publications of the 1860s and 1870s, which had captured the national imagination of the growing middle class.[8]

Indeed, Custer himself had presented accounts of his exploits in two of these periodicals, *Galaxy* and *Turf, Field*

Custer and the Little Bighorn have become commodities as well as inspired items ranging from toys to trading cards, puzzles, games, and music. Sometimes Custer has been used to promote other products, too, including 80-proof bourbon in porcelain bottles and potatoes in burlap bags. GLEN SWANSON

and Farm. Thus he actively contributed to his own myth.[9] Consequently, Custer capitalized on the public's interest by self-promotion through his writings, while satisfying his own literary ambitions.

In many ways, the encounter at Little Bighorn was one of the major stories of its time. Over a century later, it's difficult to understand the far-reaching impact this event had on the country as it proudly celebrated it centennial.

Another factor was one of the most attentive members of Custer's audience, his cherished wife, Elizabeth. During their life together and after his death, she played an active part in the promotion of her spouse's cause. Surviving her husband into the 1930s, she remained committed to playing the role of the faithful wife and model Victorian woman, and in the process, she managed to draw no little income from her public appearances and writings, which also ensured that her beloved husband would be remembered as a gallant cavalier whose unblemished spirit would live on as a model for young Americans. She likewise influenced the writings of others who were friendly to Custer's memory, and she outlived most of the men who knew Custer and could have taken up the pen against him.[10]

Even during Elizabeth's life, however, two camps existed concerning Custer and his defeat, a rift that already had been evident while he was still alive. Custerphiles and Custerphobes, past and present, have written biographies, histories, and a vast assortment of literature that came to be known as "Custeriana," a veritable industry based upon what has rightly been termed "a minor episode in the history of the United States."[11]

Many of the supposedly factual studies were self-published and usually were polemical. Several of these titles also were and continue to be directed to a specific audience of fellow Custer buffs.[12] Some of these authors passed back and forth between fact and fiction, the line between the two often being blurred. A few even turned their efforts toward the dime novel and other pulp publications, early avenues of bringing Custer to a broader audience than articles in military journals or more academic books might reach. In August and September 1876, only weeks after Custer's death, no fewer than five dime novels came off the press related to the defeated cavalry commander at Little Bighorn.[13]

Custer also inspired poets and songwriters,[14] and his final moments aroused hundreds of illustrators and artists. In the process, this group literally invented the image of the Last Stand.[15] As early as 1876, melodramas and Wild West shows likewise made much of the tableaux of the Little Bighorn.[16] Supposedly, one of the Wild West shows even doubled its attendance after adding Custer's final engagement to its bill in 1887, thereby indicating the reputation attained by this dramatic episode within a decade after it occurred.[17]

But it was after 1909, when the budding film industry found the Custer saga a suitable theme to attract patrons, that the story achieved incredible exposure. With the passage of time, Little Bighorn and Custer became, according to script writer and fiction author Frank Gruber, one of seven basic plots for Westerns.[18] Custer already was known to potential audiences of the silver screen. In the early twentieth century, he enjoyed widespread recognition and appeal.

Within a few years, cinematic renditions of Custer fell into three primary uses that remained as the foundation for subsequent movies and later television scripts. First was the scenario that featured Custer as a central character and the Last Stand as a significant part of the story line. Second, a figure based on Custer, but with a different name, was a main character, and there was a massacre of whites by an overwhelming Indian force. And third, Custer was simply inserted to add flavor or authenticity to a costume drama or Western.[19] In some instances, Custer did not even appear on the screen. His name merely was invoked to indicate to the audience that this tale was set in the Old West and would have plenty of action between the Indians and the cavalry.

Film and television portrayed Custer and the events associated with his life in a way that was perceived as being acceptable to the core movie-going audience, who, in the early days of the genre, were viewed as white, middle-class males.[20] Throughout most of the first half of the twentieth century, the staple provided for this group was the B Western, the low-budget formula picture that was a mainstay when the impact of the Depression gave birth to double-feature bills. Here, Custer was but one of a number of "character types" who appeared from one film to the next.[21] It was these types, or repetitive images, that ultimately came to dominate B Westerns.[22] Although usually not high grossing individually, the sum total of revenue from these formula pictures long helped fill the film industry's coffers and reached viewers with a message that was repeated again and again.[23]

In the original idiom of this genre, Custer was shown as a noble warrior who fell fighting for a just cause—an archetypical figure who combated the enemies of progress. Commonly these depictions were ethnocentric at best, but all too often, they were racist at the core. The Indians usually were portrayed as skulking, bloodthirsty heathens who rained down death from hidden positions with primitive weapons. In contrast, Custer and his men were presented as stalwart Christian soldiers who gallantly exposed themselves to danger with sabers in hand, faces turned bravely to meet a treacherous enemy.[24]

These early conventions changed over the ensuing decades, especially as the studio system came into full sway. Given the commercial nature of the film industry by the 1930s, being able to predict or comprehend shifts in public tastes was critical; the studios flourished when they correctly judged new trends.[25]

Responding to a broadly based, diverse audience dictated the creation of many basic themes capable of being retooled with changing times and circumstances.[26] Consequently, transformations in mass media can be viewed as a dynamic between producers and consumers. Even then, the audience has the power to accept or reject what's being offered, thereby either reinforcing or curtailing the producers' efforts.[27]

This is evident in films related to Custer, particularly those made after World War II. Starting in the late 1940s, as growing antiwar sentiment began to take hold, Custer's screen presence shifted from the heroic model to the role of antihero or antagonist.

Films had lagged behind print in vilification of Custer and his men. A growing trend in literature of the 1930s had been influenced by the mood of post–World War I "lost-generation" writers and those who questioned the country's favored position after the Great Depression. Following on this line of reasoning, the experiences of the Second

World War led to the replacement of previous onscreen Custers with other versions of Yellow Hair, in keeping with cinema exemplified by the probing *Best Years of Our Lives*.

Later still, the momentum of the civil-rights movement in the United States contributed to a heightened sympathy for American Indians, who often had been depicted as aggressor rather than victim in Westerns.[28] That stereotype increasingly was reversed. Additionally, the Vietnam War played a large part in reshaping Custer's screen persona. These opposing interpretations exist because, as Brian Dippie says, for the most part, "Custer's Last Stand is a white myth and explanations rest on white factors."[29]

Even so, some American Indians, and non-Indians too, have taken this event and adapted its meaning to their own perspectives. Consequently, Custer has been held up as a noble swordbearer of manifest destiny or, conversely, as the embodiment of all the evils that befell the original inhabitants of the United States at the hands of the newcomers.[30] Instead of a savior, Custer appears as a scapegoat who died for the sins of white America.[31] In this guise, Custer is lampooned and the punch line to humorous tales.

Because motion pictures and television productions tend to offer popular themes, they by necessity have paralleled certain tendencies found among various elements of American society. At the same time, the diversity of the marketplace dictates multiple perspectives. In response, by the 1990s, Custer's cinematic image had became so fluid that it allowed diametrically opposing views to be presented without seeming contradictory.[32]

Accordingly, the flexible nature assigned to Custer, along with his decades of public exposure as a larger-than-life figure, assures that he will not be dismissed easily from the public eye. No longer a mere man, the unsolvable mystery surrounding Custer's final actions has turned him into a pliable metaphor—one that changes periodically yet can be resurrected when deemed reusable in a former version. Eventually, his fame went beyond almost every other historical figure associated with the American West, overshadowed only by that of a few more prominent national characters.[33]

This is because the story of Custer's Last Stand essentially was fabricated. It is not based on historical data, but instead is the product "of popular culture, which, omnivorous, feeds upon fact and fancy, history and legend, and, turning cannibal, upon itself."[34] It appears then that in this instance, "logic and history" have bowed "to the much greater power of inherited image."[35]

Tracing Custer's portrayal over the decades, with an emphasis on motion pictures and television, offers a sort of barometer of how Americans responded to various issues from era to era. Moreover, examining Custer's invention and reinvention as a symbol offers insight into how legends develop and can tell something about the times and attitudes of the nation in which he was born.[36] Understanding Custer and the Little Bighorn can open a valuable window into the perceptions of the American West and its place in the minds of the American people. By providing a glimpse into the national character, this man and his fate along the meandering banks of a river in Montana have become icons in the United States and abroad. Whether savior or villain, Custer will never die so long as he can be resurrected to provide meaning in an ongoing self-conscious struggle of a country seeking to define itself.

CHAPTER ONE

Behold the Man

His family nicknamed him Autie. After he became an officer in the U.S. Army, some of his subordinates variously referred to him as Hard Ass, Iron Butt, Ringlets, and who knows what else. To the Indians, he was Long Hair, Yellow Hair, or Son of the Morning Star. In print, he occasionally appeared as the Boy General, and over time, other writers gave him many different titles, depending upon their view of him.[1] Sometimes he wrote under the nom de plume of Nomad.[2] He was George Armstrong Custer.

Born in New Rumley, Ohio, on December 5, 1839, Custer spent most of his unremarkable early years in Monroe, Michigan. When Custer was old enough, he went off to begin his formal education, but he viewed school as more an obstacle to be tolerated or at times avoided. From early on, he was characterized by action, not contemplation. Though he was no scholar, he did manage through political connections to secure an appointment to the U.S. Military Academy at West Point.

During his days along the banks of the Hudson, young Cadet Custer spent considerable time in extracurricular activities, including those at a local grog establishment known as Benny Havens.[3] There, "Fanny," as he came to be called by his classmates, enjoyed drinking and other pastimes considerably more than spending long hours with his books. Poor grades and an incredible number of demerits caused him to graduate dead last in his class, yet one of his fellow West Pointers, Tully McCrea, remembered his ruddy-faced comrade favorably:

> He is one of the best-hearted and cleverest men that I ever knew. The great difficulty is that he is too clever for his own good. He is always connected with all the mischief that is going on, and never studies any more than he possibly can help.[4]

Not long after leaving the academy, Custer went off to the Civil War, where he began to make his military mark. One of his superiors, George B. McClellan, who never was accused of false modesty himself, described his slightly built subordinate with flowing hair as "simply a reckless, gallant boy undeterred by fatigue, unconscious of fear; but his head was always clear in danger and he always brought me clear and intelligible reports of what he saw under the heaviest fire."[5]

Recognition from superior officers, combined with bravado in battle, helped propel Custer upward from a newly commissioned second lieutenant to a brevet major general of volunteers in a matter of a few years. Now he was living the life of the bold dragoons he had read about so often as an adolescent. At twenty-three, the youngest brigadier general in the Union Army, Custer began to dress the part of a cavalier, with flowing hair and flamboyant custom-designed uniforms.

Cadet Custer, West Point Class of 1861, was at the bottom of the list upon graduation with the most demerits and worst academic standing. NATIONAL PORTRAIT GALLERY, SMITHSONIAN INSTITUTION

This new lofty position also gained Custer stature in his hometown of Monroe, where he would fare better with a young lass as a general officer than he had when he still wore the shoulder straps of a company-grade officer. During the winter of 1862–63, while on leave in Monroe, Custer met the daughter of a locally prominent judge, Daniel S. Bacon. In time, Custer joined a considerable list of suitors, and his attentions gained little ground in this campaign for Elizabeth Bacon's affection. From a different social stratum than Custer, Miss Bacon probably

would not have met the youthful soldier if it had not been for the circumstances of the war.

Dissimilarity in backgrounds was but one obstacle to this courtship. The fact that Elizabeth, or Libbie, as she was known to her intimates, had witnessed George in an inebriated state returning home from a drinking bout one afternoon did not sit well with the religious, morally motivated young woman, nor did Custer's insistence on wooing more than one lady fair while he was in Monroe. Elizabeth's chief rival was Fanny Fifield, but she was not the only one on the fickle Custer's list. He acknowledged his roving eye in a letter to his half-sister, Ann Reed, in which he confessed his growing, yet not totally complete, devotion to Libbie. He wrote that only a dozen other Monroe belles caught his fancy more than Miss Bacon, "and that is the truth."[6]

As Custer persisted, Libbie's defenses began to wear thin, perhaps in part because she perceived that she had made a conquest. She confided, "Nobody could entertain him but me for over an hour without being lonely. . . . He tells me he would sacrifice every earthly hope to gain my love and I tell him if I could I would give it to him." Soon thereafter she admitted, "I like him very well," while his appearance was pleasing too, very much like "books and pictures I've seen."[7] Yet when Custer returned to duty, she expressed mixed feelings. While she did not enjoy herself nearly as much after Custer's departure, she nonetheless thought, "It is best he has gone. I am doing my duty and away from temptation."[8]

When that temptation returned with a brigadier general's star and a growing reputation as a dashing military hero, it was difficult to stave off his next assault, which began anew with a not-so-subtle package. Delivered in person to Libbie by Custer's brother-in-law, the envelope contained a large rendition of Custer by Alfred Waud of *Harper's*, among the first of many portrayals by artists of the man whose name began to spread in a period when illustrated popular pulp publications were in flower.[9]

Such long-distance exchanges continued, often through go-betweens. In the meantime, Custer's fame gathered further luster in battle after battle. The newspapers extolled him because his exploits were the stuff of banner headlines and reader-pleasing copy, and they labeled their new superstar the "Boy General."[10] Custer gained further notice at Gettysburg on July 2, 1863, when he had his horse killed underneath him while riding into the fray at Hunterstown, several miles to the east of the main fighting. He took another mount. From then on, he seemed constantly in the saddle, facing one Confederate force after another.

Autie and Libbie, the stuff of legends and legend-makers as well, c. 1865. Both wear the corps badge of Custer's Civil War cavalry command. GLEN SWANSON

Then, on September 13, 1863, at Culpeper Court House, a shell fragment struck Custer in the leg. A surgeon determined that the cavalryman could not continue to serve until he was healed, and Custer received a medical leave.

The wounded warrior headed to Monroe for more than recuperation. It was now that Libbie began to give way to the man she often fondly called Autie. Although she acknowledged that considerable misgivings plagued her "like tormenting devils and I doubt that I love him," yet she put aside these feelings and concluded that someday she would succumb and take his hand in marriage.[11] And that she did, proving anything but a mere ornament during their dozen years as man and wife. From their February 9, 1864, wedding at Monroe's First Presbyterian Church, to her own death nearly three-quarters of a century later, she remained the ever-faithful bride.[12]

Not long after George and Elizabeth wed, she emerged as a driving force in his personal life and career. From the outset, she often accompanied him on his travels. In fact, the day after their marriage, the newlyweds took a midnight train heading east, with stopovers at West Point and New York City, where they had several portraits taken by none other than Matthew Brady before proceeding to Washington, D.C.

Once in the nation's capital, Custer returned to his command, which at that time was just south of Brandy Station. By February 28, the new husband was back in the field, raiding into Confederate territory toward Charlottesville. Near the end of March, he received another medical leave. This afforded him the opportunity to meet Libbie in Washington, where they looked for a suitable residence for her and attended theater and various social functions, often with high-ranking officials, including Abraham Lincoln, among the guests.

After this whirlwind of activities, the general reported to his new superior, Philip H. Sheridan, establishing a relationship that proved influential through the remainder of his military career. Within days he assumed command of the 2nd Brigade, 3rd Division of Cavalry. From May through early July, he continued his onslaught against the Confederates. During one of these engagements, a trooper with Custer's command felled another notable cavalryman, J. E. B. Stuart.

Not everything was campaigning, however. Custer received another sick leave beginning on July 12, which meant that he and Libbie soon were together again after she came south to meet him at City Point, Virginia. Shortly after that, the pair returned to Washington, D.C., and for the next few months they were able to be with each other on a regular basis, even after Autie returned to action in the fall.

Victory after victory came his way, and in between, there were reunions with Elizabeth. These successes culminated in Custer's promotion to a major general of volunteers. His brother, Tom, likewise earned considerable fame during the war, emerging with two Medals of Honor for his heroic exploits—a rare distinction.

While the remainder of the war found Major General Custer more often than not in the front of his troops, he enjoyed considerable benefits denied most others during the conflict. On April 9, 1865, at Appomattox Court House in Virginia, he acquired the table that Robert E. Lee and U. S. Grant had used to sign the surrender terms. Hoisting this trophy over his head, he carried off the piece to eventually give to Libbie, whom he was to rejoin on April 11 at Jefferson Davis's former residence in Richmond.[13]

By the next month, General and Mrs. Custer were off with their maid, Eliza, to New Orleans, which they reached in June. While there, they found time to have their portraits painted on a pair of vases, as just one example of a growing number of images linking the couple for future generations. Late the next month, they settled into Custer's new command at Hempstead, Texas, headquarters of his Cavalry Division of the Military District of the Southwest.

Custer's father, Emanuel, and brother, Tom, joined them. Tom was posted as Autie's aide, and Emanuel received an appointment from his son as a civilian forage master. With the family secured in the Lone Star State, all seemed well. But that situation soon changed.

For one thing, Custer proved a less able peacetime leader than he did a wartime commander. As a result, he seemed poorly equipped to deal with the problems of disciplining troops who were citizen-soldiers anxious to return to their homes. Instead of the respect he had come to bask in during his time in combat, he was held in low esteem by many of his subordinates in Texas, as one of his men recorded. The twenty-five-year-old brought with him a youthful, self-important ego coupled with an inbred "tyranny of the regular army. He did not distinguish between a regular soldier and a volunteer."[14] Custer's seeming inability to distinguish between a volunteer and a professional soldier meant he was unsympathetic to enlisted men. They were mere cogs, not humans, who must obey his every imperious command.

To make matters worse, the Union army faced a considerable reduction in force by 1866. On January 31, word arrived that Custer would be demoted from a major general of volunteers to a captain in the 5th Cavalry, his old outfit at the outset of the war. Within weeks of receiving this news, he left Texas.[15] Once again, Custer was off to Washington. This time he met with Secretary of War Edwin Stanton to try to obtain a Regular Army commission for not only himself but also for his brother, Tom, and his comrade George Yates.

Not certain whether this was his best course, Custer looked into other possibilities as well. He even visited Wall Street as part of his efforts to secure civilian employment that would ensure continuation of the comfortable lifestyle the Custers had been enjoying. During this period, Custer also considered an offer of $16,000 a year, then a princely sum and double what he made as a major general, to join Benito Juárez's forces as adjutant general of the Mexican Army. Grant, who was still serving as the senior officer of the U.S. Army at the time, and Secretary Stanton gave their blessings, but the secretary of state objected because of potential repercussions from the French.[16]

Another possibility presented itself within the American military: that of the position of inspector general of cavalry. Hedging his bets, Custer explored civilian jobs in Washington, D.C. Almost immediately thereafter, he linked up with President Andrew Johnson to tour the country on behalf of the chief executive's efforts to rally the nation around his Reconstruction policies and other planks in his platform. In the process, Custer began to think about politics, especially Congress, as another avenue for his ambitions.[17] He considered this course briefly, but on July 28, 1866, his destiny was sealed. Although the monotony of frontier service faced him, Custer accepted a commission as lieutenant colonel of the 7th Cavalry, one of several new U.S. Army units forming in 1866.[18]

Consequently, by October, Autie and Libbie, with their servant, Eliza, left the grand circle of the president and his entourage and were soon on their way to a new home—Fort Riley, Kansas, where the 7th was gathering. Because the Custer party arrived in November, military activities were at a minimum. Troops in the West traditionally remained in the garrison during the colder months and took to the field in late winter or early spring. This allowed for a certain period of adjustment.

In March 1867, however, Custer's quiet homelife ended. Winfield S. Hancock gathered his forces, including the 7th Cavalry, for an expedition against the Indians in his area of command. Theodore Davis, who was a reporter during that time, met Custer as he joined Hancock's force. He commented that the 7th Cavalry's lieutenant colonel was "endowed by nature with a confidence in himself which was never boastfully exploited, and a believer that the future would surely unfold a continua-tion of the successful past—Custer's luck, his talismanic guard was trusted by him all too blindly."[19]

In this summation, Davis seems to have been prophetic. The fact that Custer had again caught the eye of the press also was telling. Now, as before, he was continally kept in public view, a place where he seemed quite comfortable and indeed, even enjoyed.

But Davis also noted Custer's growing depression during his less-than-successful Kansas campaigning in the spring and summer of 1867. Although friendly to the lieutenant colonel, Davis indicated that Custer was never so melancholy and increasingly took on a gloomy air.[20]

One of Custer's company commanders, Capt. Albert Barnitz, who at first, like Davis, was impressed with the former Civil War general, went further in describing a man who had turned sour perhaps because something angered him.[21] In subsequent letters, Barnitz decried Custer's capriciousness, especially the number of arrests the colonel had ordered to be made of men in his command, including the captain himself.[22] This prompted Barnitz to unleash his wrath in a confidential letter to his wife, Jennie, who at that time was in camp near Fort Hays. He noted how unpleasant duty under the general had become and said that this made it difficult to maintain morale, especially when Custer seemed to go to lengths to make himself "generally obnoxious." Barnitz no longer admired his lieutenant colonel as a fellow military man or as a commander, confiding: "To speak the plain truth I am thoroughly <u>disgusted</u> with him! He is the most complete example of a petty tyrant that I have ever seen."[23] Barnitz ended his letter with a final complaint that Custer was cruel to the men and discourteous to their officers.

If it had been solely Barnitz who made such statements, this might be construed as simply a matter of personal incompatibility. Soon after Barnitz's May 15, 1867, diatribe, however, Custer's own actions tended to support the picture the captain painted of his superior. In fact, just a few days earlier, Autie had written to Libbie that he was reading *Anatomy of Melancholy,* an appropriate title given what seemed to be his frame of mind at that time. His remedy was his wife. He enjoined, "<u>Do</u> hurry and come to your boy."[24]

When, on May 12, it appeared Custer would not be able to obtain his wish until late in the year, he told Libbie he would "try to kill time by killing Indians."[25] This sanguine means of sublimation wore thin after two months.

Growing anxious to join Libbie, supposedly out of concern about his spouse's well-being, Autie decided to leave Fort Wallace. According to Custer's autobiographical *My Life on the Plains,* the post was under siege, supplies were running low, mail and stagecoaches had ceased to run, and there was an outbreak of cholera.[26] These assertions were not true, but Custer painted this picture as a rationale for leading four officers and twenty-two troopers out of Fort Wallace in July 1867 on a 150-mile, fifty-five-hour ride that ended at Fort Riley.

Pushing his escort hard, Custer even refused to halt when he discovered that one of his mounts and the trooper assigned to care for the mare had been separated from the column. He dispatched a six-man detachment under a sergeant to locate the horse and soldier. In the process, the detail came under attack by Indians. One of their numbers was wounded, and the remainder of the party fled to catch up with Custer.

Once they had rejoined the main body, Custer again forbade a discontinuance of his forced march and ordered the column to proceed without turning to the aid of the injured trooper. Nothing could dissuade Custer from his pell-mell ride to Libbie, and this single-mindedness greatly contributed to his subsequent court-martial, which began on September 16, 1867, and ended with a verdict of guilty. He was suspended from duty for one year, starting on November 20.[27]

Custer's exile ended in triumph when he received word of the early remittance of his sentence. His reprieve came when William T. Sherman determined to translate the total war he had practiced during his "march to the sea" to Indian fighting in the West, where it would become what one historian termed "savage war."[28] To carry out this subjugation of the various native peoples of the Southern Plains, including Arapahos, Cheyenne, Comanches, and Kiowas who were wintering in Indian Territory, Sherman called upon his faithful Civil War lieutenant, Sheridan. In turn, Sheridan sought out his protégé Custer and arranged for his early reinstatement to duty. On September 24, 1868, Sheridan wired that his fellow generals, Sherman and Sully, and many of the officers of the 7th Cavalry joined him in the hope that Custer would be allowed to return to his old unit at once.[29]

So it was that in early October 1868, the Custers were back in Kansas. A few days later, Custer joined his unit "with his hair cut short, and a perfect menagerie of Scotch fox hounds."[30] He also added a beard and wore a buckskin field jacket for the coming campaign, the buckskin becoming a sort of personal symbol clearly demonstrating that its wearer intended to be identified as a hunter or scout, a type found in literature who knew Indians and their ways.[31] By donning this mantle, Custer merged this literary figure of the Victorian era with another powerful hero of the time, the soldier-aristocrat, thereby becoming a hybrid of these two prominent sources of popular lore that were being promoted by dime novelists and journalists of the period.[32]

Attired in an appropriate frontiersman's outfit, on November 11, Custer led his cavalrymen southward. More than two weeks passed, when he drew his command up to attack Black Kettle's village along the Washita River. This Cheyenne leader had advocated accommodation with the whites. During the Civil War, his peaceful overtures had been rewarded by Colorado Volunteers attacking his encampment at Sand Creek.[33] Now Black Kettle and his people were to suffer again.

With buglers sounding the charge and bandsmen playing "Garry Owen," the tune that thereafter became entwined with the 7th Cavalry, Custer's troopers descended on the sleeping inhabitants. Men, women, children, and animals all were thrown into chaos as they became targets for the cavalrymen.

Ten minutes later, the din stopped almost as quickly as it had begun. The enemy village was secured. At first it appeared that the fray had cost the Indians dearly but left the soldiers nearly unscathed. That preliminary assessment gave way to another verdict, when it was later learned that Maj. Joel Elliot, who had led one of the four attack elements Custer launched against the village, had been killed along with nineteen others who volunteered to follow his call, "Here goes for a brevet or a coffin!"[34] Some individuals attributed Elliot's demise to Custer's poor handling of the battle. Because of this, an existing rift between Custer and some of his officers widened, never to close again.

Capt. Frederick W. Benteen was arguably the most outspoken among those who squared off against Custer. In an article that appeared in the *Missouri Democrat* on February 8, 1869, a letter from Benteen to William DeGress of St. Louis was published anonymously. The captain made it clear that he thought Custer was more intent on demonstrating his "sharp-shooting . . . by dropping the straggling Indian ponies" than he was in making an effort to find out what happened to Elliot and his comrades.

When Custer learned of the unflattering attack in print, he called his officers and supposedly threatened to take his quirt to the man who had written the defaming words. According to one account, when Benteen entered the tent where all were assembled, he requested the offending newspaper. He then stepped outside to read it, twirled the cylinder of his revolver, and came back inside with the words, "I guess I am the man you are after, and I am ready for the whipping promised."[35]

If Custer actually had indicated that he intended to horsewhip the author of the letter, he declined to follow through on the threat. Regardless, the relationship between Custer and Benteen was just one example of the chasm that existed between certain members of the 7th Cavalry and their lieutenant colonel. Two camps existed, with Custer's inner circle enjoying his favor, the rest being kept at arm's length.

Outside observers also tended to line up on one side or the other in their opinion of Custer. Many of his subordinates, who dealt with Custer frequently, had harsh words for their commanding officer, as did some frontiersmen. Conversely, on one of his visits to New York, Custer wrote in a confidential letter to Elizabeth, claiming he had been spoken of as the most popular officer in the army among veterans. His head was turned even more at this gathering when he learned that he was "to most people, the *beau ideal* of the Chevalier Bayard, 'knight *sans peur et sans reproche,*'" and allegedly "stood unrivaled as the 'young American hero.'"[36]

In a later letter to Libbie, he pointed out the glowing newspaper reports about his activities on the Yellowstone Expedition of 1873. He reveled in references to him in the *Chicago Post* as the "Glorious Boy," a title that harkened back to his splendid Civil War years.[37]

Similarly, William E. Curtis, a correspondent for the *Chicago Interocean*, could have been Custer's press agent. He described him as "a great man—a noble man" who abstained from drink and tobacco, did not swear, or have any vices "unless an almost inordinate love for the higher brute creation may be called such, for General Custer has the best dogs and the best horses he can procure within the limits of search. His leash of hounds is probably as large and well-bred as any in the country, and his own and the horses of his regiment, the Seventh Cavalry, are famous all over the States." Curtis concluded by boasting of Custer's reputation as "the best sportsman and the most accurate shot in the army."[38]

As with most things related to Custer, his ability with firearms drew diametrically opposing views. Luther North, a man who had achieved a certain amount of fame as a scout himself, wrote about the 1874 expedition that brought Custer into the Black Hills: "Custer was quite social and did a great deal of talking. He was a very enthusiastic hunter. . . . While General Custer was always telling of the great shots he made each day that he hunted, he didn't seem to care much about hearing of anyone else doing good shooting."[39] North's comments were made at a crucial point, because this foray into the Black Hills marked the prelude to Little Bighorn. Custer's outing into

the sacred realm known to the western Sioux or Lakota people as *Paha Sapa* ("Hills of Black") opened a road to his future from which there seemed no detour.

An Oglala named Black Elk, destined to be a holy man among his people, was a youth at the time. He summed up the impact of *Pe-hin Hanska's* (Lakota meaning "Long Hair") summer expedition in the Black Hills. From Black Elk's point of view, Custer "had no rights to go there, because all the country was ours. Also, the Wasichus had made a treaty with Red Cloud that said it would be ours as long as grass grows and water flows." Here Black Elk alluded to the 1868 Treaty of Fort Laramie, wherein a number of Northern Cheyenne, Northern Arapaho, Crow, and Lakota men had "touched the pen" to an agreement with the federal government. In return for abandoning three military posts built after the Civil War by the U.S. Army along what came to be called the Bozeman Trail to Montana's goldfields, the signatories were to take up life on reservations. The white's theory had been that once the Plains peoples were so located and confined, these roving warriors could be transformed into placid planters, but as one scholar rightly judged, the peace commissioners had achieved a victory of "theory and faith over hard reality."[40]

It is doubtful that many who signed this pivotal document fully understood its implications, although many thousands of Indians eventually reported to the reservations. Others, though, refused to sign or comply, including Tatanka-Iyotanka, a powerful Hunkpapa Lakota leader better known to the encroachers as Sitting Bull, who elected to continue the life of his ancestors, remaining free to follow game and pursue the ways of his youth.[41] When Sitting Bull and others challenged those who flowed into the Black Hills after Custer's 1874 expedition provided evidence that gold existed there, Secretary of War William Belknap reacted.

Meaning to crush the resolve of Sitting Bull and others of his mindset, Belknap wrote in no uncertain terms that the Lakotas who were not on the reservations and continued a "hostile attitude toward the whites" were to report to the reserves by January 31, 1876.[42] If not, military action would be taken against them.

Probably few, if any, of those for whom these orders were intended received the notice. Even if they had, the statement was meaningless, because this group of Indians did not share the white man's concept of a calendar with specific dates and times.

No matter, many government officials knew that this missive would be ignored. Consequently, Belknap took steps to convert his words from a threat on paper to a plan of action. He soon charged the military high command to make preparations for the necessary punitive actions that would bring in the nontreaty groups. Yet it was not Custer he had in mind for this action.

Between the Black Hills expedition and the Belknap ultimatum, much had transpired in Custer's life. For a while, he basked in the limelight of the discovery of gold, which again had his name in print in papers around the country. Indeed, three journalists had accompanied Custer during the expedition. Custer no doubt was pleased with his enhanced visibility.

Not long thereafter, he and Libbie journeyed to St. Paul, Minnesota, where, among other things, they rented a grand piano and had it shipped to their quarters at Fort Lincoln. There, during the winter, the piano became part of holiday celebrations in which family and friends gathered for music, plays, and comradeship as if they were in some feudal lord's court.

The Custers did not extend this same hospitality to Belknap when he made a tour of the West during the summer of 1875, including Fort Lincoln. Being of the opinion that the secretary was a prince among many thieves in President Grant's administration, Custer received Belknap "with official correct coolness" during the secretary's stay at the post.[43]

The Custers soon departed the scene for an extended leave, allowing George to concentrate on his writings for *Galaxy,* along with work on his Civil War memoirs. The couple lived the good life during their stay in the comfort of New York City's Hotel Brunswick, where in December they took up residence.

A month later, in January 1876, the Custers moved to less expensive quarters in the city, where they continued to enjoy their stay, although funds were running low. The two never seemed to have the money that would allow them to live in as grand a manner as they might have liked. During their New York holiday, Custer dabbled in stock speculation, but the outcome was further indebtedness. He asked for an extension of his leave in February, but the request was not approved. As a consequence, toward the middle of the month, the social whirl had to be halted. It was time to return to Fort Lincoln.

Custer barely had settled in to his command when he received a summons from Washington. He was to testify before a Senate committee investigating Belknap, who was charged with selling post traderships at garrisons in the West. Custer appeared and gave his take on the matter. The secretary rightly judged, however, that Custer offered hearsay. His testimony would not be admissible in

any court.[44] Despite Belknap's correct analysis of the matter, he finally was forced to resign as secretary of war.

Although Custer enjoyed the brief attention of Democrats intent on raking the Republicans over the coals, his deposition ultimately inflamed President Grant, whose brother Orville was implicated in the tradership scandal.[45] The commander in chief was not pleased with the 7th Cavalry's lieutenant colonel as a result of Custer's statements to the Senate committee. This unexpected consequence nearly cost the officer his field command as his unit readied for campaign duty.

Custer attempted to see Grant, but to no avail. On May 1, 1876, he wrote to the president. The text was a combination of reasons why he sought to see the president and a rather indignant call for justice. His terse missive did not move the chief executive either.[46] Once again, it took allies in high places, including Gen. William Sherman and Gen. Alfred Terry, as well as some support from the press, to prevent Grant from keeping Custer out of the fray. With this backing, he gained approval to ride out with the 7th.

After everything that had transpired, Custer was determined to achieve a dramatic standing in the forthcoming campaign. He even informed some of his Indian scouts that because this was to be his last fight against the Lakota, he "must win a great victory." [47] His future hinged on this.[48]

Custer soon was in place to carry out his design. On May 17, 1876, the 7th Cavalry, arrayed for combat, set out from Fort Abraham Lincoln with Lt. Col. and Mrs. George Armstrong Custer at the head of the column. They often had ridden together, but at the Little Heart River, the couple parted for the last time. By the morning of May 18, Libbie made her way back to the post.

Custer and his men continued southward. For the next four days, the command braved rain and pelting hail. Despite the turn in the weather, the column proceeded. As of May 27, the horsemen had logged 135 miles. They now entered the badlands on the fringe of the Little Missouri River. To find a crossing proved a challenge, and Custer took Capt. Thomas Weir and his Company D in search of a ford for the cumbersome supply wagons. Two days passed before all the rolling stock could be taken across the river. That night the men encamped, and the column's commander, Brigadier General Terry, assigned Custer a mission. With Lt. Charles Varnum and twelve Ree scouts, Custer left the main body. When Custer returned on May 31, he informed Terry that there was no sign of Indians.

The next day, the rain turned to snow, bringing a halt until June 3. Then it was still slow going as the bluecoats approached the Powder River. Once more, the supply train impeded the advance. As before, Custer led the way looking for a suitable route for the wheeled vehicles.

In the meantime, Ree scouts linked up with the steamboat *Far West* on the Powder, receiving a dispatch that they brought back to Terry. From this document, the general learned that a party of forty Indians had been reported near the Tongue River, prompting Terry to seek further information.

Maj. Marcus Reno, the next senior member of the 7th's chain of command in the field, was called upon to make a reconnaissance in force with Companies B, C, E, F, I, and L, along with a Gatling gun, leaving Custer and the remaining companies with Terry. The six troops were told "to reconnoiter the valley of the Powder as far as the forks of the river, then cross to Mizpah Creek, to descend that creek near its mouth, thence to cross the Tongue River and descend to its mouth."[49] It was this foray that brought evidence of Indian movement westward.

Armed with this intelligence, the general now had sufficient information to prescribe a course of action. Calling together his two immediate subordinates, Col. John Gibbon and Lt. Col. George Custer, he made his plan of operation known. Custer was ordered to move up the Rosebud River to determine the direction of the trail Reno's patrol had discovered, saying that "if it led to the Little Big Horn it should not be followed."[50] Gibbon was to cross the Yellowstone near the mouth of the Little Bighorn and follow that stream until June 26. There the two armies would regroup and attack together, unless circumstances made it necessary for Custer to depart from these orders.

Custer called his officers together and relayed their assignment to them. On the morning of June 22, preparations to separate from Terry and carry out the general's orders began in earnest. By noon, according to an account of Company K's Lt. Edward Godfrey, "the 'forward' was sounded," and Custer's 7th, along with Gibbon's infantry companies reinforced with cavalry, set out from their encampment "in columns of fours, each troop followed by its pack mules," the impeding wagons finally having been abandoned.[51] Terry, Custer, and Gibbon positioned themselves nearby, surveying the men as they passed in review. Except for the mules causing difficulties along the way, the rest of the day passed without incident.

At 4:00 P.M., after only 12 miles, Custer had the 7th dismount. Around sunset he ordered the officers' call sounded. As the brass of the 7th assembled, the mood was somber, with little small talk or conversation, and that in undertones, as Godfrey recollected. Once everyone had

gathered, Custer announced that until further orders, there was to be no trumpet call save in the case of an emergency. Each day, the column would set out punctually at 5:00 A.M. Custer expressed his faith in his company commanders, acknowledging that they "were all experienced officers, and knew well enough what to do, and when to do what was necessary for the troops." He reserved only two prerogatives to his direct control: when to move out and when to make camp. Then, as Godfrey recalled, "He took particular pains to impress upon his officers his reliance on their judgement, discretion, and loyalty." Custer's whole demeanor differed from the "brusque and aggressive, or somewhat curt" manner that Godfrey indicated was the lieutenant colonel's usual style. Further, Custer was candid and open, once more not typical of his conduct in Godfrey's experience. In this, "he showed concessions and a reliance on others; there was an indefinable something that was *not* Custer."

Evidently this personality shift did not have a negative impact or spread a sense of impending doom, because many of the officers spent that night in song and conversation.[52] Banter continued the next night, with Lt. C. C. DeRudio, or "The Count," as some dubbed this Italian-born officer, spinning yarns. Benteen wisely attempted to sleep, because at about 10:00 P.M. "Boots and Saddles" was sounded, "not by a bugle, as usual, but by a half smothered whisper."[53] Gathering by lantern light, the officers were told by Custer that they would move in the dark because of the proximity of the Indian encampment. At daybreak they would rest, while the scouts would be sent to locate the village preparatory to a June 26 attack.

Pulling out near midnight from the heights of the Wolf Mountains, the 7th was on its way to what would be a fatal encounter. Later in the day of June 25, Custer stopped at a place now called Reno Creek. Again he gathered his officers, dividing the contingent into three groups. Companies A, G, and M were under Major Reno; Companies D, H, and K followed Benteen; and the remaining five companies, C, E, F, I, and L, went with Custer. The pack train, under Capt. Thomas McDougall, was to remain in the rear until called upon for deployment.

Benteen was to sweep wide to the left and drive every living thing before him.[54] At that, Custer followed the right bank of the Little Bighorn, or the *Pa-zees-la-wak-pa* (meaning "Greasy Grass" or "Slippery Grass," the Lakota name for the river), while Reno's three companies rode along the left bank.

Grass, water, and other important attractions brought the Lakota, Cheyenne, Arapaho, and perhaps others, to the west bank of the Greasy Grass, where they were encamped in almost unprecedented numbers. The 7th rode on a collision course with these people. Years later, Major Reno expressed the view that the command was "being drawn into some trap" by the enemy who would certainly "fight harder, and especially as we were nearing their village."[55] Benteen underscored Reno's assessment of the defenders' resolve: "We were at their hearth and homes . . . their medicine was working well, and they were fighting for all the good God gives anyone to fight for."[56] Thus the villagers were able and ever ready to repel the invaders. When the threat appeared on the horizon, they fought as individuals but with one purpose in mind—to crush the longknives.

When or if Custer ever realized what faced him is unknown. It seems that when he ignored the exclamations of his Ree scouts earlier in the day, when they warned, "Otoe Sioux! Otoe Sioux!" (plenty, or too many, Sioux), he dictated his own death sentence. Trumpeter Giovanni Martini arrived with a dispatch written hurriedly by the regimental adjutant for delivery to Benteen. The note read telegraphically, "Come on. Big village. Be quick. Bring packs. W. W. Cooke. P[S]. bring pacs." Galloping off with this summons, Martini can be considered the last survivor from Custer's immediate force to see the lieutenant colonel alive, although Pvt. Peter Thompson and Pvt. James Watson of Company C claimed they had spied him on their way to join Reno. Thompson wrote years later that he and his comrade saw Custer from a distance. "It being a very hot day he was in shirt sleeves; his buckskin pants tucked into his boots; his buckskin shirt fastened to the rear of his saddle; and a broad brimmed creamed colored hat on his head, the brim of which was turned up on the right side and fastened by a small hook and eye to its crown."[57]

What transpired next is anything but clear. In fact, the events that followed became the source of considerable speculation, contrary points of view, and heated debate. One thing seems indisputable, though: Custer had accomplished one of his greatest ambitions that day. He once had written: "In years long-numbered with the past, when I was verging upon manhood, my every thought was ambitious—not to be wealthy, not to be learned, but to be great. I desired to link my name with acts and men, and in such a manner as to be a mark of honor—not only to the present, but to future generations."[58] Custer had succeeded beyond his wildest dreams.

CHAPTER TWO

Custeriana's Many Faces

On July 6, 1876, the adjutant general of the Military Division of the Missouri received a telegram from Alfred Terry. This report, dated June 27, announced, "It is my painful duty to report that day before yesterday . . . a great disaster overtook Gen Custer & the troops under his command."[1] Almost immediately, this news was forwarded to the War Department and confirmed Custer's death.[2]

Even before military officials learned of the clash through channels, accounts of the battle had reached print. One of the first sources of this intelligence was an extra edition of the *Bozeman Times* that came off the press on July 3. Based on dispatches out of Fort Ellis, the article reported that a village "of from 2500 to 4000 warriors" had been attacked. The result was short and to the point: "General Custer and fifteen officers and EVERY MAN BELONGING TO THE FIVE COMPANIES WAS KILLED. Reno retreats under the protection of the reserve. The whole number killed was 315." The following day, as the nation celebrated the centennial of the Declaration of Independence, the Helena *Daily Herald* put out its own extra with banner headlines, "Gen. Custer and his Nephew Killed, The Seventh Cavalry cut to pieces," followed by a short second article about "the defeat of Custer and the massacre of his entire command" in the next day's edition.

Similar sensational stories appeared in the *Bismarck Tribune* for July 6, 1876, and on it went from there to reach national and international audiences over the next

weeks. Sometimes the articles were brief and contained basic facts, or what passed for facts. Others were lengthy and included information that went far beyond verifiable data available then or now.

Some readers denied the news at first, including Sheridan and Sherman, who both dismissed the earliest reports as absurd, rash rumors.[3] Others who believed the news sought to establish blame for this devastating defeat, a polemic that began for political reasons but took on a life of its own with the passage of years.[4] Indeed, after hearing of Custer's demise, news reporters, military officers, and an assortment of other curious inquirers began to ponder and publish their versions of what they believed took place on June 25, 1876.

The fact that Custer's death in Montana was more than just another clash between Indians and whites was apparent to a number of individuals. One of the earliest of those who saw significance in the Little Bighorn defeat was British-born Frederick Whittaker, a sometime dime novelist, which is indicative of how literature related to the Little Bighorn often hovered between fact and fiction, given the backgrounds of many of those who published on the subject. Whittaker hurried to pen two brief pieces.

The first was a poem, "Custer's Last Charge," for the July 16, 1876, issue of the major unofficial military periodical of the time, *The Army and Navy Journal*. A prose article by Whittaker appeared several months later in *Galaxy*, the same publication that had serially published Custer's

In this July 23, 1876 image, a newspaper artist used Custer's defeat as a background to chide government representatives (particularly those from the South who are depicted here as entering into an alliance with the Indians and thus viewed as traitors) for the reduction of the size of the U.S. Army out of political motivation. From the day of Custer's death to modern times, the Little Bighorn has offered grist for political cartoonists and commentators. GLEN SWANSON

articles that became *My Life on the Plains*. Whittaker's *Galaxy* submission faulted Alfred Terry for splitting his command and failing to maintain close communication between the two columns. In this version, Whittaker painted Custer as a brilliant "meteor flashing from the multitude" but also opined that the fallen cavalryman was inclined from birth to be brash and was possessed by a certain degree of conceit.[5]

Smitten by the Little Bighorn, and perhaps aware of potential financial rewards, Whittaker quickly turned toward a more ambitious project: a full-scale biography, *The Complete Life of Gen. George A. Custer*. In the process of preparing this first of many Custer biographies, Whittaker abandoned much of his impartiality, becoming a staunch Custerphile. This likely was due to one individual who assisted him immeasurably in his work—Elizabeth Custer.

The grieving widow opened a trove of personal papers to the biographer and cooperated extensively with Whittaker, who came to Monroe to conduct his research. Whittaker reversed his former estimation that Custer was brash, now seeing his subject very much through Libbie's eyes as "a remarkable quiet, thoughtful man . . . who never became flurried and excited in the hottest battle."[6] If anything, this valiant warrior had been defeated because of a vindictive president who refused to give Custer command of the expedition, thereby placing his fate in the hands of lesser military leaders. More immediate fault was laid at the feet of Marcus Reno, who did not support his superior, but instead held back, causing what should have been Custer's final and preeminent victory over the Indians to be instead a last stand that cost the battle and the lives of the brave men who fought it. This conclusion was ultimately at the root of Reno's calling for and receiving an open review of his actions at the engagement by a military tribunal.[7]

An advance advertisement of the biography summed up Whittaker's premise that Custer "was the best purely cavalry officer this country had ever seen. He was the ablest Indian fighter we ever had. His life is perfect romance. His name recalls nothing but brilliant deeds of daring and romantic courage, and all that is noble and charming."[8]

Here was both a challenge to pursue the truth about who was responsible for Custer's demise, as well as the gospel of early published renditions that cast Custer in the role of betrayed hero and a model for the youth of America. For several decades after Whittaker's biography appeared, most other writers likewise tended to praise the fallen frontier soldier. At the same time, they vilified the Indians who killed Custer and the whites whom they claimed brought him to the valley of death.

Arguably the most important publications to follow in Whittaker's footsteps were the three volumes of reminiscences that Elizabeth Custer began to publish within ten years after her husband's death. Not satisfied with Whittaker's tome, which she dismissed as meager prose that exploited her beloved Autie's memory, Libbie produced her own tribute. Eventually she provided a trilogy, *"Boots and Saddles"; or, Life in Dakota with General Custer* (1885), *Tenting on the Plains; or, General Custer in Kansas and Texas* (1887), and *Following the Guidon* (1890), all of which further constructed a compelling image of a dashing spouse, loving family man, bold fighter, and perfect Victorian officer and gentleman.[9]

Elizabeth dedicated her first title to "My Husband: The Echo of Whose Voice Has Been My Inspiration." While a number of elements in this and her other two books may be questioned for their veracity, this dedication certainly hit the mark. George Custer himself could not have presented a more glowing portrait had he survived to write his memoirs. In her own works, from public speaking engagements, and through extensive contact or correspondence with veterans and others intent on keeping Custer and the Little Bighorn alive, Libbie became a powerful figure in the formation of her beloved Autie's postmortem image.

While she lauded Autie, she also quieted his critics.[10] This double-edged impact cut a swath well into the twentieth century, as the long-lived widow's books, public appearances, and physical presence inspired others either to pay homage to the Little Bighorn's buckskin-clad central character or to withhold their negative comments from a public forum.

Deference to Elizabeth Custer was evident in three more early biographies, J. W. Buel's *Heroes of the Plains* (1881), Mary E. Burt's *The Boy General* (1901), and Frederick Dellenbaugh's *George Armstrong Custer* (1917). The last two volumes were written for young readers and released with Mrs. Custer's blessing. In fact, Burt's tome was a synthesis of Elizabeth Custer's three books, with Burt designating herself on the title page as editor.

Likewise, Dellenbaugh was extremely faithful to Libbie's point of view. Consequently, he secured a preface from Mrs. Custer, in which the widow proclaimed, "Were I reading of one unknown to me, I should close this book with the thought that it was the fairest and frankest story of an intrepid soldier that his greatest admirers might demand."[11]

Indeed, these respectful tones continued as the norm for writers working through the early 1930s.[12] The positive approach of these early works had much to do with

Dramatically dressed in black, the bereaved Elizabeth Custer did more than mourn her husband's death. Libbie's writings, speaking engagements, and longevity ensured that her beloved Autie's memory would be kept alive unblemished for many decades. GLEN SWANSON

the fact that throughout the years she lived, Mrs. Custer kept a vigilant eye on these chroniclers. Even a hint of rashness aimed at Custer appearing in an otherwise friendly article about his deceased commanding officer by Edward Godfrey was scrutinized, challenged, and ultimately revised in a subsequent reprint. The change was in response to Elizabeth Custer's request.

The original version by Godfrey, "Custer's Last Battle," appeared in *Century Illustrated Monthly Magazine* in January 1892; it was rewritten in 1908. This revised version became available in purged form, as part of the *Contributions to the Historical Society of Montana*, with a postscript from 1921. In the later rendition, Godfrey withdrew the remarks he attributed to another 7th Cavalry officer, Myles Moylan, indicating that Custer had erred when he split the regiment. Instead, Godfrey set forth an argument that dividing the command in and of itself was not a mistake, because that tactic had worked before. To further underscore her husband's blamelessness, Mrs. Custer wrote a preface to this reprint indicating that she had asked for Godfrey's document (without its former offending quotation) to be published "to set at rest some of the fictions that were spread broadcast . . . by the enemies of General Custer, or by friends of General Terry." She also wanted to ensure that the "story of courage and sacrifice should be retold."[13]

While Elizabeth Custer and others worked from a blueprint of a brave Boy General, Fredric Van de Water, a novelist turned biographer, released an opposing perspective. The iconoclastic *Glory-Hunter: A Life of General Custer* was on the market soon after Mrs. Custer's death in 1933. This book took an antithetical approach to previous printed versions that had lionized the fallen soldier. The author noted early on that "men, who never saw that golden head gleam in murk of battle, speak and write of him with odd personal heat."[14]

Van de Water helped fuel that heat as he torched the popular reputation of the once noble frontier cavalryman. He concluded that Custer was a "paradox; the word made flesh," who had during his brief life seemed to reveal varied personalities.[15] There were some constants, however, most notably Custer's quest for fame that "was medieval and adolescent. All his life he rode after Glory."[16] Van de Water saw Custer as a perennial cocky youth who, despite years of war, always remained a boisterous and brash adolescent. He was a perpetual dissident, and although quick witted, he was erratic. Custer could be dispassionate about taking another man's life while at the same time spare the horse of a fallen foe as a captured trophy to be ridden into further battles.

According to *Glory-Hunter*, it was not vanquishing enemies that made Custer what he would become. Instead, "death made him immortal. It is only by cryptic tragedy of his end that most men remember George Armstrong Custer ever lived." Because of this, Van de Water astutely noted, "history and controversy concern themselves chiefly with the last few weeks of his existence" rather than the broader story of his life or the context of his times.[17]

In fact, those contemporaries who shared similar views to Van de Water's tended to gloss over Custer's career and focus on the Little Bighorn, thereby giving rise to a phenomenal body of Little Bighorn publications. For example, E. A. Brininstool was a writer and reporter for various newspapers in Los Angeles. He began his association with the Little Bighorn possibly as early as 1913, predating even Van de Water by some two decades. About that time, he visited the battlefield and spoke to Curley, one of Custer's Indian scouts who survived the engagement. By 1920, his first article on the topic, "Replies to Custer Massacre," appeared in *Hunter-Trader-Trapper*, launching a lifetime of writings in the field. He communicated with many military men and students of Custer, and even purchased an important collection of letters written by Benteen to Theodore Goldin (now in the Thomas Gilcrease Institute of History and Art, Tulsa, Oklahoma), which he planned to publish after Mrs. Custer's death. Although this did not come to pass, he did allow fellow researcher Col. William A. Graham to make copies of these sources for *The Custer Myth*, while denying such an opportunity to William J. Ghent, another with whom he corresponded over the years.

Guarded in his sharing of sources, he gathered more than seventy stories of supposed white "last survivors" of the Little Bighorn (now also in the Gilcrease), all of which he challenged as being frauds. Nonetheless, considerable literature exists from purported members of Custer's column who escaped the carnage and lived to tell the true story of Yellow Hair's last actions. Usually these were whites, with at least one exception, the young Crow scout Curley.

In addition to challenging the self-proclaimed survivors of the last stand, Brininstool also took exception to the notice that Edward Godfrey drew from the press, probably because of that officer's friendly disposition toward Custer. In fact, Godfrey's attitude contradicted Brininstool's claim that he never heard a complimentary word from veterans "who were in a position to know" about Custer, except that he "was a fighter from the word go, absolutely fearless and all that."[18] Brininstool conceded Custer's ability as a cavalryman but damned him as "egotistical, headstrong, 'stuck on himself,' always in trouble on that account, and had the idea that he was a perfect angel."[19]

On the other hand, he thought Reno's Civil War record was brilliant. As such, the major was a victim of undeserved blame, a contention that appeared in some of Brininstool's dozens of Little Bighorn articles, along with such books as *A Trooper with Custer* (1926) and his privately printed *Major Reno Vindicated* (1935). Brininstool laid the disastrous outcome of this engagement solely at Custer's feet. He contended that Custer had ignored Terry's orders, was unfamiliar with the ground, and failed to believe the intelligence of his scouts about the strength of the opposition, who were well armed, unlike the untried recruits in the 7th Cavalry, with their outmoded single-shot Springfield carbines. Dividing his command, and having no plan in mind until he dispatched Trumpeter Martini, Custer made fatal errors that could have only one result—a resounding defeat. In contrast, Reno did the best that he could under incredible circumstances.

Fred Dustin echoed Reno's innocence in *The Custer Tragedy: The Events Leading Up to and Following the Little Big Horn Campaign of 1876* (1939), a limited edition that Brininstool helped finance. Dustin viewed Reno as a casualty of Elizabeth Custer's "personality, charm, and literary ability." Now that Mrs. Custer was no longer living, he believed the unvarnished truth could finally be told.[20]

One reader of Dustin's manuscript noted that the "conspiracy of silence among historians" during Mrs. Custer's lifetime had broken with a "flood of books" since her death.[21] This was much to the satisfaction of Van de Water, whose remarks appeared in an advertisement for *The Custer Tragedy*. He found the study to be "a monumental work that deserves to stand as a headstone over the interminable Custer controversy." Dustin has "said the last calm, authoritative word . . . history at its best, sober, careful, authoritative, and written with a clear and temperate pen."[22]

Dustin, whose academic background was in geology and archeology, became intrigued with the battle as a serious avocation. In the process, he went on to publish what has been called "the blackest, severest account of Custer's life ever written."[23] A later article, which appeared in the April–June 1946 issue of *Michigan History Magazine*, rankled those who were pro-Custer, to say the least, just as Brininstool's work had.

After World War I, William A. Graham, a contemporary of Dustin and Brininstool, started on his long journey into unraveling the Custer enigma. Graham was a member of the U.S. Army's Judge Advocate General Department, and his legal training reflected his approach to the topic—"to maintain a strict and consistent impartiality" in the thirty years he devoted to the subject.[24]

Graham went about his work like a lawyer preparing a brief. He weighed his data, and he attempted to steer a middle course among the parts played by Custer, Reno, and Benteen.[25] In this, he was at odds with Brininstool, although interestingly, he considered Dustin his closest colleague, praising him for his in-depth research.

Graham was of the old school in that he subscribed to the theory that the deportment of an officer and a gentleman placed an individual in a special class. Because of this, he was favorably inclined toward Godfrey, whom he thought to be gracious and reasonable except in his opinion of Reno, of which he said, "I never heard him [Godfrey] refer to Reno otherwise than with contempt."[26] Graham felt that Winfield Scott Edgerly, another 7th Cavalry officer present on the campaign, was more restrained than Godfrey, as well as "much more informative, and far more open minded."[27]

Graham, the attorney, classified his informants as one might assess friendly versus unfriendly witnesses. This tone was found in his writings, starting with articles in the *Cavalry Journal* in the early 1920s, followed by his first major tome, *The Story of the Little Big Horn*, published in 1926. Graham's approach was to provide testimony with little further comment, in order for the readers to decide the case for themselves. This resulted decades later in what perhaps was his most widely read study, *The Custer Myth*, the title of which was most revealing. The dedication to this 1953 compilation reflected his attitude in a few words: "TO THOSE PERSONS who think that Dis-solution of the Custer Myth is easy, and particularly to those who are quite sure they have Dis-solved it, This work is dedicated: (with malice aforethought, express and implied)."

In many ways, Graham contributed much to this myth, not only in his publications, but also through his influence on the efforts of others. Certainly he provoked comment from Dr. Charles Kuhlman, whose own research to decipher the Little Bighorn was more theoretical than Graham's. As Kuhlman's correspondence with Charles Dubois pointed out, "Graham is a lawyer and feels bound by the technical rules of 'evidence' in court." This was at odds with Kuhlman's style. He maintained that Graham practically had reduced "history writing to mere reprinting of sources literally and without comment or interpretation."[28]

Kuhlman and Graham also differed in methodology and background. Kuhlman held a doctorate in history from the University of Zurich and, as such, was one of the few academically trained historians to undertake serious study of the Little Bighorn battle. While his specialty had been the French Revolution and Jacobin Society, he ultimately became fascinated with military history in general, and the Custer fight in particular—peculiar interests indeed for an individual with a deep-seated pacifist persuasion. Severely hearing impaired, Kuhlman was a deep thinker who willingly shared his thoughts with others who studied the subject.

Unlike Graham, who remained distant from the site of the battle both physically and in some senses philosophically, Kuhlman spent considerable time tromping over the grounds.[29] He believed that by applying logic to the placement of markers where soldiers fell, along with careful consideration of time elements and other indicators on the field of battle, it would be possible to reconstruct what had happened to Custer. Despite a desire to solve the mystery through as many clues as the ground would yield, he rejected Indian testimony. Although he interviewed a number of American Indian participants, he concluded that the many inconsistencies of their statements made this source of information unreliable. In one sense, then, Kuhlman was a purist who contended that history could be raised to a precise science, yet he likewise put stock in "channeling"—the receiving of information from the past much as a medium supposedly does.[30]

After years of pondering all these variables from myriad sources, he released a preliminary study in pamphlet form titled *Custer and the Gall Saga*.[31] This was followed in 1951 by his *Legend into History*. Of this work, Graham said that while he admired it in a number of ways, he nonetheless felt that Kuhlman had based his arguments on meager material, which on occasion he had fashioned into "imaginary bricks without straw."[32]

While Graham remained at odds with Kuhlman and far removed from the battlefield, Edward S. Luce, another former army officer, ultimately dedicated many of the remaining years of his life to the site. Luce had served as an enlisted man with the 7th Cavalry from 1907 to 1910, then was commissioned, ending his military career as a major.

While in the army, Luce had met veterans of the regiment from its earlier days, including Godfrey. He even helped prepare a history of the regiment. Later, in 1938, he assisted in assembling the unit's records for the 1866–1910 period.[33] The following year, his key inclusion to the voluminous output in the field appeared: *Keogh, Comanche and Custer*.[34]

In January 1941, after leaving the military, he reported to the battlefield as the first National Park Service superintendent. During his superintendency, Luce communicated with many other historians, students, and buffs.

Many of them were passionate in their defense of Custer, and those of opposing views prosecuted the case against Custer with equal vigor. Both groups took the matter personally in their exchanges with the opposing camp or in justification of their own publications on the issue.[35]

Graham wrote to Luce that *Keogh, Comanche and Custer* relied too heavily on "Dr. Kuhlman's highly—indeed, wholly imaginative and conjectural reconstruction of the fight, which, while interesting, is hardly consistent with the final statement of your preface that 'the author has written history, not manufactured it.'" He concluded: "The most that can be said for Kuhlman's speculation, I think is that the incidents <u>might</u> have happened."[36]

Assuredly, the concept of writing about what *might* have occurred at Little Bighorn was at the center of another profuse outpouring that was equal to, if not greater than, the ongoing historical analysis.[37] The story of Little Bighorn, which contained drama and clear-cut characters, was the very stuff of fiction.[38] This is particularly true in regard to its main character, Custer, who originally was the incarnate "frontier hero" with added dimensions. The Custer story offered an allegory of a youth "who first becomes a soldier-aristocrat and a hero in war against a civilized power; who then goes back to the Frontier and becomes a 'buckskin' hero." He ultimately fell as a victim in a complicated showdown between "the forces of both primitive savagery and Metropolitan corruption."[39]

In this light, authors of fiction took up their pens to take advantage of this tailor-made character, and they did so with the same speed as those who purported to write the true story of Custer and his battle. This group began their labors soon after Custer's death and in many cases preceded those bent on fact finding. Many of the same writers who recounted the history of Little Bighorn turned their pens toward make-believe accounts, as did Whittaker just half a dozen years after his Custer biography. Condensing his prose, he reworked Custer's life story into a dime novel. Both publications reflect an adoring demeanor coupled with an indifference to historical facts that would become standard for later fiction, especially those aimed at juvenile audiences.[40] As one source concluded, from the year of Custer's death to the crash of the stock market, "the special features of the hero tended to become conventionalized in the 'genteel hero' vein; and these conventions in turn were exaggerated often to the point of caricature."[41]

Certainly the seeds for the pulp-fiction Yellow Hair were planted within a few months of Little Bighorn with St. George Rathborne's "Custer's Last Shot; or, the Boy Trailer of the Little Horn," published in serial form in

August and September 1876 in *Boys of New York.* Six years later, the installments were combined and reprinted as a dime novel, followed by reprintings in 1883, 1894, 1902, and 1918, as well as in facsimile edition attributed to either Col. J. M. Travers or "An Old Scout."[42] In whatever permutation, the boy hero fights and survives the Little Bighorn in a story riddled with numerous factual errors and clichéd characters. Nonetheless, Custer's representation as a "dashing spirit," even with his stubbornness and indiscretions, became the standard for years to come.[43]

Another early element in Custer fiction was the shift of emphasis from Custer to a young protégé.[44] In a variety of Custer-related dime novels as well as full-length works, this theme recurred for generations of youthful readers. Examples include Elbridge Brook's *Master of the Strong Hearts* (1898), Edwin Sabin's *On the Plains with Custer* (1913), and Zoe Grace Hawley's *A Boy Rides with Custer* (1938). The formula of a fatherly Custer figure who helps the boy hero experience his dreams of Western adventure reflects action, courage, manliness, and the appeal of the West. The young boy in these stories often becomes, as Kent Steckmesser suggests, "an embryo Custer."[45] This theme still continues in works aimed at juvenile readers, years after the heroic rendition of Custer has gone out of fashion.[46]

But in some instances since World War II, young readers have been offered alternative heroes, with American Indian figures supplanting Custer as the main character. Some deal with famous historical figures, most notably Crazy Horse.[47] Others revolve around fictional characters. In *Red Hawk's Account of Custer's Last Battle,* an old Oglala man recounts what he saw as a fifteen-year-old youth.[48] In *Only Earth and Sky Last Forever,* the Cheyenne Dark Elk must prove his manhood on the eve of Little Bighorn. And in *Life and Death of Yellow Bird,* the illegitimate Cheyenne son of Custer and an Indian princess tells of the battle in which his father was killed.[49]

Similar patterns are found in adult fiction. Early works geared to adult readers, such as Herbert Myrick's 1905 *Cache la Poudre: The Romance of a Tenderfoot in the Days of Custer,* perpetuated the heroic Custer. Randall Parrish's *Bob Hampton of Placer,* published the next year, introduced a new stock figure in Custer fiction: the cashiered 7th Cavalry officer trying to restore his tarnished reputation. This novel also contained another character often found in historical discussions, the lone white survivor of the battle, a device that recurred in many instances when claimants came forward in the late 1800s and early 1900s asserting that they had been with Custer but managed to escape his fate.[50]

The white survivor figure also appeared in Cyrus Brady's *Britton of the Seventh.* Written in 1914, this novel continued the theme of the disgraced officer while describing Custer as a mature and level-headed commander whose defeat could only be due to the failure of subordinates, namely Major Reno.[51]

By 1933, the trend to vindicate Custer was drawing to an end, as Frederick Van de Water's *Thunder Shield* presented Custer as a flawed character whose ambition led to disaster. Van de Water echoed the same conclusions in his biographical *Glory-Hunter.* Consequently, Van de Water had banished Custer from the hallowed Valhalla of "deserving heroes."[52]

Van de Water's stinging portrait of an intensely ambitious egotist had a lasting impact. Other writers followed his model. Three of the most significant novels were Ernest Haycox's *Bugles in the Afternoon,* Will Henry's *No Survivors,* and Thomas Berger's *Little Big Man.*

Published in 1944, *Bugles in the Afternoon* centered on the familiar character of the disgraced officer who joins the 7th as an enlisted man wishing to redeem himself. Considered by many to be one of the best historical Westerns, as well as one of the finest Custer novels ever written, *Bugles in the Afternoon* successfully blended fact and fiction into a smooth story.[53] The author gave a vivid characterization of Custer—much of it lifted from Van de Water—describing him as "an elemental complex of emotions and hungers and dreams never cooled, never disciplined, never refined by maturity; for he had never grown up."[54]

No Survivors, published in 1950, offered another stock player, the white renegade and former Confederate officer living with the Indians. At the last moment, he deserts the Indians and attempts to warn Custer of the trap they have set. Custer is too stubborn to heed this warning, and the author resolutely states, "In the light of what did follow, the charges could be no less than criminal negligence, dereliction of duty, professional incompetence, and moral guilt of murder—all in search of personal glorification and aggrandizement."[55] It is interesting to note that if Custer is guilty, Major Reno is vindicated from the culpable role assigned him in many pro-Custer publications. Finally, the hero, who is at the Last Stand with Custer and yet survives, hears Custer accept full responsibility for the disaster—so that even with his flaws, Long Hair dies a hero.[56]

Thomas Berger's 1964 *Little Big Man,* one of the best-known Custer novels, was viewed by at least one prominent reader as providing "a good idea of Indian attitudes toward life."[57] The story revolves around the firsthand narrative of yet another survivor of the Little Bighorn, 111-

year-old Jack Crabb. Using satire, the author looked at the legends of the Old West by "creating a new legend."[58]

Custer now, as analyzed by Brian Dippie, becomes "a balding former hero, entrapped in a legend largely of his own devising, who looked much older than his years on the last campaign, but showed the stuff of which legends are made when it came his time to die."[59]

Some more recent fictional approaches might be classified as the "twilight zone" Custer,[60] or his appearance in science fiction; the "resurrected" Custer, as found in the "what if" genre of historical fiction; and even the "supermarket" Custer, or the romance novel.

Most notable among the science fiction entries is Steven Utley and Howard Waldrop's short story entitled "Custer's Last Jump," published in 1976 in *Universe 6*. An example of "alternate world" science fiction, the narration provides a picture of Custer's defeat as the final battle against the "Plains Indians' Air Force." Because aviation already had been invented and was used during the Civil War, Crazy Horse and the Indians learned how to fly with the aid of Confederate Mosby's Raiders. The Indian Wars then become air battles with planes, balloons, and even paratroopers. Of special note is the humorous bibliography at the end of the story, with works cited such as Brininstool's *A Paratrooper with Custer* and Elizabeth Custer's *Chutes and Saddles*.[61]

A time-travel entry is Allen Apple's 1988 book, *Twice upon a Time,* that continues the adventures of Alex Balfour, a modern-day student of history who is mysteriously transported back in time to the 1876 Philadelphia Exposition. There, befriended by a young black man, he comes into contact with an elderly Indian and a young Indian woman, both captured by Custer and soon to be sold by him to P. T. Barnum. With the help of writer Mark Twain, they escape, and their journey parallels Twain's later novel *Huckleberry Finn.* Eventually the hero, the black man, and the Indian woman find themselves at the Little Bighorn. There is also a parallel subplot in which Alex's modern-day girlfriend, a journalist for the *New York Times*, is sent to investigate reports about a deranged Indian claiming to embody the spirit of Crazy Horse, only to be kidnapped by him. All meet at the Little Bighorn for the obvious rendezvous of past and present.[62]

The idea of the "resurrected" Custer is the subject of Douglas Jones's 1977 book, *The Court-Martial of George Armstrong Custer.* The novel speculates, "What if Custer had survived the Little Bighorn—as the only survivor?" He is nursed back to health, only to face court-martial by a vindictive president and a seething army bureaucracy. Jones then allows his witnesses' testimonies to sort out the many

charges that history has leveled at Custer for the disaster at Little Bighorn. Jones's characterization of a mad Custer, whose scheming wife wants to attain final justice, certainly reflects how far the image has been tarnished from the hero worship of late-nineteenth-century writers.[63]

Though Custer was no longer the dashing cavalier in literature, he still had a place in romance novels.[64] The lurid covers of such paperbacks provide plot summaries typical of this genre, in which Custer serves as a background to the story. A prime example is the 1980 work *The Tender and the Savage,* by Paula Fairman. The heroine, Crimson Royal, is a young artist who is traveling through the West with her artist father. In the process she meets Joseph Two Hearts, "a loyal Sioux with the blood of a white man running in his veins," who rescues Crimson from a fate worse than death. He spares the Victorian maiden's virtue, and she falls in love with the man who saved her, despite the differences in their cultures. But Crimson resists this emotion. She "seeks another love— the brother of General Custer" and is "caught between two warring camps, the Sioux and Custer's army, torn between two desperate and conflicting loves—an army captain and a white man with an Indian soul."[65]

In *The Tender and the Savage,* Custer is a petty man driven by presidential ambitions. He forbids his brother, Tom, to marry Crimson. At the Little Bighorn, Crimson and the renegade find themselves in the village just as Long Hair and the 7th attack. She even has a chance to speak with Tom, who then rides back across the river to certain death. After the battle, Crimson and Joseph are brought to the fort, and the renegade's freedom is assured when Crimson agrees to paint a heroic picture of the battle for no less than Mrs. Custer.

Other honorable mentions in this category include 1982's *Savage Beauty,* by Rebecca Drury, in which "a woman discovers love on the eve of Custer's Last Stand."[66] Similarly *White Squaw,* published in 1985 by E. J. Hunter, claims: "Only the White Squaw knows her enemy's weakness and it will take more than the Big Horn to force her to her knees . . . she finds no man's challenge insurmountable—and no man's saddle too hard to ride."[67]

While such escapist fare has been aimed predominantly at women, counterparts exist for men. For example, Terry C. Johnston's writing tends to be aimed at a male audience. In his highly successful "Son of the Plains" trilogy, Johnston provides multiple perspectives on Custer and the Little Bighorn while adding a romantic twist.

The first title in the series, *Long Winter Gone,* recounts Custer's receipt of a summons from Sheridan to subdue the Indians of the Southern Plains. In the process, one of the prisoners taken at the Washita attracts Custer. This "raven-haired firebrand of only seventeen," Monaseetah, although a captive, holds Custer "hostage by her charms," and he risks his "marriage, reputation, and career for her. For in love, as on any other battlefield, Custer would never know retreat."[68]

There is one exception to this contention in that Custer abandons the woman before their son is born, leaving her behind as he did Major Elliot. He eventually pays the price in Johnston's next title, *Seize the Sky.*[69] This account brings Custer to the Little Bighorn, but rather than riding to what should have been "his greatest triumph," he instead experiences "an utterly devastating defeat that would ring through the ages and serve as a turning point in the Indian wars."

Johnston's final part of the saga, *Whisper of the Wolf,* concludes with an emphasis on Custer's son by Monaseetah. In a story somewhat reminiscent of an earlier novel, *Life and Death of Yellow Bird,* the young man takes the name of Iron Eagle when he reaches maturity.[70] Eventually he rejects the white man's road and dies at Wounded Knee. He thus shares a common bond with his father in his "warrior's spirit." Johnston ends with a synopsis of Custer's "complex personality," summarizing: "Never one to think or brood on matters, Custer took control and charged ahead. With his particular brand of luck, brash and youthful Custer landed again and again at the right place and at the right time, to become a war hero not by his skill but by his wit and courage." This conclusion echoes Van de Water, but with somewhat more sympathy for Custer.

Michael Blake, author of *Dances with Wolves,* also was more supportive of Custer in his *Marching to Valhalla: The Last Testimony of George Armstrong Custer.*[71] As the subtitle implies, the narrative gives a first-person Custer perspective. Believing that his career as a soldier is drawing to a conclusion, his marriage is on less than perfect ground, and he is probably riding on his final campaign, Autie begins to write an honest account of his life. The document is no apologia, but a labor that derives from Custer's love of writing. Nor is he motivated by a desire for material gain or to achieve further fame. Thus, for the first time, Custer candidly sets down a true record reflecting upon a career where there are few regrets. He realizes that he has been blessed, but he feels his luck is about to turn. While he harbors no death wish, Custer nevertheless finds the prospect of a warrior's end not unwelcome. Blake attempts to offer a Custer who is stripped of the myth and accessible to the reader as a man.

Regardless of whether Custer is shown in sympathetic hues or in dark tones, the Battle of the Little Bighorn con-tinues to compel fiction writers more than a century later.[72] Over these same decades, other individuals have set down their words in verse or even to music.[73] In fact, more than 150 poems have been published. No less than thirty of these were printed in 1876 alone, by both obscure and notable poets, including Henry Wadsworth Longfellow, Walt Whitman, and John Greenleaf Whittier. Perhaps one of the earliest of these outpourings, however, came not from whites, but from an Indian survivor of that June battle who, after learning that Custer had been killed during the battle, composed a "kill song." The words proclaimed:

> Long Hair has never returned,
> So his woman is crying, crying
> Looking over this way, she cries.
> Long Hair, horses I had none.
> You brought me many and I thank you.
> You make me laugh!
> Long Hair, guns I had none.
> You brought me many. . . .[74]

Such songs offered only one means used by the victorious Indians to convey their side of the story, albeit mostly for an audience of family, friends, and descendants. Oral tradition was a means of keeping the individual accounts alive for the victors.[75] But while some researchers turned to "Indian eyewitness reports," they generally eschewed this testimony in favor of conventional white sources.[76]

Even as eyewitness accounts regularly were ignored or dismissed as sources of information by the larger public, so too were American Indian visual representations of the battle.[77] Instead, the works of those who had not been on the battlefield that day gained the widest exposure and influence. In point of fact, white artists created the instantly recognizable icon that came to embody the whole Little Bighorn mystique—Custer's Last Stand.[78] Artists have produced no less than 1,327 prints, paintings, drawings, and sculptures to render this dramatic episode, as if it were as compelling a theme as the crucifixion.[79] Truly, the triangular composition of many of these works, with the focal point regularly being Custer, is reminiscent of countless depictions of the Christ suspended on the cross at Golgotha, a leitmotif perpetuated in various art forms from the Middle Ages to present times.

As might be expected, the quality of the artistic efforts varies, although this issue seems secondary to some critics, who are more focused on how accurate the images are.[80] But because there were no white survivors, the images were based only on speculations on what occurred.[81]

THE INDIAN WAR—DEATH OF GENERAL GEORGE A. CUSTER, AT THE ... OF THE LITTLE HORN RIVER, MONTANA TERR...

Within weeks of Custer's death the first of hundreds of renderings of his final moments would be created, this image appeared in The Police Gazette *for the week of July 13, 1876, and evidently is the first representation by an illustrator of what came to be known as "Custer's last Stand."*

Arguably the most famous illustration of the Little Bighorn because of widespread distribution by Anheuser-Busch. F. Otto Becker's oil on canvas Custer's Last Fight *(1895) was the basis for the mass-produced prints made of this picture. Becker borrowed extensively from another artist, Cassilly Adams.* GLEN SWANSON

Nevertheless, the first renditions of the battle were less fixed on presenting a precise history lesson and more oriented toward creating an impression about Custer's final moments. Scarcely weeks after the engagement, *The Illustrated Police Gazette* for the week of July 13 carried a front-page image with the title "The Indian War—Death of General George A. Custer." The July 19 *New York Daily Graphic* followed suit with "The Battle of the Little Big Horn River—The Death Struggle of General Custer," by William M. Cary.

These two pictures offered opposing views. The first depicts Custer's fall early in the fight, while the Cary ren-

dition shows the brave soldier as the last to stand, meeting his "fate head on, proving worthy of the mythic end that life has scripted for him."[82] It was William Cary, bolstered and refined by Alfred Waud's *Custer's Last Fight* for Whittaker's biography, that set the pattern for scores of images that followed. In fact, subsequent versions tended to be repetitive to the extent that they verged on ritualism, with Custer generally being the immediately identifiable hero.[83] Erect and assuming a spread-legged stance, Custer typically is the dominant figure, surrounded by his predestined circle battling to the last, without hope of winning, rescue, or flight, but resolute in their "determination to go down with honor."[84]

Of all the pictures that fit this formula, the so-called "Anheuser-Busch Barroom Custer," a lithograph derived from Cassilly Adams's *Custer's Last Fight*, rendered between 1878 and 1886, and F. Otto Becker's 1895 painting, no doubt gained the greatest circulation. More than 150,000 of these prints were distributed to the public by the famed St. Louis brewing company.[85]

Moreover, the appearance of this mass-produced image and previous lithographs dating as early as 1876 signaled the beginning of a long line of commercial uses for Custer and the Little Bighorn that, in terms of product and tourism promotion, continues to this day. Thus, the fact that the Becker-based interpretation achieved the greatest distribution and probably was seen by more people than any other artistic effort, including some traveling giants (such as John Mulvany's monumental 11-by-22-foot *Custer's Last Rally*, which went on tour starting in 1881), is a significant milestone in the use of Custer as a marketing tool or a commodity in and of himself.[86]

Over the years, however, painters themselves and the public seemed to have inspired fresh interpretations.[87] In part, this has been responsible in certain instances for the disappearance of Custer entirely from the plane of reference, or his relegation to a minor figure. Notable examples include Charles Russell's 1903 watercolor *1876—The Custer Fight;* W. Herbert Dunton's *The Custer Fight,* first reproduced in 1915; and William Robinson Leigh's 1939 oil on canvas, *Custer's Last Stand.*

Removing Custer as the focal point of such compositions in some sense coincides with Custer's fall from grace as a heroic icon when twentieth-century sensibilities gradually eroded Victorian ideals. Harold Von Schmidt's 1976 *Here Custer Fell* embodies the trend toward deemphasis and can be viewed as a visual counterpart to Van de Water's writings.

Despite this, even without Custer's presence, the shorthand of outnumbered whites engaged in a life or death struggle with overwhelming Indian forces has become so pervasive that the validity of such a thing as "the last stand," not just Custer's, could not be denied. This was a commonly held view that was at the very essence of what has come to be called "the Old West." The validation was in the sheer quantity of likenesses depicting such an event. How could so many pictures of the same thing not be real?[88]

So it was that by the early twentieth century, Custer and the West had become so enmeshed through many popular forms that Custer's mystique had not been exhausted. In fact, promoted by an array of wholly fabricated yet compelling images, the central figure of Little Bighorn was ripe for exploitation in other ways not previously imagined.

CHAPTER THREE

Dynamic Depictions: Melodramas, Wild West Shows, and Early Motion Pictures

Custer and the Little Bighorn were elevated to nationally recognizable symbols not long after the smoke of battle had cleared. But the drama of the man and this event went beyond static written words and pictorial works. Indeed, live action was called for to capture the dynamics of Custer's deadly duel. Consequently, it was not surprising that in 1876, four melodramas were played out on stages in the East, which capitalized on recent headlines about faraway Montana.

Among the shows was William F. "Buffalo Bill" Cody's "Red Right Hand; or, Buffalo Bill's First Scalp for Custer." This production exploited Cody's much touted hand-to-hand duel with Yellow Hair, an event that allegedly took place in the campaigns immediately after Custer's death and helped propel the frontiersman's image as the heir apparent to the stricken Yellow Hair.[1]

Soon Cody took his theatrics from the stage to the arena. In so doing, he continued to elevate the Custer saga. His motives must have included a belief that the crowd would immediately recognize the import of Little Bighorn and be induced to buy tickets. Cody settled on a bold means to bring about this result when he put none other than Custer's old nemesis, Sitting Bull, under contract. During the 1885 tour, the purported architect of Little Bighorn was paraded around in both the United States and Canada. Later audiences even had a chance to see Rain-in-the-Face, claimed to be "the man who killed Custer."[2]

Additionally, Cody included a sequence called "The Last Charge of Custer," with Buck Taylor standing in for the 7th Cavalry's heroic lieutenant colonel, as part of *The Drama of Civilization* pageant, which he incorporated into the show in late 1886. This addition commemorated the tenth anniversary of Little Bighorn.[3] For several seasons, both American and international audiences saw this action-packed rendition unfold before them. By 1893, Cody went one step further and staged a reenactment of the Last Stand as a spectacular centerpiece among the "epochs" of his traveling show.[4] This came to form the hub of his program's pageantry.[5]

With the passage of time, Cody assumed a new role and look relative to the Little Bighorn.[6] Abandoning his earlier "first scalp for Custer" rendition in vaquero outfit, he set aside the velvet jacket of dime novels and donned the buckskins dripping with fringe, cavalier boots, and wide-brimmed hat so often depicted in renderings of Custer, even trimming his hair, beard, and mustache to resemble the artists' portrayals. Thus Buffalo Bill was transformed from avenger to the reincarnation of the courageous soldier.[7]

The effect was not lost on the public. Even Elizabeth Custer commented that their maid, Eliza, having seen Buffalo Bill in the new guise, remarked, "Well, if he ain't the 'spress image of Ginnel Custer in battle, I never seed anyone that was."[8]

BATTLE OF THE LITTLE BIG HORN

FOREPAUGH'S EQUESTRIAN SPECTACULAR TRAGEDY

The years are but half a score,
And the war-whoop sounds no more
With the blast of bugles, where
Straight into a slaughter-pen,
With his doomed three hundred men,
Rode the chief with the yellow hair.
—*Whittier.*

AVIL PRINTING CO. PHILA.

DEATH OF CUSTER

Wild West shows readily drew upon the widespread name recognition that Custer had achieved by the late nineteenth century. For instance, ticket sales for Forepaugh's Wild West benefitted greatly from the addition of the Custer fight as part of the program early in the twentieth century. AUTRY MUSEUM OF WESTERN HERITAGE, LOS ANGELES

While Cody perhaps was the individual most linked with promoting Yellow Hair—after Libbie Custer, that is—others were intent on drawing upon this prominent, crowd-pleasing historic figure for their productions. Captain Jack Crawford, known as "the Poet Scout," who sometimes costared with Cody, managed to weave Custer into *On the Trail,* a "border drama" that was pronounced "historically . . . correct, and the picture of life and death in the region of the Big Horn in the year of the Custer massacre."[9]

Besides Captain Jack, one of Buffalo Bill's rival operations, Adam Forepaugh's New and Greatest All-Feature Show, incorporated its version of the same theme into a spectacle using "Custer's Last Rally" as part of *The Progress of Civilization* extravaganza. This scenario evidently continued after Forepaugh's death and the subsequent continuation of his company by James A. Bailey and James E. Cooper, with Bailey carrying on the tradition until 1911. Thereafter, the act became part of Charles H. Thompkins's

Beginning in the late 1890s, reenactments of the last stand were staged on the battlefield, as well as elsewhere, to commemorate the event and to draw tourists. In the latter instance, sometimes other locations within "Custer Country" took advantage of audience recognition of this event and performed the ritual battle, as evidenced by this early twentieth-century South Dakota version. VINCENT A. HEIER

production through 1914.[10] Evidently, even Pawnee Bill's show, which began in 1888 and merged with Cody from 1909 through 1913, included the Custer fight and eventually added Wounded Knee to the performance as well.[11]

The inclusion of this later 1890 event paralleled Buffalo Bill's own periodic overhauling of his program by inserting timely material taken from current events. In fact, Cody even replaced "Custer's Last Fight" with the "Battle of San Juan Hill," starting with the 1899 season, and went on to add "The Allied Powers at the Battle of Tien-Tsin and the Capture of Peking" for 1901 and 1902.[12] Nevertheless, by 1905, a rendition of Custer's final moments found its way back into Cody's lineup as part of the Continental tour.[13]

Wild West shows were not the only popular vehicles for re-creating the last stand. Once again, the theater was deemed ready for another show. By 1907, Charles Ulrich penned an unlikely light melodrama with comic overtones titled *On the Little Big Horn,* a script he published in Chicago.[14] At that time, the Windy City was one of the early moviemaking centers, where "Colonel" William Selig, George Kleine, and George K. Spoor actively churned out one-reelers.[15] Because Westerns had started to become box-office draws in these fledgling years of the motion-picture industry, the Custer story offered potential as a feature. Additionally, Selig may have learned about a

South Dakota reenactment of the Battle of Little Bighorn and conceived of a plan to take advantage of the cast that had been assembled for the event.[16]

This was not the first time an effort at re-creating the engagement had occurred. As part of a July 4, 1891, commemoration of Custer's death, a sham battle was played out within a mile of the present "Last Stand Hill" monument. But Indian fought Indian, because the U.S. troops were played by a company of Crow cavalry from nearby Fort Custer, while officers and their ladies from that post and civilians from Billings participated only as spectators. Subsequently, during many anniversaries of the Little Bighorn battle, troops and American Indians participated in various ways, most notably in 1909 and 1926.[17]

As part of the 1909 observance, the Burlington Railroad ran a special excursion train from Billings to the battle site for individuals who wanted to attend the performance.[18] The railroad had gone to considerable lengths to promote the ease by which travelers could reach this destination, which, advertisements claimed, was "not remote from transportation lines."[19] It was no more than 40 miles from Billings the copy continued, no farther than Washington, D.C. from Baltimore. Consequently, there was no reason for anyone not to visit the place that had become "the epitome of all that had gone before" and had come to stand for Indian warfare. Travelers were urged to visit this site, which was a worthy pilgrimage that could be made in comfort and with ease because of the railroad.[20]

Over the years, others promoted tourism to Custer Country. Whether individual entrepreneurs, organizations, or government agencies, the potential for luring tourists was worth their marketing efforts. By 1965, almost 190,000 people had come to the battlefield in one twelve-month period. Just five years later, an estimated 500,000 flocked to Custer Country.[21]

These growing numbers represented both promotion and ease of travel, as the automobile allowed visitors to easily trek to the site. The 1919 creation of the 1,500-mile Custer Highway from Omaha, Nebraska, to Glacier National Park, Montana, was just the beginning of ever-improved routes that made access possible.[22]

With this route in place, the state of Montana stepped up its program with the theme "Custer's sacrifice was not in vain." Beckoning newcomers through a promotional pamphlet that played on Yellow Hair's last written message, the publicity read, "COME ON—Montana will welcome you."[23]

With such tremendous interest in the battlefield evident even in the late nineteenth and early twentieth centuries, it's not difficult to appreciate Selig's move to make a film about an already popular subject. For one thing, he was in the process of relocating his company from Chicago to the West, where he could take advantage of both good weather and varied scenery. Indeed, this short, heavyset man of about forty, who had been a traveling salesman and magician before organizing his movie company in 1897, would help change the course of motion-picture history. In the decade after starting his business, he sent Francis Boggs to Colorado. Boggs, alongside actor-director Gilbert "Bronco Billy" Anderson, sought to use the environment and scenery of that state as a backdrop to Westerns.

By 1909, this temporary arrangement had worked so well that Selig sent Boggs to California, where he set up one of the first production companies in Hollywood. During the early silent era, Selig worked from what was then a backwater rather than the movie mecca it was to become.[24]

The public enjoyed Selig's work, which had, according to one critic of the time, a certain assurance of quality. Once he started working in the West, he turned out such titles as *In the Badlands, Pet of the Big Horn Ranch, Stampede, On the Border, Pine Ridge Feud, An Indian's Gratitude, In Old Arizona,* and *Boots and Saddles.* The last two featured the military on the frontier and might be looked upon as dress rehearsals for his most ambitious undertaking to that date, a multireel movie that bore the same title as Ulrich's play, *On the Little Big Horn,* and the alternate title of *Custer's Last Stand.*[25]

In this, the original silver-screen treatment of Custer, Selig accomplished what few future productions ever repeated, sending his company on location to Montana, as well as helping introduce future cowboy star Tom Mix into the genre, albeit in a minor capacity.[26] This 1909 effort constituted an ambitious undertaking because of the rather extensive cast Selig employed. Indeed, the picture was on a grand scale by standards of the period. Hundreds of local Crows, along with a number of national guardsmen as the cavalry contingent, assembled as reenactors for Selig's interpretation of Custer's activities on the Plains. The crew and actors intrigued local newsmen sent out from Billings. One of the reporters noted that Custer, played by Capt. Paul McCormick, a Montana national guard officer, was the last one remaining alive, throwing away his saber to keep fighting with the twelve rounds left in his pair of revolvers. At the final moment, with only a single shot left, he placed one of the pistols to his temple. He then squeezed the trigger, and the discharged blank "fairly lifted him off the ground."[27]

It is uncertain whether Selig's version, now lost to history, as is the case with most nitrate movies, used this sequence or another one filmed in the studio back in Chicago. It is known that the story opened with the arrest of Rain-in-the-Face for the murder of two civilians. This event then provided the background for the battle along the banks of the Greasy Grass.

Later Custer movies followed Selig's lead but often turned this incident into a set piece, molding it indiscriminately to fit their plot lines. As a result, such films helped perpetuate and further distort the already dubious Rain-in-the-Face account, which first appeared in a sensational newspaper article of July 1876. According to this account, Rain-in-the-Face sought revenge on Yellow Hair's younger brother because of supposed wrongs perpetrated by that member of the Custer clan. Henry Wadsworth Longfellow's highly dramatized poem *The Revenge of Rain in the Face* helped fix the purported incident in the public mind.[28] Screenwriters hastened to include this popular saga in their plots, and with each successive telling, the legend gained further strength.

Besides setting the stage for future imitators, Selig adopted a pro-Custer stance, characterizing him as a soldier of "proven dash, courage and bravery." Moreover, the script blamed Maj. Marcus Reno for Custer's undoing. The film presented Reno as a coward, who was distrusted by some of Custer's loyal officers. They had warned their leader not to rely on the major. Reno was not the only one to be vilified, however. According to one review, Selig's Indians were a "band of naked painted devils." Portraying the Indian participants as savages further indicated Selig's reverent view toward Custer.

From this point to nearly the end of the silent era, Custer was portrayed as a hero. Likewise, Selig's introduc-

The Indians triumph in Selig's 1909 On the Little Big Horn. VINCENT A. HEIER

Custer first came to the silver screen in 1909 as a brave and noble role model worthy of the youth of America, a depiction which was found in other popular forms prior to On the Little Big Horn's *premier.* MOTION PICTURE ACADEMY OF ARTS AND SCIENCES

tion of a romance—here between a fictional 7th Cavalry officer, Lieutenant Glenn, and the post commander's daughter, Dollie—was repeated in various forms throughout many of the Custer films.

In Selig's case, Custer interacts with Dollie, who induces him to send her young suitor back to safety as soon as danger arises. This intercession thereby spares the young officer from sharing Custer's fate. In the next scene, Custer and some of his subordinates observe the village through field glasses. Custer leads the attack, with the undependable Reno taking command of the supporting column instead of taking the advance assault toward the village. This action suits Rain-in-the-Face, who draws the cavalry into a trap.

Knowing the aggressive enemy leader cannot resist, the Indians tantalize Long Hair. Custer orders the charge as the enemy flees. At the gallop, the 7th goes after their quarry, who use the terrain to elude their pursuers. The troopers spur their mounts and close, but as they crest the bluff, the men realize too late what is in store. There, "stretched away as far as the eye can reach, upright and naked on their ponies they sit, three thousand Sioux warriors, waiting for the handful of white soldiers to be brought to the slaughter."[29]

Undaunted, Custer rallies his command. While he makes for higher ground, Reno's officers hear the volley that greets Custer's cavalrymen. They beg Reno to ride in support, but he does not. The Indians overpower Custer's detachment, stampeding the troopers' horses, which are left without a means of retreat. Soon "the brave little band" is cut down to forty-one men.[30] News of the defeat reaches Fort Lincoln two days later, as does Lieutenant Glenn, after the young officer is captured by the Sioux on his way back to the post but manages to escape.

Selig's 1909 effort, then, incorporated much of the classic lore of the Last Stand from previous literature, thereby establishing a model for future cinematic renditions.

Three years later, director Thomas H. Ince decided to try his hand at dramatizing the Custer saga.[31] In 1912, he brought out *Custer's Last Fight* for Bison Films, an independent New York production company.[32] This midsummer release coincided with the thirty-sixth anniversary of the battle. It resembled its predecessor in numerous ways, especially by attempting to follow certain incidents leading up to Custer's ill-fated actions. These included the killing of a pair of whites whom Ince cast as "two quiet and inoffensive . . . amateur naturalists." The men manage to stray into Indian territory by accident, only to become victims of Rain-in-the-Face. Later, the warrior boasts of this deed at the agency. Learning of the matter,

Custer sends his brother, who arrests the "powerful savage." Rain-in-the-Face eventually escapes imprisonment and makes his way to Sitting Bull's village, where he plans his revenge.

The plot jumps to 1876, with Custer heading into the field with orders "to drive Sitting Bull and his hostiles back to their reservation." Mrs. Custer accompanies her husband for a while, then turns back to Fort Lincoln. She will never see her beloved Autie again. The scenario then moves forward to Custer's splitting of his command and preparation for the attack.

After the first contact with the enemy, an "incompetent" Reno falters. His retreat leaves Custer open to the overwhelming forces of Gall's warriors. The 7th Cavalry's commander falls in a noble effort to repel overwhelming odds.

Thus Custer continued to be seen in a favorable light. Elizabeth Custer also has a more prominent place in Ince's treatment.[33] Ince attempted to pay attention to details Selig had ignored. This was in keeping with his style and a general trend in the early film industry, which claimed that its products provided education and enlightenment as much as entertainment.

Custer's Last Fight embodied costume dramas in that this genre is pedantic from its earliest appearance. Ince sought to create a look or feel rather than concern himself with accuracy. Instead, he and others strove for authenticity to convince the audience that what they were seeing rang true in order to carry the storyline. Another common element represented by this type of approach was the contest "between the opposing forces of history, biography, and fact against authenticity and the free-thinking, freehanded, movie-to-movie exchange of generic modes," all of which is influenced by a tendency to employ the past as a platform to explore present issues.[34] Such films then depended upon creating images that appeared authentic to the viewers of the period when the movie was made, and not the era being represented. In fact, the farther away in time the production was from the actual event, the more it tended to stray from the historical basis for the story.

Custer's Last Fight offered many examples of this. For instance, the Sioux were "terrible fighters, but aside from their bravery were as destitute of nobility as other savage races. They were merciless to the weak, inhuman in their outrages on white women and children and incapable of gratitude."[35]

Custer's long, flowing hair was one of Ince's other concessions in keeping with a commonly held stereotype. Likewise, Ince obviously drew upon F. Otto Becker's painting of the Last Stand, using this image as a model

Promoters of the 1912 release of Custer's Last Fight *used publicity stills that drew directly from the famed Anheuser-Busch "Barroom Custer" and a side panel from Cassilly Adams's circa 1886 oil on canvas rendering of Custer in death.* GLEN SWANSON

for the heroic saber-slashing demise of the Boy General. This detail contradicts the fact that sabers generally were not carried into the battle by the 7th Cavalry that day.[36]

Nonetheless, the ready identification of this scene, which graced many saloons and homes at the time because Anheuser-Busch had made prints available through widespread distribution, was good showmanship, if poor history, on Ince's part. No matter, this image was fixed in the minds of many of the viewers as reality. Including such recognizable elements helped give credence to Ince's production as far as the general audience was concerned.[37]

Others may have disagreed with Ince in this regard, but certainly they saw the potential for ticket sales from the popularity of the Custer tale. David W. Griffith began work on his own version of the story the same year as Ince.[38] Destined to become famous himself, Griffith, a

romanticist, used many of his budding cinematic skills in *The Massacre*—skills that would be honed in *Birth of a Nation* and *Intolerance,* as well as many of the other 450 titles he made for Biograph from 1911 through 1913. The plot took a new twist in that the story did not deal with the historical figure of Custer. Instead, his presentation alluded to the date 1876 and "one of the most deadly massacres and Indian fights of the period."[39]

In addition, *The Massacre* contrasted with previous representations in its general antiwar overtones, and Griffith tended to be somewhat more sympathetic in his views of Indian people. Above all, Griffith's pictures carried morality messages as an integral part of the story.[40]

In this sense, some have faulted Griffith as being sentimental or maudlin. He has been accused of seeing "life through Victorian opera glasses." His fair-haired heroines were frail and his dark villains depraved. Though he was known for his personal "kindliness and consideration," Griffith held strong convictions and prejudices. His firmly fixed viewpoint, coupled with the tendency to "set himself up as historian-philosopher," resulted in film subtitles that pontificated or were overly authoritative.[41]

Whether any of these alleged faults contributed to the delayed release of *The Massacre* cannot be determined. Whatever the reasons, the picture did not reach theaters until two years after its completion. In fact, other productions used the Custer figure before that: *Campaigning with Custer* and *Camping with Custer,* both from 1913, and possibly the same film.[42]

Then, in 1914, the first of many satires about Custer was released as *Colonel Custard's Last Stand.* In this light fare, Indians besiege a fort, and Colonel Custard's daughter Molly escapes to find help, which "her comic lover" eventually provides.[43]

A 1915 release, *Custer's Last Scout,* likewise revolved around a romantic entanglement, but with more serious overtones.[44] This rather jumbled scenario concentrated not on Custer, but on one of his scouts, Alfred A. Chapman, a character loosely based on one of many claimants who vied for the title of sole survivor of Little Bighorn.[45] The film version of this frontiersman competes with one of the 7th Cavalry's captains for the affections of the heroine, Marjorie Woodruff.

The pair of characters top the list of suitors at the fort, and Marjorie's brother, a lieutenant himself, favors his fellow officer, Captain Bates. Woodruff sees Bates as an equal, while he views his sister's possible union with Chapman as a misalliance. Ultimately her brother's wishes take precedence. She accepts Bates's proposal. Marjorie writes a note with this news, sending it along with a trooper to inform Chapman of her decision. Her brother intercepts the message and confiscates the important document.

At the same time, Lieutenant Woodruff and another officer by the name of Kane set out with two enlisted men to hunt antelope. The Indians come upon them and kill the group, save for one enlisted man. Hiding in the underbrush, he makes his getaway.

Captain Bates, en route to Fort Rice, finds the bodies of the three other men and discovers the note to Chapman. Bates suspects Chapman of foul play and rushes to Custer with an accusation. With the note as evidence, Custer calls for the scout's arrest.

By chance, the lone survivor from Lieutenant Woodruff's party is found alive. He explains everything and clears Chapman, who then goes along with Tom Custer to apprehend Rain-in-the-Face for his part in the

hunting party incident. This move enrages the local Indians, and an uprising erupts. Washington orders Custer to put down the outbreak. Chapman joins the expedition, only to be captured and tortured, but he manages to flee his captors in order to warn Major Reno's besieged contingent about the fate of their lieutenant colonel. Here, he finds Bates severely wounded and personally conveys him back to Marjorie. She "weeps as she thanks the faithful scout." In true Western hero style, Chapman grins and rides off into the proverbial sunset.[46]

From this point forward, subsequent motion pictures on the subject tended to stray from the facts with equal abandon. For instance, in another 1915 feature, *In the Days of '75 and '76,* Custer appears momentarily as part of a formula, giving scouting assignments to two of the main characters, "Wild Bill" Hickok and "Calamity Jane," in the first of many cinematic links of this trio.[47] Here was the progenitor of linking historical Western personalities together as a means of providing a means to give a feel of reality to fictional film portrayals.

The next year, *Britton of the Seventh,* the first Custer film to be taken from a novel, once more assigns Yellow Hair second place in a romantic melodrama, with the Little Bighorn as a backdrop to lend authenticity to the plot.[48] Designed to be projected one reel a week for four consecutive weeks, this early serial, or forerunner to the miniseries, revolved around the central character, Lt. Tony Britton.[49] In flashback form, Britton, as a grandfather, tells of his thrilling life some forty years earlier when Rain-in-the-Face, after killing two troopers from Fort Lincoln "for the love of Otonawah, an Indian maiden," is sought for murder. Britton is sent to take the accused man into custody. In so doing, he deprives Tom Custer of his usual place in previous plots. In fact, subsequent films seldom mention Custer's younger brother. Later, Britton is forced to resign his commission to avoid a court-martial after being wrongfully accused of becoming involved with the wife of one of the captains at the fort. This poor women, Frances Grason, loves Britton but is doomed to remain with her worthless, brutish husband.

Tony, now a civilian, returns to the army as a scout. In this capacity, he comes to the aid of Custer with a warning about "a horde of over a thousand Indians on the warpath." Custer responds, deploying his troops. Because of Reno's hesitancy, Custer's brave command is annihilated.[50]

Again a scapegoat is found for Yellow Hair. Once more the hero manages to avoid the fate of his commander, because Britton survives. Cleared of past accusations, he regains his commission, thereby enabling him to win the leading lady, Barbara Manning.[51]

Often Custer was cast more as a father figure than a dashing romantic lead, in some respects as an outgrowth of many juvenile fiction works that were written in the Victorian era and thereafter. Dwight Crittenden's Custer in Bob Hampton of Placer *(1921) was one such example of this aging process for the films.* AUTRY MUSEUM OF WESTERN HERITAGE, LOS ANGELES

In reality, this 1916 interpretation represented little more than a hybrid of the films made prior to this time. With few exceptions, this proved the case for the remainder of the silent era and the decades that immediately followed.

One has only to look at the next release, *Bob Hampton of Placer* (1921), to demonstrate this point. The script, based on Randall Parrish's 1910 novel of that title, revolves around the main character, former army officer Bob Hampton, who has been charged with a crime he did not commit, the murder of Major Brant. The convention of false accusation harkens back to many Charles King novels about the frontier army and found its way into numerous later theatrical works about the military in the West. After serving a prison sentence, he heads west to become a gambler and gunfighter. Later, he helps save a wagon train from destruction by attack. In the caravan, he finds a young woman known as "The Kid," who turns out to be his daughter. Shortly thereafter, a man who was responsible for the misdeed confesses, thereby exonerating Hampton. This means that his daughter may now marry Major Brant's son, who is also an officer. Hampton rides off to join Custer as a scout at the Little Bighorn.[52]

If this all sounds faintly familiar, it's no coincidence. The rudimentary story had become a convention by this point. As such, *The Massacre, Britton of the Seventh,* and *Bob Hampton of Placer* shared main basic plot devices in keeping with the derivative nature that had come to characterize the Western even at this early stage.

Another familiar device, the cameo use of Custer, was evident in the 1923 feature *Wild Bill Hickok*. This picture also related the 7th Cavalry's leader to other personages of the American West, including not only Hickok and

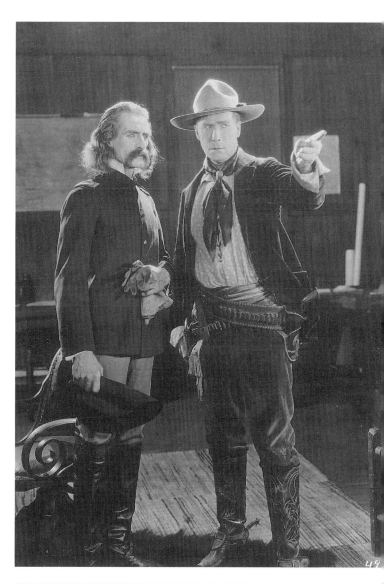

TOP RIGHT: *Charles Dudley performed as Custer opposite William S. Hart, who took the title role in* Wild Bill Hickok *(1923), as one of the several instances where screenwriters brought together major historical characters as part of the cast. Once again, Custer was presented as a much older man than the historic persona being portrayed, but the long hair and enormous mustache signal the audience that this is nonetheless a recognizable rendition of the Little Bighorn's defeated cavalryman.* SEAVER CENTER FOR WESTERN HISTORY, LOS ANGELES COUNTY MUSEUM OF NATURAL HISTORY

BOTTOM RIGHT: *The title character of* Bob Hampton of Placer, *portrayed by James Kirkwood, is found alive after Custer's Last Stand. The lone white survivor is a recurring role in both literature, film, and television, in order to provide the audience with an eyewitness account of what took place at Little Bighorn.* AUTRY MUSEUM OF WESTERN HERITAGE, LOS ANGELES

Ince's 1912 feature was repackaged and released in 1925 just prior to the fiftieth anniversary of Little Bighorn. AUTRY MUSEUM OF WESTERN HERITAGE, LOS ANGELES

Calamity Jane, but also "Bat" Masterson. The sprinkling of such famous names continued in a number of subsequent films in which fictional characters mingled with famous individuals on screen. These historical personages were transportable personalities that allowed the viewers to feel as if they were "insiders who know more than others on the screen" or served as "an *aide-memoire* for the time travelers in the audience."[53]

In this show, Wild Bill Hickok (William S. Hart) hangs up his shooting irons when he arrives in Dodge City. Hickok finds the town so lawless, however, that he asks Custer, who has held Bill's weapons for him, to give him back the six-guns so he can cleanse the town of its lawless element.[54]

Even as Hart employed Custer as a set piece, the time approached for consideration of the forthcoming seventy-fifth anniversary of Little Big Horn. With this in mind, Ince's *Custer's Last Fight* was resurrected, and with reworked title cards and some additional footage, it was reissued in 1925.

That same year, *The Scarlet West* also found Custer a place in movie theaters. But in *The Scarlet West,* Custer was not the hero but played a minor role. Instead, the audience followed the tribulations of Captain Cardelanche, an American Indian. After being educated in the East, Cardelanche returns to his home in the West. There he is shunned by his people, despite the fact that he is the son of their chief.

Cut off from his family and former friends, Cardelanche sets out to carve a niche for himself elsewhere. One day he saves a detachment from nearby Fort Remington (perhaps so named in the script as a tribute or nod to the Western artist), which earns him a commission in the cavalry. Cardelanche takes his station at the fort, where he falls in love with Miriam, the post commander's daughter, played by the "It" girl, Clara Bow.

Another officer, Lieutenant Parkman, also wants to marry the young woman, and the two suitors clash. Parkman's superiors reduce him to the ranks because of the fight.

When Cardelanche's people join in the fight against Custer, he realizes that he must abandon hope of winning Miriam. He resigns his commission and adopted way of life and returns to help his people.[55] In so doing, he fits into the tradition James Fenimore Cooper established in his "Leatherstocking" tales, in which the hero cannot marry the heroine because of the convention that frowned on mixed marriages.[56] Cardelanche struggles against prejudice. Like Cooper's Uncas, he cannot fit into white society or marry someone of another race.

The artifice of regaining a lost love resurfaced in the next Custer-related release, *The Flaming Frontier,* a picture Universal Studios' 1926 advertisements boasted of in terms of "historical accuracy," which supposedly elevated this film to the level of the 1923 blockbuster *The Covered Wagon.*[57] Because that epic picture had demonstrated the power of big-budget Westerns during a period when the genre had temporarily waned, making such claims must have seemed good advertising.[58]

In reality, it's difficult to imagine how accurate the film could have been when the locations were in Pendleton, Oregon, and the San Fernando Valley, near Universal Studios headquarters. Regardless, Universal hired Col. George S. Byram, West Point Class of 1885, to oversee military details and, according to the spin doctors at the studio, even interviewed Indian scouts and veterans.[59] Despite these supposed efforts at veracity, *The Flaming Frontier* was a hodgepodge of almost every conceivable facet of the West, including the blending of the Pony Express and Custer's Little Bighorn expedition, although these elements took place a decade and a half apart. Such errors were unimportant to the studio officials, who were more intent on promoting the movie's star, Hoot Gibson, than realistically portraying the past.

This was so because Gibson, as Bob Langdon, a former Pony Express rider turned West Pointer, was at the peak of his career. Usually known for his combination of comedy and contemporary story lines, Gibson set aside his regular screen persona to appear in this costume drama, an occasional departure from character allowed by Universal for their successful cowboy star and leading man. In fact, the studio lavished money on publicity for the production and for battle scenes directed by Edward Sedgwick, who also wrote the story.

The opening-night program for the show set up the central conflict: "In 1876 the tide of civilization is steadily pushing Westward. The Indians are growing restless and jealous of the advancing whites."[60] The two sides were going to clash on the plains as settlers and soldiers headed westward, while "politicians and profiteers" in Washington sold liquor and weapons to the Indians. Enter Bob Langdon, a devil-may-care Pony Express rider whom Custer has befriended.

Through Custer and Senator Stanwood, Langdon secures an appointment to West Point. There he meets the senator's son Lawrence. He also is introduced to the senator's daughter Betty, with the immediate and predictable result that the two become infatuated with each other.

The Scarlet West *(1925) rendered Custer's Last Stand in traditional form, with pistol packing Yellow Hair standing in the center of the fray blazing away with his revolver.* BRIAN W. DIPPIE

Publicity for Universal's Flaming Frontier *(1926) styled Custer (played by veteran silent actor Dustin Farnum) as "The Bravest Man That Ever Lived" and invited movie-goers to "See His Sublime Courage . . ."* UNIVERSAL PICTURES. MOTION PICTURE ACADEMY OF ARTS AND SCIENCES

As Langdon's new life in the East unfolds, Custer is seeking to bring peace in the West. He clashes with the profiteers who attempt to discredit him with President Grant. Senator Stanwood assists Custer in his cause.

The senator is singled out by the plotters. They send Lucretia Bleden to West Point. She is able to create a scandal, once she brings Stanwood's son under her spell. To shield the senator's family, Langdon takes the blame and is expelled.

He returns to Custer's command, where by this time tensions have increased. The Indians, aided by renegade whites, unite under Sitting Bull. Custer, misled as to the Indians' strength, attacks their village with 400 men against the enemy's thousands.

He dispatches Langdon with a message for Reno to come at once. Reno fails. Custer and his command are wiped out, to the joy of the profiteers.

Of course, good triumphs in the end. Custer's death will not be in vain, as Langdon rights the wrongs and wins the hand of the leading lady, Anne Cornwall, whom studio publicists claimed was an army brat born at Fort Hamilton, New York, and in real life was married to 7th Cavalry officer Capt. Charles Maigne. Additionally, copy claimed, "over two thousand Indians, cavalrymen and scouts were used in this one big scene [the Last Stand] alone."

Recognizing the importance of the jubilee of Little Bighorn, Dustin Farnum agreed to come out of retirement from films to be in *Flaming Frontier.* In preparation for his role as Custer, he read extensively on the general and the massacre. He would be paired off against Noble Johnson, a noted African American actor of the era who would portray Sitting Bull.

Supposedly, the film's producers "went to extreme measures to reproduce the Battle of the Little Big Horn, better known as the Custer Massacre, in faithful detail. . . . Military men say the resulting pictures are the most realistic ever screened of Indian-soldier struggles."[61] Other forms of promotion included glass slides with images related to the film that would be projected to announce the picture as a coming attraction.[62] As another means to entice audiences, Universal sent a "Radiomobile" across the country with calliope, microphone, and promotional posters to drum up crowds, and went one step further by a mass mailing to schools espousing the "patriotic and educational" qualities of the picture, a not uncommon ploy in future renditions of the Custer saga.[63]

If *The Flaming Frontier* had its faults, *General Custer at Little Big Horn,* which was released only three days later, on September 15, 1926, seemingly lacked any redeeming attributes. Described as having "only a slight story line, which attempts to interject some romance," the low-budget oater was destined to disappear without a trace.[64] But there are some points worth mentioning, one of which is the similarity between the main character of the film, Lem Hawks, to Langdon and Chapman. Hawks is a scout and rival suitor for the leading lady.[65] Replete with ornate frontiersman costume, he overshadows Yellow Hair not only in garb, but also because of his central place in the film. Thus Custer the hero had given way to Custer the supporting character.[66]

Of even more consequence, though, is the picture's presentation of the Indians who face Hawks, Custer, and the other whites. Attired in Plains regalia, these noble chiefs proclaim that the injustices visited upon them by the intruders have forced the Indians to take up arms to defend what is theirs.[67]

Another 1926 entry, *The Last Frontier,* made no effort to explain Indian viewpoints. This was simply a cowboy saga, with the protagonist, Tom Kirby, played by handsome leading man William Boyd in his pre–Hopalong Cassidy days, struggling with archvillain Lige Morris to gain heroine Beth Halliday's love. After failure at first, what

was he to do to be worthy of his lady fair? Join Custer as a scout, of course, while also crossing paths with Wild Bill and Buffalo Bill. Eventually Kirby overcomes all obstacles, and when Morris is killed, nothing stands in the way of a union with Beth.[68] Again, Custer is a distant second to the main thrust of "good guy defeats bad guy to win the girl."

The final entry of the decade into the Custer film cycle, *Spoilers of the West* (1927), starred another well-known cowboy performer, Tim McCoy, as Lieutenant Lang. A veteran of World War I and the former adjutant general of the national guard in Wyoming, McCoy brought a certain military bearing and realism to the screen. Among other things, he had made several films that revolved around martial topics.

In this instance, the story is set in 1868. Trappers invade Indian land. President Andrew Johnson sends out a peace commission to quiet the situation, but Red Cloud will not be placated.

Custer thinks that Lang, because of his knowledge of sign language and Indian ways, might be able to avert an uprising with a regiment in support. Gen. William Sherman tells Custer that the use of such troop strengths ended with the Civil War. Cutting Custer off in this way, Sherman informs Lang that the young officer will have to accomplish his mission with a small contingent of Indian police.

At one point, the force proves too small. Lang requires reinforcements from a cavalry patrol. Fighting continues. Finally, Lang secures Red Cloud's promise that he will cease hostilities long enough for the lieutenant to make one last effort to remove the bone of contention, a trading post run by a young woman.

The dashing lieutenant seizes the establishment. The young woman surrenders to Lang and leaves the area. Red Cloud acknowledges that Lang kept his word. He shakes hands with Sherman and signs a treaty. Lang receives congratulations from Sherman and Custer, while Lang's lovely prisoner is brought forward. After giving her a lecture, Sherman sentences her to life in Lang's custody.[69]

McCoy's film brought about what appeared to be an end of an era. Custer had become little more than a secondary element—a bit of set dressing, like the stockaded fort or other Hollywood conventions that had become routine during the silent era. By this time, Custer seemed destined to disappear or play only a minor part in future motion pictures. Several factors could have led to Custer's fading. For one thing, the silent era had used and reused him to the point of possible overexposure. Had he become a cliché for the majority of the viewing public?

Moreover, the audience's increasing distance from the actual period of Custer's life might have meant that there was less immediacy to his name and time, along with a concurrent lack of identification with him or the West. This may have been one reason why the Western experienced considerable peaks and valleys during the 1920s, when, despite the financial success of *The Covered Wagon,* followed by a high-water mark in production of no less than 227 oaters in 1925, the genre slipped into a momentary decline. Thereafter, no more than 150 Westerns per year were ever released by the Hollywood's film factories.[70]

Changing public attitudes also may have altered views toward Custer during the 1920s. Could the hundreds of thousands of Yanks who went to Europe ever regain the innocent hero worship of their youth in the wake of brutal trench warfare? Melodramas featuring Custer and Wild West shows were things of the past, when the dead lay buried under rows and rows of white markers across the sea, and the physically or emotionally maimed doughboys of the Great War became a grim reality. In such an atmosphere, the bold cavalier Custer's stock had declined. Accordingly, his place as the central figure in most pre–World War I films, such as Selig's pioneer picture, had given way to a much lesser position as supporting character, a function that began as early as *Custer's Last Scout.* Indeed, Custer could even be lampooned or made the butt of humor. And finally, during the time before movies added sound, he could be replaced entirely, a surrogate serving the same purpose as Griffith had introduced in *The Massacre.* Hence as both the decade and the age of silent films drew to parallel closes, all of Custer's cinematic functions had been established.

By that point, the country seemed torn between the old-fashioned values of sobriety and morality that gave rise to prohibition and film censorship on one hand, and the "live-for-today" approach of the flapper and speakeasy generation on the other.[71] These opposing and complex views, along with major economic downturns and technical innovations in film as the 1930s approached, meant that Custer was momentarily set adrift.

At first, this downward trend was most evident in large-budget productions, which, after the devastating stock market crash of 1929, seemed too costly for studios to consider. Ironically, that year, the best-actor Oscar went to Warner Baxter at the fledgling Academy Awards, but even this success did not persuade the large production companies to invest in expensive Westerns. One notable exception was *The Big Trail,* a 1930 vehicle that failed to propel its young main character, the former Marion Morrison, under his stage name of John Wayne, into stardom and was a disappointment to its investors.[72] Most major movie moguls wanted to avoid this same fate, even after

another blockbuster Western, *Cimarron,* took the Oscar as best picture in 1931.

But it was not just the Western that failed to attract customers to the movies. In general, the Depression caused a temporary decrease in film attendance. Even the growing number of talkies could not overcome the widespread economic woes and bring back viewers.

In fact, converting over from silent films was just one more factor that caused Westerns to slump.[73] Wide-open space was a key to the genre. Conversely, early sound technology required a controlled environment that at first could be achieved only in specially built, constricted facilities. At the outset, these sound stages were few and far between because of the high price that had to be paid for their construction. Camera and recording equipment required considerable outlay as well. Then, too, large numbers of smaller theaters had little cash to replace their old silent equipment with updated projectors, add speakers, and make other outlays to accommodate the cinema's newfound voice.

So even though movies no longer would be mute, it appeared that the Western might be abandoned. This proved only a brief setback, though. In a move to woo moviegoers back to the silver screen, the idea of the double bill was inaugurated. The main feature would be an A film, with noted leading actors and actresses, along with all the window dressing, and the opening picture would be a B film, often from one of the lesser production companies that churned out inexpensive shows, to round out the program. Now the public would get more for their money and, theoretically, would be willing to part with scarce cash to take in a double feature.

While this was only one of several schemes to attract audiences, it proved to have a lasting effect. Westerns were ideal for the B market because they were cheap to make, although this meant that the sound quality had to be sacrificed, and they had ready market appeal. As such, the genre was on the rebound. By 1932, Western production was higher than the levels experienced at the conclusion of the silent age.[74]

Perhaps this rekindled interest in Westerns also had something to do with people's desire to look to a period before the Depression when there was relative security, prosperity, and optimism. The heroes of the past and mythlike image of America's "golden age" loomed large in importance.[75] In this environment, biopictures spotlighting great figures from bygone times not only from the United States, such as Abraham Lincoln, but also from elsewhere, including Émile Zola, Louis Pasteur, and Benito Juárez, were provided by the major studios, along with other period or costume dramas. Yet Custer was conspicuously absent from the scene.

Although at first blush it seems that he should have been an ideal figure for the costume dramas that became a staple during the lean decade of the 1930s, perhaps his sullied image at Van de Water's hands made him suspect among some studio heads. But at least one of these movers and shakers, Mervyn Leroy, was a producer who knew how to package such pictures with their message tailor-made for a Depression-weary audience. He was not afraid to include Custer if he thought the character had a use. In *The World Changes,* based on Sheridan Gibey's *America Kneels,* Leroy gave viewers a lesson in the shifting fortunes of time.

Starting in the 1850s, the audience follows an adventuresome Ordin Nordholm, Jr., played by Paul Muni, who arguably was the king of the 1930s biopicture. Nordholm sets out for the promise of the West, first to Texas, then the Dakotas. Along the way, Custer and Buffalo Bill pass through Nordholm's life, which is a series of ups and downs as he attempts to achieve the American dream, only to be dashed by personal tragedy and the crash of the stock market in 1929. Here again, Custer is only a bit player—part of a stock company of recognizable historical personalities used to add credence to the story being told. More to the point, the fictional character is the focal point, not Custer or Cody, and in this case Muni's performance was praised for its breadth and seriousness.[76]

But not all films of the time delivered such sober messages. Instead, most pictures steered away from the harsh realities of soup lines, mass unemployment, and other depictions of the Depression. Escapist monster movies, gangster films, Busby Berkeley musicals, and screwball comedies were the rage.[77]

Even Custer was not immune from such lighter fare, which also included the serials that attempted to get audiences to return week after week to find out what happened to the hero and heroine.[78] The combination of Custer and the weekly cliff-hangers held promise for producers and theater owners bent on bringing back the crowds during this economically difficult period, just as the double feature had been designed to do. During the 1930s, three such serials used Custer as little more than a prop for his name recognition.

The first of this trio was RKO and Van Beuren's *The Last Frontier* (1932). This expanded version of the 1926 feature by the same name rearranged components of the plot from the earlier melodrama.[79] In the serial version, a dozen chapters allowed for nearly every cliché, including the unlikely presence of the "Black Ghost," a mysterious masked hero who provides assistance to Custer from time to time. (See appendix C for an episodic synopsis of this and the other two serials of the 1930s.) As the first episode unfolds, Custer speaks to his subordinate, Colonel Halliday, about gun smugglers who are arming the Indians with late-model weapons that are better than those carried by the soldiers. This is "a disgrace to the army," says Custer. The situation has to be stopped. Custer tells Halliday that he personally will intervene if the problem is not resolved.

One of the chief forces in speaking out against the gun runners, Tom Kirby (the same character name and basic plot from the silent version of the film), is a local newspaperman and a Zorro-like figure incognito. Kirby disagrees with Lige Morris, a local prominent citizen who secretly heads the gang. Morris tells Custer and his subordinate that the Indians do not know any better than to raid and go on the warpath. Kirby responds, "They know how to tomahawk our women and children; they know how to shoot guns and kill soldiers." Custer agrees with Kirby.

Having added the novelty of this masked avenger, the story carries on with a number of typical conventions, including an attack on a wagon train; an Indian raid against the town; wagons going over cliffs, exploded by gun powder, or turned over amidst a buffalo stampede with Kirby, (a.k.a. the Black Ghost) who narrowly escapes from death with Colonel Halliday's spunky daughter Betty. There are also a sidekick, Happy; a foundling, Aggie, whom the hero had rescued years earlier from an Indian attack; and a character called Wild Bill, presumably based upon James Butler Hickok, this last role going to stuntman and future second unit director Yakima Canutt.

Despite the efforts of Tom and Betty, Lige Morris's gang manages to continue its deadly supply to the Plains Indians, making it possible for them to strike Custer and destroy his command.[80] Hence, a white renegade betrays the troopers by providing the wherewithal for the Indians to overcome the soldiers.

The second serial to employ Yellow Hair, the fifteen-episode *Custer's Last Stand,* also issued in a feature version, had a few interesting slants, including a fairly significant role for Mrs. Custer. The picture also had its own version of the Little Bighorn fight, with Rex Lease as Scout "Kit" Cardigan, who valiantly but futilely attempts to assist Custer in the final battle.

This cliff-hanger from Weiss Productions promised to be "a significant contribution to that all-too-small film library of Americana." Once more, publicity compared the picture's quality to that of *The Covered Wagon,* claiming *Custer's Last Stand* to be "an authoritative and definitive

By the advent of early sound films, Yellow Hair (Frank McGlynn, Jr.) continued to devolve into a worn cliché and almost exclusively appeared in a cameo capacity through the 1930s, in such oaters as the fifteen-episode serial Custer's Last Stand *(1936). This production had very little to do with the 7th Cavalry's lieutenant colonel or his famous final fight, although the press book for this serial promised theater owners that the production was "An authentic dramatization of one of the most thrilling episodes in American history." Such superlatives were hype.* AUTRY MUSEUM OF WESTERN HERITAGE, LOS ANGELES

dramatization of the American Indian's last stand against the westward progress of white civilization."[81]

Despite this assertion, the product was far different from publicity promises. Kit spends much of his time rescuing Barbara Trent and her brother Bobby from the clutches of evil white men and rampaging Indians. One film historian's summary struck the mark, characterizing *Custer's Last Stand* as "a topheavy plot" with almost every conceivable Western cliché.[82]

Nearly the same assessment could be made in regard to the third serial, *Oregon Trail* (1939). This fifteen-episode thriller paralleled *Custer's Last Fight* in several ways, including the presence of Jimmie, a boy with grit, as a draw for juvenile viewers, and Margaret Mason, a damsel in distress, to provide the love interest for scout Jeff Scott.

Scott is a frontiersman who works as an undercover agent for the government. He has been sent by the authorities in Washington to stop raids along Francis Parkman's famous road. In the end, Jeff, with Custer's periodic assistance, defeats Sam Morgan and his gang of henchmen under Bull Bragg. At last, peace comes to ensure that Paradise Valley can live up to its name.[83]

Whereas these serials contained simple messages and left something to be desired in terms of production values, the next celluloid attempt, the 1937 blockbuster *The Plainsman*, achieved a more favored niche in film annals. Once again, this epic, starring Gary Cooper and Jean Arthur, was compared to *The Covered Wagon*. *The Plainsman's* significant budget, notable cast, and famed director, C. B. DeMille, provided its memorable moments, including sequences using Wyoming national guardsmen around Pole Mountain for Custer's final battle. Yet the film was no better in its historical accuracy than most and in fact was worse than some of the previous productions.[84]

One aspect that proved somewhat novel, however, was the depiction of Custer's final actions. Cooper, as Wild Bill Hickok, comes upon an Indian brave leading a trooper's horse and carrying a trophy guidon bearing 7th Cavalry markings. Hickok captures the man, played by Anthony Quinn. He questions the captive with the aid of his friend Buffalo Bill Cody (James Ellison). While a flashback provides a heroic final look at Custer, the brave tells the pair about how Yellow Hair fell, giving an account of the scene in a contrived native tongue. This is one of the few times that the battle is shown from the American Indian's point of view.[85]

As lavish as *The Plainsman* was, Custer was little more than a stock player in the plot. Another 1937 release played on the name recognition of many of same characters that DeMille had called upon in his spectacular, but

In a rare departure from playing the heavy, Roy Barcroft appeared in long hair, and donned a mustache and chin whiskers (a typical convention in films despite the fact that by the early 1870s Custer had abandoned facial hair except above the lip) to team up with the real star of the serial Oregon Trail *(1936), Johnny Mack Brown.* AUTRY MUSEUM OF WESTERN HERITAGE, LOS ANGELES

on an exceedingly smaller scale and for laughs. In *Goofs and Saddles*, the Three Stooges as "Buffalo Bilious," "Wild Bill Hiccup," and "Just Plain Bill" don buckskins to burlesque their way through the West. They play frontier scouts on a mission for "General Muster." Naturally, their zany antics land the trio in trouble, but they are rescued by Muster and his cavalrymen in true Hollywood form.[86]

By this time, Custer, under an assumed appellation or his real name, had degenerated to little more than a caricature on the silver screen. In 1940, Custer fared little better when added as a serious foil to Wallace Beery's farcical Reb Harkness in *Wyoming*. Filmed in part on location around Jackson Hole and the Tetons, Beery mugs it up along with his partner, Pete Marillo (Leo Carrillo), as the duo ineptly try their hands at train robbery. The law

sets out to capture the pair of lovable bandits and comes close to doing so before the two flee Missouri for the safety of the High Plains.

Along the way, Reb meets Steve Kincaid, an ex-Confederate also headed to Wyoming, where he has a small ranch. Harkness and Kincaid become friends, although they part company at Angel City. Reb wants to go on to California, but when he finds that rustlers have murdered his new comrade, he vows revenge.

Harkness guns down four of the outlaws. Then he gives the money the rustlers made from the stolen cattle to Kincaid's orphaned daughter and son, Lucy and Jimmy. Thus Beery continues the tradition of the reformed bad man that had been popular in Westerns from the time of "Bronco Billy" Anderson and William S. Hart.

The Plainsman offered another opportunity for Custer (John Miljan) and Hickok (Gary Cooper) to meet again on screen. Just to make certain the audience understands that this exchange is in the mystic past, Custer hold a quill pen, long outmoded by the 1870s, the time period for this C. B. DeMille Western. PARAMOUNT PICTURES. AUTRY MUSEUM OF WESTERN HERITAGE, LOS ANGELES

A captured warrior, played by DeMille's future son-in-law, Anthony Quinn, narrates as a rear projection depicts the "hordes of hostiles" who brought Custer (John Miljan) to his dramatic demise in The Plainsman. *The composition of this scene drew directly from Alfred Waud's illustration for the 1876 biography,* A Complete Life of General George A. Custer, *as did a number of other last stand film vignettes.* PARAMOUNT PICTURES. AUTRY MUSEUM OF WESTERN HERITAGE, LOS ANGELES

Reb carries on in an effort to find the rest of the gang, headed by a man named Buckley. The villain decides to do away with this thorn in his side, just when Custer arrives to arrest Reb for his past crimes. Buckley concocts a scheme to draw Custer out of town so that he can get into the jail and silence Harkness. Mehitabel, a woman blacksmith in the town, foils the plan by helping Reb escape.

This does not halt Buckley's activities, however. He gains political power as he moves to take over Angel City. Reb tries to block him by organizing the citizenry. Custer reappears. For the moment, he restores calm. He directs

Wallace Berry in one of his many "good-badman" roles upstaged even Custer (Paul Kelly) in Wyoming *(1940).* MGM. AUTRY MUSEUM OF WESTERN HERITAGE, LOS ANGELES

Buckley "to cease his lawless activity" and orders Harkness out of the area.[87]

Not to be stopped, Buckley incites an Indian uprising. A war party attacks the Kinkaid ranch. They burn the buildings and are about to close in for the kill, when Custer comes to the rescue, relieving Harness and his wards from the siege. Reb becomes a hero and marries Mehitabel. Lucy weds one of Custer's soldiers, Sergeant Connolly.

In another pre–Pearl Harbor offering, *The Badlands of Dakota,* Custer again assumes a cameo role as local peacemaker, this time for the rough-and-tumble town of Deadwood. The community is a haven for criminals, including Bob Holliday, a man who has become embittered over the news that his brother Jim married his intended bride, Anne Grayson. Custer tells the townspeople to elect a marshal to put a stop to lawlessness. Bob realizes the danger this man will be in once in office, so he does everything possible to get his brother the position in order to see Jim killed.

The younger Holliday is elected but turns out to be no easy mark. He forms a posse and captures or kills a number of the bandits, although Jack McCall, the main desperado, remains at large. McCall and Bob team up to rob the bank under the cover of an Indian attack. Jim stops this plan and also avoids being murdered when Calamity Jane shoots Bob just as he is about to gun down his brother. She once loved Jim and has come to his aid. Custer arrives at the same time to quell the attack on Deadwood. Jim, with Calamity Jane and others, finally clean up the town.[88]

Restoring law and order likewise was an element of still one more Custer film made before the United States' entry into the Second World War, *Santa Fe Trail* (1940). Inspired to some degree by the success of Fox's *Jesse James* (1939), Warner Bros. decided to capitalize on the talents of Errol Flynn, the swashbuckling hero of many adventure films and two other Westerns, *Dodge City* and *Virginia City.* This time the studio decided to transport Flynn across the Mississippi for a picture casting the dashing Tasmanian as James Ewell Brown (Jeb) Stuart. The female lead, Kit Carson Halliday, went to Olivia de Havilland, who frequently appeared opposite Flynn. The pair were involved romantically offscreen, and this relationship came through on camera, giving the couple a special appeal.[89]

In addition to Stuart, *Santa Fe Trail*'s producers decided to include an entire litany of later Civil War generals. They had the future Confederate cavalry commander (class of 1854) graduate from West Point with such notables as James Longstreet, Phil Sheridan, John Hood, George Pickett, and George Custer. Though these men all left the Military Academy at different times, the script depicted them receiving their diplomas together.[90] The comrades then reported to Fort Leavenworth, Kansas, where John Brown was at the center of violence.

The plot further diverges from historical reality once the young "shavetails" make their way West. Among other fictional elements, Stuart and Custer both fall under the spell of de Havilland in the role of the tomboy daughter of a Leavenworth entrepreneur and visionary, who dreams of a railroad spanning the continent. Other than this allusion to a transcontinental form of transportation, there is no reference to the Santa Fe Trail itself, despite the film's title, a point underscored by both contemporary reviews and more recent discussions of the picture.

Nevertheless, this romp through antebellum history remains a classic example of formula escapism costume

dramas produced just before the outbreak of the Second World War. Moreover, it gave Ronald Reagan added exposure in the role of Custer and was one of his first forays in a Western.[91] But more to the point, *Santa Fe Trail* became one of the most famous renditions of the Civil War in the West.[92] In this, the picture's negative portrayal of John Brown depended heavily upon the Southern causation interpretation of the Civil War that was then in vogue, following, among other sources, Claude Bower's influential *Tragic Era.*

With the success of such genre period pieces holding strong, the next year Warner Bros. decided to reunite Flynn, this time as Autie, and de Havilland, as Libbie, in what was to be the couple's final film together. *They Died with Their Boots On* became the most famous of all the depictions of the cinematic Custer couple. This block-

Advertisements promised "a thousands thrills" for Santa Fe Trail *(1940), one of many features starring the offscreen lovers Olivia de Havilland and Errol Flynn as onscreen romantic interest. Flynn portrayed J. E. B. Stuart.* WARNER BROS. VINCENT A. HEIER

In Santa Fe Trail, *George Custer, played second string to "Jeb Stuart." Nonetheless, young Ronald Reagan (right) enjoyed being cast as the fresh from West Point cadet, who would later make history at Little Bighorn.* WARNER BROS. AUTRY MUSEUM OF WESTERN HERITAGE, LOS ANGELES

buster recalled a few of the earliest films in its introduction of biographical elements about George and Elizabeth, but it even went further back in Custer's career, taking the story to his entrance as a plebe at West Point, where he crosses paths with a fictional fellow cadet, Ned Sharp.[93]

The story then moves to his Civil War days, when Custer finds time to woo Elizabeth Bacon and win her for his bride, as well as to hobnob with Phil Sheridan and Winfield Scott, between daring charges reminiscent of scenes from Flynn's *Charge of the Light Brigade*. After a brief but restless period as a civilian, during which Custer takes to heavy drink for a time, the saber-wielding cavalier obtains an appointment to the 7th Cavalry. This turns Custer around. He heads west to Fort Abraham Lincoln.

En route, he manages to capture Crazy Horse, thereby incurring the warrior's wrath. In so doing, the stage is set for revenge that once had been the domain of Rain-in-the-Face in prior pictures.

Such liberties with history were more than just poetic license. With World War II threatening to involve the United States, Warner Bros. was "generous to a fault in paying their respects to the hero."[94] The country would need people of this stature to carry on the fight against fascism. Indeed, one character, who in an earlier version of the script represented a combination of Myles Keogh and William Cooke, was transformed into an Englishman, "Queen's Own" Butler, for the sake of making the con-

nection that England and the United States had been allies in many other causes during the past.[95]

Additionally, a "third-column" element, in the person of Sharp, who had been Custer's superior for a time early in the Civil War, played a conspicuous part in the plot's development. Now Sharp, at the center of a group of exploitative white politicos and businessmen, attempts to drive the Indians out of the Black Hills through underhanded dealings designed to incite a war.

They Died with Their Boots On not only served as a patriotic vehicle and a means of strengthening Anglo-American ties, but also represented a pinnacle of pro-Custer depictions. Although early in the script, Flynn speaks with great

The quill pen (stock props of costume dramas) this time in the hands of Custer, who writes a letter on the eve of battle exposing the corruption in high places that caused him to fight the exploited Indians under Crazy Horse, or so the audience is led to believe in They Died with Their Boots On. WARNER BROS. AUTRY MUSEUM OF WESTERN HERITAGE, LOS ANGELES

bravado and arrogance and is much the egotistical Van de Water glory-hunting Custer, he evolves into an "idealist, a man willing to surrender his life for the common good."[96]

These later characteristics are seen when Custer exposes corruption in U. S. Grant's administration by attempting to reveal Sharp and his cronies. He is removed from command but regains the 7th at the eleventh hour by personally appealing to the president as a former soldier. Grant relents. Custer returns to Fort Lincoln from Washington.

At the post, Custer confronts Sharp. Custer agrees to break his oath of abstaining from alcohol and joins Sharp in several rounds of drinks. As they match shot for shot, Sharp reflects about their earlier times on the Hudson, when Custer enthusiastically spoke of glory and statues to heroes. Sharp says that this was foolish talk; only money meant anything in the scheme of things. Custer disagrees. He retorts, "You can take glory with you when it's your time to go." Then Sharp realizes that Custer has been leading him on in order to get him intoxicated. In his stupor, Sharp is taken away in one of the wagons on Custer's ill-fated expedition against the Indians.

Before he leaves, Autie and Libbie have one final touching moment in their quarters. Emotionally, she begs, "You can't go. You'll be killed. I won't let you go." To this, Custer responds that he must do his duty as an officer in the U.S. Army.

This issue of duty over personal feelings settled, Libbie reviews the list of things he must not forget, including his watch. Autie breaks the chain on purpose so as to leave it behind rather than risk its loss, because he believes he will not return. He tells Libbie he does not want to lose the timepiece. She replies that it will be the first time he has not carried it with him into battle. She too has a premonition, which he discovers in her diary. Custer assures his wife that nothing will happen to him and that he will return soon so they can grow fat and old together. Autie professes, "Walking through life with you ma'am has been a very gracious thing." Then he takes Libbie into his arms and gives her a passionate farewell kiss. As soon as he leaves the room, she collapses.

From here, Custer rides out to his date with destiny. The Indians observe his approach. Crazy Horse calls for a council of war. On the night before the two sides are about to meet, Custer calls his adjutant, Butler, to him. He tells the Englishman that he wants him to carry an important letter back to Fort Lincoln. The man respectfully declines. He knows that Custer is attempting to keep his old comrade out of the fray because he is a foreigner. Butler says that the only real Americans are the Indians.

In a sense, then, he is no more a foreigner than the rest of the regiment.

Next, Custer learns of Gen. George Crook's defeat from his scout, California Joe. With this intelligence, Custer decides he must strike the hostile force before it can ride down on Alfred Terry's infantry.

He goes to Sharp, who still is tied up in the supply wagon. Custer tells Sharp that he will release him, but because they are in the midst of the Indians, Sharp has no choice but to accompany Long Hair. A frightened Sharp asks Custer where they are going. He is told, "To hell or to glory. It depends on one's point of view."

Willing to march into hell for a heavenly cause, Custer rides forth that day with the intention of offering himself to protect Terry's column. He will stand as the last survivor before being killed by Crazy Horse. Here Custer embodies the brave American ready to make the ultimate sacrifice in defense of what he thinks is right. Even Sharp is at his side, being won over to the cause and thus giving up his life for his past sins. After the battle, Sheridan tells Sharp's father and the crooked Indian commissioner Romulus Taipe that Custer saved not only Terry, but the entire frontier by his noble deed. Custer also left behind a letter that as a "dying declaration" was admissible as evidence. In this document, he denounced the two men and their greedy plot.

Libbie says she will destroy the paper if Taipe resigns and dismantles his crooked ring. She likewise states that the government must agree to provide a fair deal for the Indians, as this was her husband's wish. All agree. Custer's defeat turns to triumph. His spirit marches on. Consequently, *They Died with Their Boots On* epitomized the first three decades of Yellow Hair on the silver screen. It was to become the pinnacle of Custer's celluloid image.[97]

They Died with Their Boots On also provided expensive stock footage and segments of the soundtrack for a 1945 Warner Bros. short subject, *Law of the Badlands*. This short subject nearly replicated the silent *Bob Hampton of Placer,* changing little more than the name of the lead character, in this case to Robert Tate Fleming (played by Robert Shayne), an army officer who has been cashiered for causing the death of a comrade. The charge is contrived, the crime having been committed by another man. Close-ups of Custer, for purposes of dialogue and similar reasons, employed an actor who essentially was a clone of Flynn insofar as costume and flowing hair with mustache and chin whiskers were concerned. For distant shots, Flynn and the extras from *They Died with Their Boots On* were spliced in to allow for large numbers of cavalry and Indians to be on hand for the Last Stand, including

Flynn faces his heroic end, saber in hand, regardless of the fact that these edged weapons were left with the pack train during the fateful battle. Symbolism is what counted—a brave knight of old boldly faces the overwhelming foe with cold steel. WARNER BROS.

Anthony Quinn full on camera riding to deliver Custer's death blow.

While Custer is but a cameo in this brief show, as he often was in the past, he still played a central part in the message of the movie, which concluded with a tribute to "that glorious regiment, the Seventh Cavalry." As the scene shifted from the battle, the film's narrator announced, "Far off in the Black Hills of the Dakotas the plains of Little Bighorn will live forever as a monument to those men who so valiantly went down in victorious defeat."

These diametrically opposed concepts of defeat and victory sum up the Last Stand mystique that had held sway for so long. Whether Custer was the central figure, as in *They Died with Their Boots On,* or a background player, as in *Law of the Badlands,* his death was an event readily understood by the audience to hold deep, diverse meanings, but in all instances it had been treated in a positive and often reverential manner, from the days of the first melodramas through the conclusion of the Second World War. That one constant could no longer be counted on in the years following the end of World War II.

CHAPTER FOUR

Hero to Villain:
Post–World War II Features

World War II had ended, but the nation soon found itself facing another enemy as the wartime alliance with the Soviet Union collapsed. The Cold War had begun. While a face-to-face confrontation between the two superpowers never erupted, the threat of the bomb hung heavy. As fears of the possibility of global destruction or world domination by the Red menace took hold, the cinematic pendulum began to swing from depictions of Custer as a peerless paladin to a version that was in keeping with Van de Water's egotistical glory hunter—or worse.

The change was not immediate, nor at first was it blatant. Beginning in 1948, veteran director John Ford oversaw the creation of *Fort Apache*. Taken from James Warner Bellah's short story "Massacre," and rewritten by one-time *New York Times* film critic Frank Nugent under the working title of "War Party," Ford's drama was set in 1870s Arizona Territory rather than the Little Bighorn. So he returned to his familiar Monument Valley, the locale for *Stagecoach* and many of his subsequent films, where the famed stock company of actors he regularly employed for his films (including John Wayne, Victor McLaglen, and Ward Bond) toiled for forty-four days to complete the more than $2 million project.[1] There Cochise, not Sitting Bull or Crazy Horse, was the foe. Despite these and other changes, Ford intentionally drew upon the Custer story, demonstrating once again that the script need not be a literal re-creation of Little Bighorn to drive home the meaning of this battle to an audience.[2]

Although other films as far back as Griffith's *The Massacre* had followed a similar path, Ford's vision was unique. Not bound by minutia, Ford's rendition of the Custer saga achieved considerable heights, proving an excellent example of "the dignity, grandeur, and romance of the best" of his Westerns. Moreover, his film was ambivalent in that it upheld "the nobility of white and red men who must engage in combat."[3]

But Ford's originality rested in great part on the treatment of *Fort Apache*'s Custer figure, Col. Owen Thursday. Thursday is a realistic character with flaws. He is all too human but brave. The death of Thursday and his troops could have been avoided, but the sacrifice was not in vain. His replacement as commander, Kirby York (none other than John Wayne, in a role somewhat akin to Frederick Benteen), a man who had previously opposed the fallen cavalry officer, now defends his late superior. York maintains: "No man died more bravely nor brought more honor to his regiment." He likewise contends that Thursday's actions made the men of the command better soldiers, providing them with a heroic model to follow. These words serve as "a powerful endorsement of Ford's belief in the glory of defeat."[4] Custer's longevity as an element of popular culture had long rested on this complex foundation, which achieved strong resonance with the

The few against many awaiting their fate . . . John Ford's interpretation of the Last Stand from Fort Apache *(1948) where Cochise's warriors engulf the blue clad troopers who die to a man.* RKO/TURNER ENTERTAINMENT. AUTRY MUSEUM OF WESTERN HERITAGE, LOS ANGELES

American public, as witnessed by the passionate attachment to the Alamo and Pearl Harbor.

Additionally, as one historian noted, despite York's hatred of Thursday, he understood that "if the massacre is to have any value it must be made a myth. The myth, even if false, can provide an ideal of courage and sacrifice for the cavalry (and the nation)."[5] Certainly Ford comprehended the power of myth, and its ability to become fact,

and he explored this theme again in *The Man Who Shot Liberty Valance.*[6]

Consequently, despite Thursday's fatal pride, his charge is given meaning. Unlike earlier Custer-related films, the character's fatal flaw surfaces in relationship to the commander's actions. The cavalry officer dies for his own sins rather than as a victim of betrayal, but his blood sacrifice redeems him and nurtures those who come after.

Ford's surrogate Custer then was not without merit, because he was an honorable warrior. In a 1951 Republic release, however, Custer's stand-in was stripped of most of the redeeming qualities so long associated with Yellow Hair. Comparable to *Fort Apache*, Republic's *Oh! Susanna*, set in the Black Hills during 1876, was a derivative of the Little Bighorn tale and to some extent rolled the Fort Phil Kearny and Fetterman story into the mix as well.[7]

The feature revolves around a lieutenant colonel by the name of Unger (Forrest Tucker), who is overbearing and dictatorial but, unlike Colonel Thursday, not entirely a man of integrity. Unger is a greedy cavalry officer who wants to instigate an Indian outbreak as an excuse to invade their land to obtain gold. One of his underlings, Captain Calhoun, is a rival for the leading lady's hand. Moreover, Calhoun attempts to respect the treaty with the Sioux.

Unger's partner in crime arranges for a raid, with his henchmen disguised as Indians. In supposed retaliation, Unger is to launch an attack against the Plains Indians and ignite a war. The Indians take advantage of this action to assault the fort in Unger's absence. Like Thursday, he must return and fight, but he ends up being defeated. Unlike Thursday, his heroic death cannot undo the damage caused by his contrived war.

While the Custer figure was making its descent from the onetime heroic pedestal, films still did not seem ready

"When the legend becomes fact"—Despite his personal animosity toward Owen Thursday, Kirby York maintains that "no man died more bravely" as he discusses his former commander's death with a group of reporters. It is more important to give credence to a lie than tell the truth and negate the symbolism of "Thursday's Last Stand." RKO/TURNER ENTERTAINMENT. AUTRY MUSEUM OF WESTERN HERITAGE, LOS ANGELES

to assail Custer per se. One way to avoid presenting a negative characterization of Yellow Hair was to leave him out entirely, as did *Little Big Horn,* one more 1951 entry into Custer's celluloid cycle. Although he remains at the center of the drama in name, the real focus is a detachment commanded by a young Lloyd Bridges. This early-day

"dirty dozen" set out to inform their lieutenant colonel about the fate that awaits the 7th. They fight among themselves, while constant strikes by war parties reduce their numbers, similar to *Lost Patrol.* Finally the survivors arrive, too late to do anything, but in spite of their less-than-sterling performance on the way to Little Bighorn,

In another take off of the Custer story with the names changed "to protect the innocent" Lieutenant Colonel Unger (Forrest Tucker) supported by Rod Cameron (left) and Chill Wills (right) dies with saber in hand. His final moments are more valiant than his previous actions as an egocentric, self-serving opportunist. In some respects, Tucker, who actually had served a stint in the U.S. cavalry, assumed a comedic version of this type of character as Sergeant O'Rourke in television's F Troop. REPUBLIC PICTURES. AUTRY MUSEUM
OF WESTERN HERITAGE, LOS ANGELES

Despite the title Little Big Horn *(1951), a doomed patrol led by Lloyd Bridges and John Ireland are never seen near that battleground, nor does the audience even catch a glimpse of Custer.* LIPPERT PICTURES/SCREENGUILD. AUTRY MUSEUM OF WESTERN HERITAGE, LOS ANGELES

once confronted with the inevitable, they rise to the occasion.[8] Although they could have fled, and they know that their small numbers will do little good, the men charge to glory—fulfilling their mission, even though their fate is to join the list of fallen troopers.

In another 1951 picture, *Warpath,* Custer rescues a besieged patrol but figures little more in the film. The main character, John Vickers, is a former army captain. Vickers heads West, bent on revenge. His quest is to find the three men who murdered his wife. Having found the first of the trio and killed him, he sets out to join the 7th Cavalry, where he is told another of the killers will be found.

Vickers enlists. At Fort Lincoln, the new recruit soon crosses swords with Sergeant O'Hara (Forrest Tucker), both men attempting to win the favor of Molly Quade. The young woman falls for Vickers, but her father turns out to

be one of the men the hero has been trailing. Of course, O'Hara is the third member of the gang. When Vickers discovers this, he sets out to complete his vendetta. Before he can accomplish this mission, O'Hara deserts and must be apprehended. Sam Quade, in turn, dies in an attempt to save his daughter and other settlers. In the end, O'Hara is brought to justice, and Molly and John are free to marry.

The film, although derivative in many ways, still had elements that set it apart. For one thing, as a critic of the time discerned, the depiction of "a natural animosity between soldiers and civilians" and the implication "that life in the Seventh Cavalry was on the thorny thankless side" were novel.[9] Another interesting sidelight was the casting of C. W. Brice, a grandnephew of Custer, as one of the troopers in the regiment. Because the modern 7th Cavalry was fighting in Korea at the time, and because

In Warpath *(1951) Custer and the Little Bighorn play an inconsequential part because most of the fighting is between two white troopers in the 7th Cavalry—Edmond O'Brien and another screen persona for Forrest Tucker.* PARAMOUNT PICTURES. AUTRY MUSEUM OF WESTERN HERITAGE, LOS ANGELES

Winchester '73 *(1950) typified many features released in the decade immediately following the end of World War II. In such movies Little Bighorn and Custer were mentioned but not depicted, thereby simply providing some historical context for the fictional script. This release gave a young contract player named Anthony Curtis (center) a bit of extra exposure as he made his way toward stardom.*

UNIVERSAL. COURTESY AUTRY MUSEUM OF WESTERN HERITAGE.

Colonel Brice had commanded the outfit earlier, this was director Nat Holt's tribute to the unit's heritage during the seventy-fifth anniversary of Little Bighorn.[10]

The Korean conflict was still being waged when Custer returned to the silver screen in *Bugles in the Afternoon.* This 1952 feature was taken from Ernest Haycox's novel of the same title. The two forms were very different, though, in that Haycox closely followed the Van de Water school in his book, but the film used the oft-repeated formula of a disgraced former cavalry officer in the classic *Britton of the Seventh* mold. This time, the maligned soldier is Kern Shafter, who has lost his commission in a scuffle with Captain Garnett. The cashiered Shafter departs from the East to start a new life in the West. He enlists as a private, but his commander turns out to be his old foe.

Josephine Russell, the "pert, blond daughter of the local storekeeper," complicates matters because she takes a fancy to Kern despite Garnett's interest in her. The captain uses his position to send Kern on every hazardous mission. Such events seem to have no limits. Garnett's efforts to eliminate his rival indirectly lead to Custer's defeat. In the end, Shafter triumphs and wins the girl. Custer, this time with the honors going to Sheb Wooley, rides in toward the end of the story. He takes the command to the field amidst calls from the garrison's women to bring back their men safely.

These well-wishers do not carry the day. As the audience knows, Custer will be faced by overwhelming odds, but again, the implication is that one of his subordinates is actually at the root of the 7th's defeat.[11]

Thus Hollywood was not prepared to topple Custer as Haycox had done. Instead, the Little Bighorn debacle was explained as the doing of a dishonorable subaltern, as it had been in many previous film interpretations.

As with many other films, Custer figures only as a background character in Bugles in the Afternoon *(1952), a tangled tale of revenge and love in the 7th Cavalry starring Ray Milland (center).* WARNER BROS. AUTRY MUSEUM OF WESTERN HERITAGE, LOS ANGELES

Custer's desire to provoke an Indian war comes home with a vengeance in Sitting Bull. *He no longer is heroic martyr, but instead is a self-serving militarist.* UNITED ARTISTS. AUTRY MUSEUM OF WESTERN HERITAGE, LOS ANGELES

By 1954, the tone had changed. It was no longer important to be cautious about who was responsible for the 7th Cavalry's annihilation. *Sitting Bull,* with J. Carrol Naish as the mystic Lakota, openly made Custer the villain. In this version, Sitting Bull, as a sort of Hunkpapa Hamlet, wrestles with the question of whether he should remain friendly to the whites or take up arms against them. He asserts, "I will try to make peace with the white man. If that fails, then they will hear our war cries and the shouts from our fighting braves." Even after the troops kill his son, Sitting Bull does not respond to Crazy Horse's question, "Now will you make war?" He calls upon the Great Spirit for guidance, asking, "Must there be war? Is this land not big enough for all people? War or peace? War or peace?"

One member of the 7th Cavalry echoes these words when he speaks to President Grant. A hero of the Civil War, in which his bravery had been recognized with a Medal of Honor and high rank, Major Parrish (Dale Robertson) wants the two peoples to live together. In this he is at odds with his commander, Custer. Yellow Hair forces the Indians into battle because of his duplicity and blind hatred of Indians.[12]

The pacifists fail to avert bloodshed. Custer charges headlong into the valley of death. Despite Custer's brashness, Sitting Bull orders his followers not to mutilate the body of this brave fighting foe. He then goes off to Canada with the help of Parrish, who knows how to avoid Gen. Alfred Terry's pursuing column. The mighty Lakota soon returns, however, when Parrish faces a firing squad for what a court-martial deems treasonable actions. Sitting Bull enters the fort, where he finds President Grant. He defends his white benefactor, a man who has helped point the way to true understanding between the white and red peoples. After Parrish is exonerated, Sitting Bull rides off nobly.

Clearly, *Sitting Bull* had become part of a growing interest in Hollywood to reverse past negative images of the American Indians in film—an important thrust found in some pictures dating from the silent era. After all, the public had been exposed to two versions of American Indians—the noble savage and the bloodthirsty "hostile"—since the earliest literary traditions.[13] Though the civil-rights movement had not yet gained its full strength, the environment after World War II had made certain elements of American society more sensitive to the country's diversity. Perhaps the approach taken in *Sitting Bull* was intended not to replace negative characterizations but, as some observers contended, to draw audiences.[14] And that the film did. *Sitting Bull* became one of the first Westerns to make a substantial financial showing, taking in some $1.5 million in comparison with the top moneymaker of the year, *White Christmas,* at $12 million.[15]

Whatever the motives for *Sitting Bull,* the approach was not to be ignored, nor were the economic figures. Following a show-business maxim that you can never give the audience too much of what they are willing to pay for, another famous Lakota leader seemed prime for the big screen. With this in mind, *Chief Crazy Horse* was 1955's addition to the growing list of pro–American Indian treatments. Again, a non-Indian played the title role, in this case Victor Mature.

Most of the action focused on Crazy Horse's efforts to court and win Black Shawl and the bad blood that resulted from this romance. But Black Shawl's selection of Crazy Horse over Little Big Man sowed the seeds for her husband's downfall. In fact, the romance assured the fulfillment of a prophecy that a great warrior would appear to lead the Lakotas against their enemies, but even at the pinnacle of his victories, the man was destined to be killed by one of his own. Thus Crazy Horse attains the stature of a savior of his people who dies as the result of betrayal by one of his own, a theme that had more than once been applied to Custer.

Now Crazy Horse, not Custer, was a sacrificial victim. Custer was demoted to minor a figure, riding onto the scene for a scant few moments before being overcome by

Crazy Horse's superior generalship. Indeed, the actor who portrays Long Hair does not even receive a credit and is treated as little more than an extra.

This role reversal did not spark enthusiasm on the part of the critics, however, who panned the feature. One review considered it little "more than a pedestrian concept of the great man" Crazy Horse.[16]

Another writer noted that three clashes between the army and Crazy Horse—the Fetterman Fight, Rosebud, and Little Bighorn—were shown, but by the time the script reached the point for the last battle, the budget was not available to martial sufficient extras to depict Custer's final fight. In fact, the picture nearly ignored what so often had been a pivotal event in previous films,[17] instead jumping abruptly from Custer cresting the hill with his immediate command to the bodies of the white soldiers being stripped in the aftermath of the fight.

But perhaps this departure was not just based on costs. After all, if Crazy Horse was the main figure, what importance did just one more victory over this particular white man have to add to the victor's laurels? One thing is clear, however: After *Crazy Horse,* there was no turning back for the use of Custer as an all-purpose film antihero—the ugly American in the flesh. The literature of the 1930s finally had come to the screen.

The absence of the Last Stand was not a matter of speculation in the next feature. *The Seventh Cavalry,* starring Randolph Scott, had a reason for not depicting

What ever happened to Randolph Scott? Among other things he played an officer wrongly accused of cowardice in The Seventh Cavalry *(1956).* COLUMBIA PICTURES. AUTRY MUSEUM OF WESTERN HERITAGE, LOS ANGELES

Custer. Scott, as Capt. Tom Benson, arrives at Fort Lincoln. After meeting his fiancé, Martha, her father, the post commander, Colonel Kellogg, opposes the upcoming marriage. To make matters worse, Benson has reported for duty in the wake of news about Custer's death. Those who are at the fort and the survivors of the Little Bighorn blame him for not accompanying his command or sharing the fate of his men. Additionally, the captain cannot produce a written order that permitted him to leave the column in order to fetch Martha.

Shortly thereafter, Colonel Kellogg holds an inquiry. The hearing turns into an inquisition branding Benson a coward. No substantial evidence is introduced against Tom, but the stigma remains. The inhabitants of Fort Lincoln ostracize Benson. Only Martha remains by his side.

Colonel Kellogg does all within his power to get the captain to resign. When this tactic fails, he sends Benson on a suicide mission. Tom must lead a patrol of "drunks, misfits and malcontents" released from the stockade to rebury the hastily interred bodies of Custer and the men of the 7th. To ensure Benson's undoing, the colonel sees to it that Sergeant Bates, a man who detests the captain, accompanies the group. Another snag is that the Indians, who still lurk about the area, regard the battleground as sacred. Naturally, they would not take kindly to whites entering this place of "good medicine."

Benson's men learn of the situation and threaten mutiny. The problem intensifies. Tom must remain awake at night for fear of being murdered by one of his own command.

The Searchers (1956) originally contained a scene which was John Ford's version of the Washita while a Custer character, played by Peter Ortiz, also formed part of the original plot before ending up on the cutting-room floor. WARNER BROS. VINCENT A. HEIER

Tonka's last stand scene is one of the most elaborate ever filmed, but unlike previous renditions Custer does not remain as the final one to fall, nor does he assume the heroic upright stance. Instead he uses a dead horse for cover as he desperately fights for survival.

WALT DISNEY STUDIOS. AUTRY MUSEUM OF WESTERN HERITAGE, LOS ANGELES

While all this is taking place in the field, Corporal Morrison (Harry Carey, Jr.) rides into the post after completing a courier mission. He learns of Benson's dilemma and informs Kellogg that he heard Custer give Tom verbal permission for his absence. Having cleared the hero's name, Morrison sets out on Dandy, twin to the mount Custer had ridden at the Little Bighorn, carrying a message for Benson to return to the fort.

Just as Benson and his men brace for their own final stand, the corporal appears on the horizon. He is shot, but the horse comes galloping into the valley minus its rider. The awestruck attackers see the charger and flee in the belief that this is Custer's spirit returning to take revenge.[18]

Another famous 7th Cavalry mount gave rise to the next Little Bighorn motion picture, Walt Disney's *Tonka,* a fanciful tale based upon David Appel's juvenile-oriented

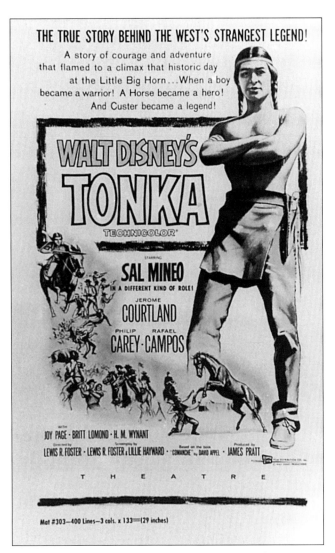

THE TRUE STORY BEHIND THE WEST'S STRANGEST LEGEND!

A story of courage and adventure that flamed to a climax that historic day at the Little Big Horn...When a boy became a warrior! A Horse became a hero! And Custer became a legend!

WALT DISNEY'S
TONKA
TECHNICOLOR

STARRING
SAL MINEO
IN A DIFFERENT KIND OF ROLE!
JEROME
COURTLAND
PHILIP   RAFAEL
CAREY · CAMPOS

JOY PAGE · BRITT LOMOND · H. M. WYNANT
LEWIS R. FOSTER · LEWIS R. FOSTER & LILLIE HAYWARD · "COMANCHE" by DAVID APPEL · JAMES PRATT

T H E A T R E

Mat #303—400 Lines—3 cols. x 133==(29 inches)

Tonka's pressbook promised the film was "a story of courage and adventure that flamed to a climax that historic day at the Little Big Horn . . . when a boy became a warrior! A horse became a hero! And Custer became a legend!" WALT DISNEY STUDIOS.
VINCENT A. HEIER

novel of how Capt. Myles Keogh obtained his horse Comanche, and the biography, in effect, of the steed before life with that officer.[19]

Most of the early scenes focus on White Bull (Sal Mineo), a Lakota who is coming of age. He finds and tames the wild horse around which the story centers. When his cousin Yellow Bull demands that the young man turn over the mount, White Bull complies. The older warrior mistreats the horse, thus prompting White Bull to set the horse free.

Tonka then comes into the hands of Keogh, played by Philip Carey. The Irish captain and his friend Lieutenant

Nowlan (Jerome Courtland) serve under Custer, a role assigned to Britt Lomond, the actor who also portrayed the heavy-handed *comandante* in Disney's *Zorro* television series. In *Tonka*, Lomond carries on in that same tradition but now sports a bleached-blond shock of hair and postures as a megalomaniac.[20]

Custer reacts to an Indian attack on a wagon train that included the kidnapping of two women. He informs Keogh that there will be considerable action ahead for the 7th as the unit takes to the field to drive the Indians onto the reservations. Then he concludes, "It is more important to teach these red savages a lesson than to rescue the white women. They [the Indians] must be exterminated."

Custer sends an ultimatum to the Lakota, who by now are preparing to meet the white onslaught. He tells them that his troops, "will march and burn every Sioux village to the ground" if they do not return to their agencies. Custer also tells Keogh that there is "no way to separate the good from the bad. They burn—pillage—they're all bad." With this idea firmly fixed in his mind, Custer leads his command to its doom.

His threat backfires. Approaching the encampment, the column moves forward for the final scene, one of the two most ambitious attempts to re-create the Last Stand between the 1940s and the early 1960s. As the battle opens, the bluecoats face overwhelming odds. Rather than standing heroically to the end, Custer fires from a seated position on the ground behind his horse as a shield. He soon falls as an early casualty. Keogh, however, continues to fight bravely and is the last to die.[21] Thus he is the hero, while the formerly spotless Boy General has his reputation tarnished and his luster dimmed even more.[22]

After *Tonka's* release, the Custer theme departed the big screen for several years, but it was resurrected with a vengeance by the following decade. In fact, four companies competed to obtain Leon Fromkess's script, which eventually became *The Great Sioux Massacre*. This 1965 release gave Sidney Salkow, who directed both this picture and *Sitting Bull,* a chance to recycle some footage from his earlier production.[23]

The Great Sioux Massacre focuses on Custer through the eyes of Major Reno and Capt. Frederick Benton (the film inexplicably changed the name of Captain Benteen). The two men detest each other. Reno is an alcoholic and an unreconstructed former Confederate general who hates Benteen, a fellow Southerner, for throwing in his lot with the North during the Civil War. The only thing they have in common is Reno's daughter, whom Benteen wants to marry. Eventually Reno reforms and ends his estrangement with his daughter and the men are reconciled.[24]

As Reno and Benteen resolve their differences, Custer (Philip Carey, who played Captain Keogh in *Tonka*) undergoes changes as well, but not for the better. Early on, he is a no-nonsense, candid soldier who sympathizes with the Indians and detests politicians and agents bent on gain from these people.[25]

His views on the matter lead him to trouble with high-placed members of the government in Washington, D.C., and to his "unofficial exile." An embittered man, he returns to the West, but not before succumbing to a pow-erful senator's schemes to make the officer into a political hero. With dreams of the presidency in mind, Custer transforms into a sadist. His blind ambitions lead him to seek nothing less than the total destruction of the Lakota people in order to wrest away their lands.[26]

This portrait is little different from the one painted in the other 1965 release, *The Glory Guys,* a film based on Hoffman Birney's *Dice of God,* a relatively well-crafted novel published a decade earlier. In this takeoff from the Custer theme, similar in approach to *Fort Apache* and *Oh!*

Darren McGavin and Joseph Cotton (center left and right) assumed the characters of Benteen and Reno, the central players in the drama The Great Sioux Massacre *(1965), while Philip Carey was to don Custer's buckskins as a politically driven man on the make.* COLUMBIA PICTURES. AUTRY MUSEUM OF WESTERN HERITAGE, LOS ANGELES

Ad No. 401—448 Lines—4 Cols. x 8 Inches

The Credits

enplay by Fred C. Dobbs; Story by Sidney Salkow
Marvin Gluck; Music by Emil Newman, Edward
well; Director of Photography, Irving Lippman; Art
tor, Frank P. Syles; Production Manager, Howard
er; Assistant to the Producer, Rita Fromkess; Assist-
Director, Abby Berlin; Make-up Artist, Beau Wilson;
Stylist, Doris Kurkus; Wardrobe, Frank Tauss;
erty Master, Ted Cooper; Technical Advisor, Iron
Cody; Film Editor, William Austin, A.C.E; Music
r, Edna Bullock; Sound Effects, Milton Mann; Sound
r, John Bury, Jr.; Script Supervision, C. Duane Toler;
al Effects, Jack Erickson; Sound by Samuel Goldwyn
d Department; Produced by Leon Fromkess; Directed
Sidney Salkow; A Columbia Pictures Release in Cine-
cope and Columbia Color.

The Cast

Major Reno	Joseph Cotten
Capt. Benton	Darren McGavin
Col. Custer	Philip Carey
Libbie Custer	Nancy Kovack
Caroline Reno	Julie Sommars
Sitting Bull	Michael Pate
Crazy Horse	Iron Eyes Cody
Dakota	John Mathews
Senator Blaine	Don Haggerty
General Terry	Frank Ferguson
Tom Custer	John Napier
Mr. Turner	Stacy Harris
Presiding Officer	Blair Davies
Miner	William Tannen
Mrs. Turner	Louise Surpa
Military Aide	Dean Casper

The Story

(Not for Publication) Civil War hero and famous Ind
fighter, General Custer welcomes the arrival West
Captain Benton, whom he grooms to succeed him
command of the post over Major Reno. Benton
Reno's daughter Caroline are in love. A group of rut
political lobbyists persuade Custer to kill off the S
tribes so their lands can be confiscated; the Indian
forced to fight back to preserve their treaty lands. Cu
with a chance at the Presidency at take, and with
encouragement of his wife Libbie, ignores the advice
his officers, and rides to the battle field at Little
Horn where he is overwhelmed by superior Indian for
led by Chiefs Sitting Bull and Crazy Horse.

Running Time: 101 min.

COLUMBIA PRESSBOOK

Susanna, General McCabe, (Andrew Duggan, of the later "Lancer" television series) is yet another officer bent on a victory against the Sioux regardless of the costs in suffering and human life. His unrelenting loathing of Indians and all-consuming ambition know no bounds.[27]

To relieve McCabe's oppressive sobriety, the film adds a three-way romantic interest between a local woman, an officer in the general's command, and a scout serving at the fort. From there on, the events leading up to the destruction of McCabe vary little from those in earlier pictures written along the same lines.

Nevertheless, this did not prevent others from considering the idea. Dino De Laurentis toyed with a Custer-based film. So did David Weisbart for Twentieth Century Fox,[28] who envisioned a costly blockbuster, spending $1 million in preproduction, which included considerable costume design work and some advance casting. The script

LEFT: The Great Sioux Massacre *'s pressbook contended the drama as depicting "The one battle no Indian warrior or cavalry hero could ever forget."* COLUMBIA PICTURES. VINCENT A. HEIER

BELOW: *Andrew Duggan as Major General McCabe (center right) was a Hollywood Custer clone for the feature* Glory Guys *(1965).* UNITED ARTISTS. AUTRY MUSEUM OF WESTERN HERITAGE, LOS ANGELES

Despite being filmed in color, the 1965 remake of The Plainsman *paled by comparison to the original C. B. DeMille casting, with Don Murray and Guy Stockwell (right and left) being the central characters along with love interest Abby Dalton. In this production, Custer (Leslie Neilsen in his pre-comedic career) only made token on-camera appearances.* UNIVERSAL PICTURES. AUTRY MUSEUM OF WESTERN HERITAGE, LOS ANGELES

by Wendell Mayes (whose credits in the 1950s through 1960s included *Spirit of St. Louis, The Hanging Tree, Anatomy of a Murder, Advice and Consent, In Harm's Way,* and *Von Ryan's Express*) concentrated on the events directly leading to the 1876 campaign not only from the military's point of view, but also from the perspective of the American Indians who won the battle. In fact, the Lakota were to speak in their own language with subtitles, Crazy Horse and Sitting Bull being the main figures. All the major and many of the minor characters of the 7th Cavalry also appeared in this narrative, which drew heavily upon historical research, more so than any other effort to that time.[29]

Fred Zinnemann was slotted for director, an excellent choice, based upon his triumph in *High Noon*. Richard Zanuck approached Charlton Heston with an offer to

play Custer.[30] Although Heston had been in three frontier military-related pictures (*The Savage* and *Arrowhead* in 1953 and *Major Dundee* in 1965) and was not averse to taking on famous characters, from Moses to Michelangelo to Buffalo Bill, he nevertheless rejected this part. He wrote in his diary that the idea did not seem very sound. Heston indicated that his recollection of history made it impossible for Custer to be a protagonist. In Heston's estimation, Custer was an inept soldier and not much of a human being. He concluded, "I don't see how you can make a serious film about a man who seems to have been not only egocentric, but muddleheaded."[31]

Other actors were considered to fill Custer's boots, but despite extensive development of the project, the production never became a feature. Instead, it was trans-

George Armstrong Custer

Libbie Custer

Preproduction sketch for some of Autie's and Libbie's costumes for "The Day Custer Fell," a proposed big budget Fox film that never reached the screen. TWENTIETH CENTURY FOX. VINCENT A. HEIER

formed into an ill-fated television series that had little of the promise found in Mayes's story.

Outside Hollywood, Robert Haggiag and Albert Sordi proposed an Italian production, *General Custer's Bugler,* possibly inspired by one of the few Italian-born 7th Cavalry members associated with the battle, Giovanni Martini.[32] Though it appears that this concept never left the drawing board, two other Italian movies at least bore titles that indicate a link with the topic: *La Carica Del 7 Cavalleggeri (The Charge of the Seventh Cavalry,* 1964) and *Due Sergenti Del Generale Custer (Two Sergeants of General Custer,* 1965). Their titles aside, neither of the pictures really had anything to do with the Little Bighorn. Both were set during the Civil War in the West, years prior to the formation of the 7th Cavalry.[33]

One might think that by this time the potential had been exploited to the fullest for Custer in the cinema, but not so. In one of many remakes, *The Plainsman* gave him a brief new appearance in 1966.[34] Former B movie leading man Leslie Neilsen assumed Custer's flowing locks, long before he switched to yet a third career in various farces from *Airplane!* to *Mr. Magoo.*

A year later, in *Red Tomahawk,* Howard Keel was a cavalry officer sent to protect Deadwood from a pending attack by Indians who were flushed with victory after the Little Bighorn. This was the last of A. C. Lyles's many oaters for Paramount.[35]

In 1968, another European foray into Little Bighorn territory, *Custer of the West,* called for a complex characterization ably handled by Robert Shaw. *Custer of the West*

Howard Keel, better known for his singing abilities, nevertheless donned a cavalry captain's costume for Red Tomahawk *(1966) in order to save a town from attack after the Little Bighorn.* PARAMOUNT PICTURES. AUTRY MUSEUM OF WESTERN HERITAGE, LOS ANGELES

With more than the hint of a brogue, Robert Shaw rendered a version of Custer who was an anachronism. Rather than live in a world without honor, he readily embraced a warrior's death at the conclusion of Custer of the West. *For some reason, the pressbook for this feature indicated that Custer's horse was the famed "Comanche" despite the fact that the steed in the film is the wrong color, while the actual mount of that name belonged to Capt. Myles Keogh. Adding such details, albeit erroneous ones, is but one example of how filmmakers attempted to woo the audience into thinking that what they see on the screen is based on fact.* SECURITY PICTURES. AUTRY MUSEUM OF WESTERN HERITAGE, LOS ANGELES

prompted one critic to note an ambitious foundation for the film, which attempted to view "the Indian Wars through a contemporary sensibility, and Custer as a thoroughly modern man who would have liked Camus."[36] Nevertheless, the picture was marred in that it relied too heavily upon cineramic gimmicks and such stock clichés as casting the blame for the debacle on Major Reno (Ty Hardin, the star of Warner Bros. "Bronco" on television)—

not unlike renditions of some forty years earlier.[37] Indeed, *Custer of the West* clearly was influenced by *They Died with Their Boots On* and was very much a homage to that film.

Like Flynn before him, Shaw's Custer is one of the few instances where foibles and strong convictions exist side by side, offering a characterization of some substance. An anachronism, as is the case with George C. Scott in *Patton,* the Boy General refuses to bend to the political will. He speaks out against corruption in high places and falls from grace with Grant. Libbie, played by Shaw's wife, Mary Ure, tries to aid him in his darkest hour. But even her strong love cannot save the husband she adores, because he rejects a scheme to endorse a Gatling gun–bristling railroad car designed as a superweapon of war against the Plains Indians. Custer clings to a chivalric code that a warrior must face his foe man-to-man. He will not hide behind superior technology or advocate its use under any circumstances. Realizing that his thinking is outmoded, Custer takes to the field for a final fight in the traditional way, and after a valiant effort, his command is destroyed. The Indians surround him and, out of respect for a brave enemy, give him the opportunity to escape, but Custer will not run. He accepts his fate and dies, not so much for his shortcomings as for the evils of a society that has rejected honor in its headlong race toward manifest destiny.

The bittersweet conclusion of *Custer of the West* might have indicated that the time for noble warriors had come to an end. Soon the war in Southeast Asia strengthened that message and carried it further when it came to the military in general and Custer in particular. A prime example of this change of the 1960s can be found in director

Little Big Man's *insane Custer (Richard Mulligan) raves about a corrupt U. S. Grant as his fate is about to be sealed. In this version of the story, the long-haired egomaniac, and the government he serves, are both guilty of a racist war of conquest—a message inspired by the conflict in Vietnam.* NATIONAL GENERAL. AUTRY MUSEUM OF WESTERN HERITAGE, LOS ANGELES

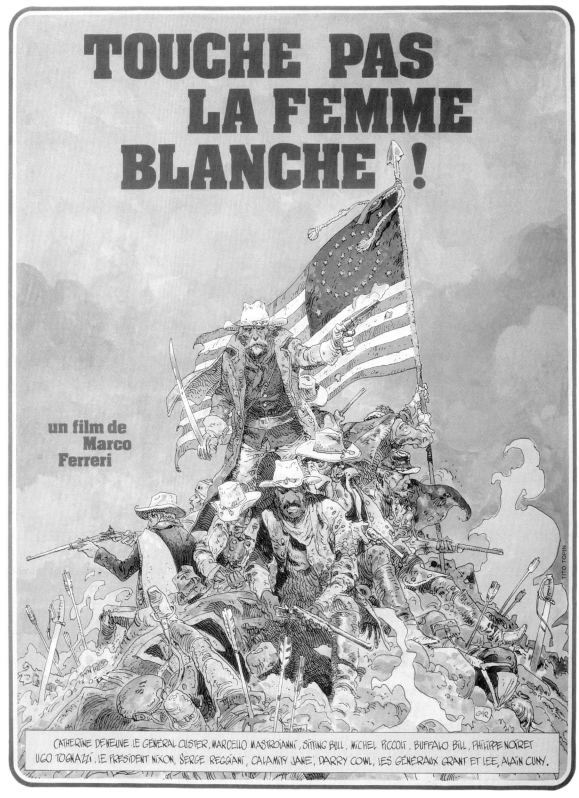

In the French production Touche pas la femme blanche *(1974), Custer epitomized the imperialistic ugly American military industrial establishment. Frederic Remington's* The Last Stand *(1890) inspired this one-sheet poster lampoon as just one indication of relationship between various popular forms that have been combined to form the Custer myth.*

In the post-Vietnam era, Custer as slapstick buffoon was an accepted satiric figure in Won Ton Ton, the Dog Who Saved Hollywood *(1976). Given the tenor of the times, about the only cinematic rendition of the Boy General during the centennial of his last stand predictably was a comedic one.* PARAMOUNT PICTURES. COURTESY OF THE MOTION PICTURE ACADEMY OF ARTS AND SCIENCES

Arthur Penn's reinterpretation of Thomas Berger's best-seller, *Little Big Man.*

Whereas the original novel was a comment on myth, Penn's adaptation took a different course. Following the example of *Soldier Blue,* Penn rendered an image of the army, personified by Custer, in keeping with sentiments generated during the war in Vietnam.[38] Though Richard Mulligan, as Custer, turned in a noteworthy performance, the movie was not on the same plane as Berger's literary work.[39]

Shortly after its premiere in 1970, one critic summed up the movie's major flaw: "Penn has juggled history to suit his purposes—while purporting all the while to be telling it like it is."[40] Nevertheless, the message seemed in keeping with the times. Not only did the lunatic leader suffer for his actions, but the "Christian" nation that con-

doned such militarism bore equal culpability, as evidenced by a scene cut from an earlier version of the script. In this deleted plot element, President U. S. Grant appears in the West to underscore the point that the country's guilt for mistreatment of the Indians reached to the highest government levels.[41]

Marco Ferrei's *Touche pas la femme blanche* of 1974 went beyond Penn to carry a similar message. Ferrei transformed his Custer, through the international star Marcello Mastroianni, into a vainglorious, dandified Milquetoast.[42] Custer fancies himself a lady's man but performs as dreadfully in lovemaking as he does in battle. One of his scouts, Buffalo Bill, is depicted as a spoiled, haughty closet homosexual, while "the half-breed Mitch, whom Custer has ordered, 'touche pas la femme blanche,'" is jealous of Yellow Hair and "runs a shop for Indian artifacts using white women as sweatshop labor."[43]

The president is not Grant but Richard Nixon, who sends the CIA into the picture. To make certain that the audience does not miss the point, displaced Vietnamese play the oppressed Sioux, under Sitting Bull (Alain Cuny), who leads his warriors into modern Paris, fighting their way through rush-hour traffic to engage Custer and his command, who are relaxing at a sidewalk café.[44]

There is no mistaking the attempt to equate Custer and the treatment of the American Indian in the nineteenth century with the United States' involvement in Southeast Asia in the twentieth century. So far as Ferrei's vision was concerned, the two episodes were all part of a continuation of America's long history of imperialistic designs.

For many years, Penn's and Ferrei's visions were the dominant silver-screen renditions of Custer. Then, in the early 1980s, Custer accompanied President Grant, Wild Bill Hickok, and Buffalo Cody West as a minor character in *The Legend of the Lone Ranger.* Custer appeared in but two scenes, one on a train, where the president tells him to move over for a guest at breakfast because he is such an inconsequential person. Grant prods Custer to obey with the threat that he will send him to Montana if he fails to do so. Later, when Grant has been kidnapped and is making good an escape with the Lone Ranger's assistance, Custer again comes into the picture, heading a cavalry charge to ensure the president's return to safety.[45]

In this, Custer finishes a poor second to the handsome pistol-packing hero and appears only to lend a degree of historical flavor to the "Wild Wild West" style

Art imitating art . . . Richard Mulligan returns as a caricature of Custer in Teachers. *In this case he is an escaped mental institution patient who dresses the part of figures from America's past to teach history at a inner city high school.* MGM/UNITED ARTISTS. COURTESY OF THE MOTION PICTURE ACADEMY OF ARTS AND SCIENCES

At least Custer was permitted to ride to the aid of the Lone Ranger in the concluding fight against the good guys and bad guys in classic Hollywood cavalry charge style in The Legend of the Lone Ranger *(1980).* UNIVERSAL PICTURES. AUTRY MUSEUM OF WESTERN HERITAGE, LOS ANGELES

production. Ironically, by the 1980s, Custer is less real, and perhaps less recognizable as a persona, than the fictional Lone Ranger with whom he rides.

It seems that *The Legend of the Lone Ranger* finally put Custer to rest, so far as the big screen was concerned, although an egotistical Custer-based character, Maj. General William Larchmont, reminiscent of the *Little Big Man* model, heads up the 7th Cavalry in *Wagons East,* a 1994 farce starring John Candy as a down-and-out wagon train master. In another 1994 film, a Chevy Chase vehicle called

Man of the House, a cardboard cutout of Custer appears as a comic foil for a youth group who uses the figure as a target for tomahawk-throwing practice. In both of these comedies, the message is clear. The once heroic cinematic Custer had become an instantly recognizable icon of vainglory. He now was a loser, whose name did not even have to be summoned to drive home the point. Only a quick caricature needed to flash across the screen to provide the necessary reference that all could readily understand. A similar fate lay ahead for Yellow Hair in yet another media form—television.

CHAPTER FIVE

Little Bighorn and the Little Screen

Many technical marvels were introduced after the Second World War, but few had greater impact than television. Beginning in 1948, following some two decades of experimentation, the new broadcast form aggressively invaded the living rooms of America. At first, four networks, which were to a great extent outgrowths of radio, launched the new vehicle over only thirty-seven channels. These were all clustered in less than two dozen metropolitan markets on the East Coast of the United States.[1]

As the new entertainment form spread, the appetite for shows grew. Producers reacted in many ways. The original news, sports, and variety offerings soon were joined by live drama, game shows, and comedies. As such, television from the outset was derivative, drawing upon many sources, including cinema, theater, vaudeville, and radio. In particular, it resembled radio because of the episodic basis of numerous TV shows. Like radio, too, television was geared for a national audience, who would tune in within hours of each other from New York to Los Angeles, thereby creating a homogeneous public experience.

On a more specific level, in 1949, television found Westerns to be yet another option for the growing lineup, when William Boyd bought the rights to his *Hopalong Cassidy* films, reformatted them, and televised the programs on Sundays. Gene Autry, Roy Rogers, and a host of others soon saddled up as well in an effort to capture the youth market whose parents once had been their fans at the Sat-

urday matinee. Unlike Hoppy, however, these shows were newly made productions.

If juvenile viewers could be enticed by a host of good guys on weekends, would not older buckaroos, who had been raised on the genre, desire to return to those thrilling days of yesteryear? The answer seemed strongly in the affirmative. Consequently, dozens of cowboys, lawmen, hired guns, gamblers, and even an occasional cavalry officer populated adult Westerns, which, from the late 1940s through the 1960s, formed a core of prime time.[2] Over time, numerous television oaters were churned out predominantly for a male audience in the evening, just as soap operas were being pitched to women during the day.

With Westerns holding their own in the ratings during this period, the prevalence of the genre assured that Custer would have at least an intermittent place in the evening lineups, but for the most part he was not a main player. Rather, he once again was relegated to a supporting role, much as he had been in many releases that were produced before the advent of TV. And just as in the past, sometimes only Custer's name was evoked rather than his appearing on the scene.

For example, in the 1956 *Gunsmoke* episode "Custer," Joe Trimble, a deserter from the 7th Cavalry, is apprehended as a rustler and brutal murderer. Matt Dillon, the fictional marshal of Dodge City, brings the man to trial, but because of a lack of evidence, he must relinquish the criminal to the military.[3] This plot was identical to that of a 1951

Custer found his way into the many Western television series of the 1950s and 1960s, including the "Longhair" episode of Yancy Derringer *(1958) where Grant Williams assumed the guise as he menacingly confronts one of the show's regular characters, Pahoo-ka Ta Wah, an Indian played by X. Brands.* CBS. NEIL SUMMERS

In *Bronco,* another Warner Bros. Western, the protagonist, Bronco Layne (Ty Hardin), does not witness Custer's defeat, but he does agree to find Sitting Bull in the mistaken belief that he is assisting a U.S. Army officer on a secret mission. In reality, the major is an impostor who wants to retrieve the payroll taken from the dead 7th Cavalry troopers at the Little Bighorn.[7]

In *Have Gun Will Travel,* Paladin (Richard Boone) rides past the site of Custer's defeat not long after the fight. The black-clad gun-for-hire, a former officer himself, does not dwell on this incident and simply rides on to his next encounter.

Barry Atwater was another actor cast as Custer, in this case for a two-part show on the popular Cheyenne *series.* WARNER BROS.

DAN GAGLIASSO

In a two-part episode of Branded *called "Call to Glory" (1966), Autie (Robert Lansing) and Libbie (Kathie Browne) are resurrected in a pale imitation of the Olivia de Havilland–Errol Flynn casting for* They Died with Their Boots On.

NBC. NEIL SUMMERS

show of the same title on the radio version of *Gunsmoke.*[4] Here the former trooper turned desperado is linked to the ill-fated Custer as one means of informing the audience that poetic justice is served. After his release, Trimble is escorted back to duty just in time to rejoin the regiment as it rides to the Little Bighorn.

During the 1957 season, the hero of the Warner Bros. *Cheyenne* series, Cheyenne Bodie (Clint Walker), attempts to make peace with the Sioux. In so doing, his path crosses that of Custer.[5] The next season, in a two-part episode, Bodie undertakes a secret mission to halt Custer before his advance to doom. While working undercover, he is captured and held prisoner. In the concluding segment, he is branded as a deserter but comes back to recount the fate of the 7th Cavalry.[6]

As such, Little Bighorn was the hook for viewers, not Custer, who was, during the immediate post–World War II years, restricted to features. It was Walt Disney who brought Yellow Hair to American viewers at home. Disney's theatrical release *Tonka* was renamed *Comanche* and shown as one of the many offerings from Frontierland on the popular, long-running Sunday TV show.

Another one-time cavalryman, Jason McCord (Chuck Connors), the cashiered West Point graduate of *Branded,* finds himself associated with a military disaster other than his own fictional Bitter Creek when he becomes involved with the Little Bighorn in a multipart episode, "Call to

Glory." Asked by President Grant and General Sheridan to investigate allegations that Custer's political ambitions might stir up trouble among the Indians, McCord at first refuses. He subsequently finds that Custer disdains the Indians, calling them "dog eaters" who are savages living "twenty thousand years behind our civilization." Fearing that rumors of Custer's interest in the White House may be the fuse to ignite a war, Jason visits Autie (Robert Lansing) at Fort Lincoln, where McCord's old friend receives him warmly.

The hero soon discovers that Yellow Hair is being wooed as a presidential candidate by "Indian Ring" oper-

The Twilight Zone's "The 7th Is Made Up of Phantoms" was another instance where twentieth century characters were transported back to June 25, 1876. CBS. AUTRY MUSEUM OF WESTERN HERITAGE, LOS ANGELES

atives bent on using the officer's popularity for their own greedy ends. In the process, Crazy Horse (Michael Pate) enters the picture. White maltreatment of the Indian warrior adds fuel to the hatred that grows between the two peoples.

McCord pretends not to care for Custer, whom he pronounces a moronic fop. Working his way into the confidence of the scheming politicos, he exposes their plot and returns Custer to his senses. In the end, the two West Pointers are reconciled. Like schoolboys, they end the three-part episode with a race from Fort Lincoln, North Dakota, to a hilltop. After their mad dash, the two halt to overlook the valley below. It is the Little Bighorn. Regardless of this preposterous situation, the audience knows, unlike the two men, that this parting presages another

Joe Morros was Custer for a Warner Bros. Time Tunnel *episode. The studio mingled footage from* They Died with Their Boots On *for large scale scenes in this 1966 TV production.* ABC. DAN GAGLIASSO

event in Custer's life. There Autie and his old comrade meet for what will be the last time. He gives Jason a watch that plays "Garry Owen." McCord then bids his friend farewell and rides off to further adventures.

Other television characters were destined for an unexpected adventure in Custer country. They were not riding forth in the 1870s with the 7th Cavalry, however; rather they were late-twentieth-century national guardsmen on maneuvers in Montana. Two of the men, Sergeant Conners and Private First Class McCluskey, are familiar with the minute details of the Custer battle. A third member of their crew, Corporal Langsford, is not. He thinks his comrades are crazy as they begin to link certain present-day events to that fateful day in 1876. In the end, the two amateur historians prove all too correct as Rod Serling informs: "Past and present are about to collide head-on, as they are wont to do in a very special bivouac area known as . . . the Twilight Zone."

Caught in an unexplained time warp, the trio ultimately attempts to reach Custer and save him. As they near the site of the Last Stand, the men abandon their tank and join in at the last moment with their M-1 carbines and Colt M1911 semiautomatic pistols for a provocative *Twilight Zone* version of Little Bighorn, "The 7th Is Made Up of Phantoms." At the episode's conclusion, the three men's names appear on the monument alongside the fallen troopers who rode with Custer's command.[8]

Time travel also lands two scientists from the 1960s, Dr. Tony Newman and Dr. Douglas Philips, of *The Time Tunnel*, in the midst of the 1876 campaign.[9] Crazy Horse and some of his followers capture the pair of time travelers, who are part of America's most "secret experiment." One of the visitors from the future escapes. The second one remains in the hands of the Sioux and speaks to Sitting Bull. He wins the wise elder over, persuading him to parley with Yellow Hair. All the while, their colleagues in the 1960s are attempting to extract the pair from their plight with the technical assistance of a professor from the local university, Dr. Charles Whitebird, an American Indian who specializes in the history of government relations with his people.

The modern-day rescuers fail in their mission, as do Newman and Philips as they try to induce Custer to treat with the Sioux and Cheyenne. Yellow Hair refuses. Because Custer has learned of Gen. George Crook's encounter, he believes that the warring tribes must be engaged at all costs. Custer divulges to Dr. Philips that he will be on hand to witness the 7th Cavalry's greatest victory. Custer rides forth to the Little Bighorn. Philips and Newman escape and disappear into another era. History remains unchanged.

Wayne Maunder had considerable help from the supporting cast of Custer, *including scout California Joe (Slim Pickens), Capt. Myles Keogh (Grant Woods), and Sergeant James Bustard (Peter Palmer) on a television series that lasted only a single season (September to December 1967). Evidently Custer had run his course as the stuff of heroic daring for most TV viewers whose evening news was filled with real warfare in Southeast Asia.* ABC. NEIL SUMMERS

For the remainder of the 1960s, Custer's TV appearances were fleeting and tended to offer a one-dimensional character or a cartoon, such as in one episode of *F Troop*, a sitcom that opened each week with a clip from the charge in *They Died with Their Boots On*.

Bumbling Capt. Wilton Parmenter (Ken Berry), commander of Fort Courage, meets Custer. Impressed by what he sees, he adopts the legendary lieutenant colonel as a role model. Parmenter takes on the airs of his idol, complete with riding crop, swaggering, and long hair. The results of this hero worship are anything but positive. The troops begin to call their once beloved, albeit ineffective, leader "Old Ironpants." Eventually, Parmenter returns to his former ways as a lovable, naive pawn of his two manipulating noncommissioned officers, Sgt. Morgan O'Rourke (Forrest Tucker) and Cpl. Randolph Agarn (Larry Storch), who actually control the fort.[10]

Despite the fact that the town of Monroe, Michigan's favorite son had been reduced to the level of an unflattering TV parody, he became the main character in a short-lived series, *Custer*. During the 1967 season, David Weisbart, who never gave up hope for *The Day Custer Fell*, was able to sell ABC on his pet project. After spending $1 million in preproduction, Weisbart's feature was shelved because *Cleopatra* had proven so costly that Fox did not have the $18 million required to make a Western version of *The Longest Day*. By the time funds became available from that studio's all-star World War II blockbuster and the financially successful *Sound of Music*, the executives decided not to continue the enterprise. One compelling factor was that Robert Shaw's *Custer of the West* had beaten them to the punch. Once that occurred, Weisbart found it "almost impossible to revitalize" his own vision of Little Bighorn.[11]

Not willing to scrap the enterprise, he converted the concept into a television show that was to cover the decade after the Civil War. The show's producers envisioned action as the central force of what they promised to be a dramatic and suspenseful series, with limited romance.[12] Just in case, however, Wayne Maunder, in the title slot, was to be a bachelor. That way, an occasional love interest could be interjected. So much for poor Elizabeth.

In the first episode, Custer rides into Fort Hays, Kansas, on a dark and stormy night. He finds the sentry asleep and the enlisted men gambling in the stables. The ringleader is an ex-Confederate, James Bustard, the actual name of an enlisted man who served in Company I of the 7th from 1875 to 1876.[13] In his TV persona, Bustard is a muscular, tough private who has no love for Yankees or officers. Custer removes his shoulder straps and challenges the man to a fight. He defeats the trooper, but rather than sending

him to the guardhouse, promotes him to sergeant. On the spot, Bustard becomes a Custerphile.

Meanwhile, Captain Keogh has come in during the fight, yet having observed the fisticuffs, says nothing, then departs. Bustard reveals to Custer that the cigar-chomping Irishman is Captain Keogh, who can be counted on to keep quiet about the incident. Keogh joins Bustard as a pro-Custer man, as does the scout California Joe. This foursome spends the rest of the season in various adventures that have little to do with Custer's real life or the Little Bighorn. For instance, a meeting of Custer and Crazy Horse in Kansas and Oklahoma in an early episode was one of many complete fabrications.

Whether because the plots were so improbable that they were unacceptable or because of changing attitudes among a good many Americans, *Custer* was canceled after only a season. Despite his flowing hair and rebellious manner, Maunder's Custer lacked appeal to the youth market of the 1960s and did not ring true with older viewers brought up on Errol Flynn or previous versions of this historic figure.[14]

Indeed, Maunder's portrayal and the premise of the series were at odds with a growing shift in public opinion in a number of areas. First of all, the show ran into opposition from several groups, including the Tribal Indians Land Rights Association, which worked to have the show taken off the air. Lobbyists depicted Custer as a nineteenth-century Nazi in trying to oust him from the ABC lineup. Another tactic was to insist on equal time from the various network affiliates at the local level, which would have been costly.[15] Also, a strong antimilitary trend had developed among various sectors of the American public during the Vietnam War.[16] All of these factors, combined with the decline in the Western not only on TV but also in the theater, meant that *Custer* could not contend for primetime ratings.[17]

Nonetheless, the series was to television what *They Died with Their Boots On* had been to films, in that Custer was a positive central character rather than a minor character or antagonist. There were vast differences between the two, however, as the feature proved a financial success that was remembered for years to come, whereas the small-screen version enjoyed neither distinction.

Little wonder then that nearly a decade passed before Custer had a television comeback. This time he was to be tried for his crimes rather than hailed as a hero. "The Court-Martial of George Armstrong Custer," a 1977 *Hallmark Hall of Fame* entry, opened with Alfred Terry's column arriving on the scene in the aftermath of June 25, 1876.[18] They find a lone survivor—Custer. In death, he would be

What if Custer had been found alive on the battlefield? This scenario was the basis of an alternate history novel, The Court-Martial of George Armstrong Custer, *and the television program adapted from this book as part of the* Hallmark Hall of Fame *in 1977, with Blythe Danner as Libbie and James Olson as Autie.* NBC/WARNER BROS. AUTRY MUSEUM OF WESTERN HERITAGE, LOS ANGELES

a hero. Alive, he represented a major embarrassment to the Grant administration.

Custer must be dealt with rapidly and made to bear the burden for the defeat to block Grant's political enemies from turning the Little Bighorn debacle to their advantage. All must appear fair and aboveboard so critics could not claim that this was a whitewash. Sheridan is ordered to testify on Custer's behalf to ensure that the proceedings cannot be construed as a vendetta.

The plan fails. Grant and his circle do not reckon with Autie's two powerful allies, his defense attorney (Brian Keith) and his charming Libbie (Blythe Danner). In the end, Custer is vindicated, but through no action of his own. He has lost his mind and is in no position to refute any of the charges against him. Thus the star witness to one of the greatest historical mysteries of all time cannot shed any light on what actually happened. Nonetheless, he emerges a hero. Elizabeth Custer manages to extort a Medal of Honor for her husband while wining the love of the prosecutor (Ken Howard), who is reduced in rank and exiled to a far-off Western post after losing the trial.

This Pyrrhic victory again pointed to the conclusion that the responsibility for a nation's actions rests on the shoulders of both those who carry out a policy and those who made the policy, a moral that was timely, given the outcome of Vietnam on one hand and Watergate on the other. Moreover, Elizabeth Custer emerges as the power behind her spouse, which was in keeping with the growing feminist movement. Of equal importance was the recognition that Libbie actually played an extremely influential part during and after Autie's life.[19]

Further, to a certain extent, "The Court-Martial of George Armstrong Custer" offered Yellow Hair as a tool of inept politicos, a version of the past that fit with the post-Vietnam period. The halcyon days of Camelot had been upstaged by assassination, divisive war, racial unrest, and the resignation of a president. Custer could not withstand these factors when he again came to television, this time in *The Legend of the Golden Gun*, a 1979 NBC release. The tongue-in-cheek scenario transformed him into a Victorian-era Douglas MacArthur, complete with sunglasses and corncob pipe, perhaps to demonstrate that all professional military men are cut from the same unsavory cloth. An egotistical, boastful bungler, Custer is at odds with the pure motives of the story's main character, a youth who has donned the gleaming white outfit of a champion of right, a pseudo Lone Ranger. Custer, an antihero, attempts to thwart the lad at every turn but is no match for the protagonist.[20]

Having been brought back to life, Custer was ready to perform again, but he was not to come back into the limelight for many years. As an example, Raquel Welch's TV performance in *The Legend of Walks Far Woman* (1982) takes place in the aftermath of the Little Bighorn. Welch was in the village during this battle, but the audience sees nothing of Long Hair or his troopers. Instead, the focus is on her tribulations after this great but short-lived victory for the Plains Indians.

Likewise, a made-for-cable Sam Elliott vehicle, *The Quick and the Dead* (1987), has leading lady Kate Capshaw heading west in 1876 to join a brother who is an officer with the 7th Cavalry, only to learn that he has been killed at the Last Stand. Here again, the incident is dropped into the story line as a minor plot element to establish time and place, but as in *Walks Far Woman*, Custer does not appear. In fact, it is not necessary for his physical presence at all. The mention of his name and the place of his final battle are adequate to send a signal to the audience, which immediately recognizes the implications of Custer and Little Bighorn.

Many years passed before a more serious and concerted effort to draw upon this notoriety was considered. Then, Melissa Matheson's miniseries script, based on Evan Connel's best-selling *Son of the Morning Star*, made the rounds of the networks.[21] The teleplay finally landed at ABC, where the financial success and acclaim accorded *Lonesome Dove* (1989) and the subsequent triumph of *Dances with Wolves* (1990) ultimately worked in favor of the venture.

Before this, casting experienced ups and downs, as various preliminary choices for Custer were rejected. Early in the process, a pre–*Dances with Wolves* Kevin Costner was considered, but executives felt he did not have enough name recognition to draw viewers, so they sought another actor. The search went on, with Tom Berenger and even Sean Penn being mentioned, before Gary Cole, the star of television's *Midnight Caller*, gained the title role long before he played the father in the tongue-in-cheek *The Brady Bunch Movie* (1995).

With the main actor selected, Hollywood once more reshaped the Custers. They became the nineteenth-century equivalent of the young, upwardly mobile couple. Some genuine attempts at accuracy were made by taking pieces of Connell's work as story elements, thereby returning to similar efforts made by Selig, Ince, and Walsh, as well as incorporating many characteristics contained in Mayes's *The Day Custer Fell*. And based on circumstantial evidence, there even seems to be a case to be made that Stephen Ambrose's *Crazy Horse and Custer* had a strong influence on the teleplay.

Elizabeth Custer also enjoyed the same prominence as her counterparts in *They Died with Their Boots On, Custer of the West,* and *The Court-Martial of George Armstrong Custer.* In fact, much of the dramatization depended on Libbie's voice-over narration to carry the plot during the decade that began with Custer's post–Civil War transfer to Kansas and ended with his death in Montana. To offset Libbie's adoring prose about her Boy General, a Cheyenne woman, Kate Big Head (voice-over by folk singer Buffy Sainte-Marie), offered what supposedly was representative of the Indian point of view.[22]

In certain respects, George Custer almost is secondary in the story—a character of relatively little consequence in the broader sweep of things. Grant, Sherman, and Sheridan maneuver their headstrong subordinate not as a knight, as Custer might believe, but as a mere pawn in the final game to complete manifest destiny. A postscript about Crazy Horse and Sitting Bull told how they came to their ends,[23] Sitting Bull coming off as "far more noble" than Custer, Grant, and the other self-serving whites of the miniseries.[24]

Promotions for *Son of the Morning Star* stressed the extensive research that had been conducted to produce the show. The show's historical consultant, as might be expected, made much of these efforts, praising the costuming and production design as superior for the most part, and the use of reenactors and Plains Indians for the extras as added pluses.[25]

On the other hand, one knowledgeable reviewer concluded that "director Michael Robe tries too much historical veracity with little or no explanation." He then went on to list a string of details, all of which added little or nothing to the story, even when they were based on some factual underpinning. In fact, it appeared as though "the director hoped to include every incident and viewpoint but many depictions are unfortunately off base."[26]

So much for efforts to depict history in miniseries form.[27] In attempting to capture so much minutia, *Son of the Morning Star* seemed to have fallen short of delivering a compelling story. Problematical casting of the main characters detracted from the entertainment value as well.[28] The leads seemed to walk through their parts with little enthusiasm, thereby even reducing the romance between Autie and Libbie to an unconvincing melodrama. They certainly lacked the on-camera magic of Flynn and de Havilland!

A more telling reflection on "this latest paean to G. A. Custer" was the remark that even "Uncle Tomahawks" among American Indian people liked *Son of the Morning Star,* a depiction that one writer held up as a prime example of the "New Custerism" that replaced the former stereotypes of the "Old Custerism," which depicted the Indians

Gary Cole's Custer waits between takes on the set of Son of the Morning Star *(1991).* MOUNT PRODUCTIONS/REPUBLIC/ABC/PRESTON FISHER PRODUCTIONS. AUTRY MUSEUM OF WESTERN HERITAGE, LOS ANGELES

as savages. Instead, *Son of the Morning Star* and other more recent productions painted a picture of "sentimentality and romance" when it came to the American Indian.[29] Critic Judith Crist's analysis for the February 2, 1991, issue of *TV Guide* was somewhat more enthusiastic, as well as perceptive in finding the story to be a "big, brawny but flawed accounting of a man who continues to fascinate and explain America."

Whatever its shortcomings, *Son of the Morning Star* had reintroduced Custer to the viewing public in more than a passing way. Though long absent from movie theaters, he found steady albeit cameo roles on television, not unlike his use as a secondary stock player for serials, features, and short subjects in the 1930s and early 1940s.

His intermittent appearances as a merciless Indian hater in five episodes of CBS's *Dr. Quinn, Medicine Woman* provide one example of how he had become the quintessential white supremacist of the Indian wars. Conversely, NBC's *Class of '61* (1993) presented him as a youthful, raucous cadet heading bravely off to duty in the Civil War.[30] At the end of the twentieth century, Custer's on-screen personas formed a whole symbolic continuum,

In three of Custer's five appearances as a recurring character on Dr. Quinn Medicine Woman *Jason Leland Adams was the Indian-hating Yellow Hair and archvillian worthy of a nineteenth-century melodrama.* CBS. AUTRY MUSEUM OF WESTERN HERITAGE, LOS ANGELES

ranging from bigoted, corrupt megalomaniac to youthful, dashing cavalier.

Nonetheless, during the decades following Vietnam, the prevalent portrayal was that of an all-purpose antihero, as seen in *Buffalo Girls* (1995), a miniseries based on Larry McMurtry's novel (although it is notable that Custer was not included in the book). Broadcasting Custer into the living rooms of America gave one of the characters, Bartle Bones (Jack Palance), a chance to exchange words with the cocksure Custer. Bones tells Long Hair that the cavalry faces a large Indian village with many men who are brave warriors, as opposed to only 200 or 300 troopers (the number in the command actually was more than 600). To this, Custer (John Diehl) replies, "We're the Seventh Cavalry" and can beat any adversary.[31]

At this statement, Bones declares Custer a madman. He warns his friend Calamity Jane (Anjelica Huston) to get away from the 7th Cavalry as soon as she can. Calamity follows this warning but manages by accident to be present at the Little Bighorn, where she observes the battle from a distant vantage point in the model of many of the previous eyewitness survivors' stories scattered throughout print, film, and television.

During the week following *Buffalo Girls'* television premier, Elizabeth Custer made her return in "Custer's Next to Last Stand," an episode of *Legend* on the United Paramount Network. Libbie (Ashly Laurence) and Autie (Allen Hyde-White) were reunited once more in a fanciful show in keeping with a series that lampooned Western heroes.[32]

Custer flatters his supportive spouse with the words that she would "make a lovely first lady" as they ride together on a mission to gather evidence against War Department bureaucrats who endanger the lives of U.S. troops through corruption. Libbie pursues the show's main character, Ernest Pratt (Richard Dean Anderson), a former newspaperman turned dime novelist with his fiction creation and alter ego, Nicodemus Legend. She believes that her friend Pratt can help find evidence to support their case, although her husband looks rather askance at the fiction writer.

When Pratt points out that the general needs resounding facts to present to Congress, the reply is, "They have the voice of George Armstrong Custer. What could be louder than that?" Pratt retorts that it will take more than Custer's "wonderful charisma" to convict the wrongdoers, to which Custer responds, "What you mean to say is my ego."

Despite such overtones, Custer's efforts are to attack corruption in government, thereby showing a side that for the most part had been suppressed after *They Died with Their Boots On.* This positive motive seems less important, though, than the tag line of the episode. At show's end, Custer enthusiastically embraces his next assignment on the Plains. As always, the audience knows what Custer does not: Little Bighorn will be his final scene.

In yet one other short-lived new-age Western, the 1996 syndicated series *The Lazarus Man,* Robert Urich wanders the immediate post–Civil War frontier in search of his lost identity. After being buried alive and left for dead, he emerges from the grave with amnesia. He knows nothing of his friends, enemies, or anything about himself.

In his quest to discover who he is, he comes upon a sergeant waiting in ambush to kill Custer. Lazarus saves the Boy General, although he does not know who the man in the buckskin is. Others ride up while the two converse. One of the riders is Tom Custer, who lets Lazarus know that the man with whom he has been speaking is the "golden cavalier"—Custer.

The party rides back to the post, where Autie passionately greets Libbie as Tom looks on intently. Later the audience discovers that Tom's interest is far from fraternal. Regardless, the key is that Libbie is as much center stage as Autie in this version, somewhat as had been the case in "Legend" the previous season. This increasing emphasis on Elizabeth Custer in television programming was indicative of heightened sensitivities growing out of the women's liberation movement.

In this light, Libbie is an important presence when Lazarus joins the Custers in their quarters for dinner soon after he has arrived at the post. Tom is present with a pair of Medals of Honor pinned to his frock coat, one of the several details to cue the knowledgeable viewer that what they are seeing is authentic.[33]

The conversation is cordial, and Lazarus regales the party with a tall tale. After the supper concludes, Custer and Lazarus withdraw to the general's study, where he confides that he sometimes wishes he were a king so that he would not have to be held back by his superiors. He then offers Lazarus a position under Chief of Scouts Will Comstock, in the main as a bodyguard and an undercover agent to discover who is behind the murder attempt.

Looking for leads, Lazarus inquires what the motive for the shooting might be. Custer replies that he was a brigadier general at the age of twenty-three. He goes on to cite that during the last six months of the war, "[I] captured ten thousand prisoners, including seven generals, and during that time I never lost a color, never lost a gun, and certainly was never defeated." With this sort of enviable record, Custer egotistically concludes that the killer could be anyone "who wishes he were me."

The next day, Lazarus takes up his inquest, but after discovering the prime suspect and reporting the finding to Custer, he is told that there is another mission to be carried out that is more pressing at the moment. This is to take Libbie on a carriage ride, because Autie has military matters to attend to. Lazarus agrees.

During the ride, she tells Lazarus how General Sherman sent her the table on which Lee signed the surrender at Appomattox, with the explanation that no individual did more to win the war. She rhetorically asks, "What women would not love a hero such as him," and indeed, "What women wouldn't perish for the privilege of being in that man's arms?"

As soon as they halt, however, Libbie makes advances toward Lazarus. She bluntly states that when you marry a Boy General, you live with a man who is sometimes a

Allen Hyde-White was on hand for "Custer's Almost Last Stand" episode of Legends *(1995).* TL PRODUCTIONS/UPN. AUTRY MUSEUM OF WESTERN HERITAGE, LOS ANGELES

Maxwell Caulfield made a number of costume changes reflecting the popular images of the Civil War cavalier and Custer as buckskin-clad frontiersman that had come to personify the man who had been transformed into a myth. These renditions were for the "Boy General" episode of the short-lived Lazarus Man *series.* PHOTOGRAPHS BY FRANCES HAYS AND TOM DAWSON. CASTLE ROCK ENTERTAINMENT. AUTRY MUSEUM OF WESTERN HERITAGE, LOS ANGELES

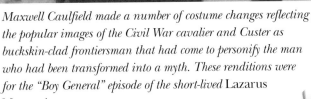

dashing Galahad, and at other times a "stubborn, self-absorbed, and frankly reckless" child. He is a great man, she acknowledges, but they never will have children of their own. She longs for an adult relationship, even if only a fleeting one.

Lazarus rejects her because they are both trusted by Custer. To violate this trust would be dishonorable. Frustrated, Libbie exclaims: "I am sick of honor, valor, and patriotism! Don't men ever think about love?"

Though nothing comes of this, Tom Custer has been observing through field glasses. Eventually he reveals that he loves Elizabeth and is capable of killing for her, just as his brother Autie is. Nothing comes of this potential threat.

Instead, Lazarus saves the general's life a second time, when he foils an assassination plot led by Comstock. Custer kills the scout in cold blood, then intends to dis-

patch the other four assailants, despite the fact that Lazarus has disarmed them. He is furious when Lazarus keeps him from cutting down the other conspirators. The general orders Lazarus's arrest, but later he relents in deference to the two times he has been saved by this mysterious stranger.

He still is not content, however, and decides to punish the man who twice rescued him. Custer does so by gunning down yet another member of the group that sought to murder him. Lazarus looks on helplessly as this trooper dies. The victim is the only man who can reveal Lazarus's true identity.

In frustration and anger, Lazarus calls out: "You're running up quite a debt Custer! I wonder on what stricken field you'll be asked to pay for it?" Custer does not respond, but the viewer knows the answer.

Lazarus, who earlier had told Libbie, "There are not many women in the world like you Mrs. Custer," writes in his diary at the conclusion of the episode that Custer is court-martialed for the death of the trooper who held the key to his past. Despite this, he confides in his journal: "Gallant Libbie. Lucky Custer."

In another 1996 outing, Custer once again is painted in unflattering hues, in this case portrayed by Peter Horton, from the popular "thirtysomething" series. He is every bit as haughty as the man-who-would-be-king character of *Lazarus Man.* But in the TNT made-for-TV production, *Crazy Horse,* the famous Lakota warrior again is spotlighted as the prototypical American Indian leader. The Last Stand in this show is but a required ritual to execute Custer for the transgressions of greedy white expansionists.

Though trampled by Crazy Horse, Custer refused to remain in the grave. He arose the next year as a younger, pre–Little Bighorn nemesis in CBS's *Stolen Women, Captured Hearts.* The buckskin-clad Custer, this time personified by an alumnus of *Dr. Quinn*—William Shockley—rides rampant in 1868 Kansas. He is opposed by a proud warrior, Toklah (Michael Greyeyes), whose family has been killed by the hated whites. Toklah's capture of two white women, a newly married redhead, Anna Morgan (Janine Turner), and her friend Sarah White (Jean Louisa Kelly), has an unfortunate consequence.[34]

Anna's groom and her brother set out with a grizzled, Benteen-like cavalry officer, Captain Farnsworth (Dennis Weaver), to rescue the two women. They fail, but word of this story has reached Custer, and "Old Goldy Locks," as Farnsworth refers to his commanding officer, takes an interest in the matter. His motives are less than altruistic, however, because, as the captain quips, Custer "hasn't been in the newspapers since he massacred all those Cheyenne down on the Washita. I reckon he's starting to feel ignored."

Bent on publicity, Custer comes into town to the strains of the "Battle Cry of Freedom," his long, unbound hair flowing under a wide-brimmed black hat, his costume *du jour* of 1990s television. He theatrically boasts, "We'll

Peter Horton had a cameo role in Crazy Horse, *indicative of Yellow Hair's fall from grace and his replacement as hero by others.* TURNER ENTERTAINMENT. DAN GAGLIASSO

dash across the plains; rescue the damsels; and be back in less than a month." This is not bombast, however, because Custer's command finds the prisoners. He demands their return, but in true romance formula, Anna has fallen in love with Toklah and does not want to leave him. For the moment Custer seems sympathetic, remarking, "I often thought I was part Indian myself."

His response is mere rhetoric. Once the two women are safely home, Custer informs Anna's husband not to worry about the "damned savages." He vows to find them again, and when he does, "it will be like clearing out wasps."

Here one can discern what Custer has come to represent in and through popular culture. After generations, he can be manipulated much like the plastic characters in Dungeons and Dragons style role-playing games, invested with whatever attributes or idiosyncrasies the player might desire from a stockpile provided by the game's creator.[35]

Custer's elasticity contributed to his endurance. Like several other larger-than-life personalities associated with the American West, including Buffalo Bill, Wild Bill Hickok, Billy the Kid, and Davy Crockett, he is an instantly identifiable international celebrity who offers an easy means for varied media to convey a range of themes.[36]

Consequently, with the passage of time, the historic Custer and the details of his life might be seen as being superseded by his utility as a malleable myth.[37] The remarkable niche carved in the main by film and television has afforded him a certain immortality. This especially seems true in light of the voracious appetite for programming brought on by the advent of home video, cable and direct TV, the information superhighway, and additional electronic forms, which were ushered in during the last two decades of the twentieth century.[38] With all these forums, the various faces of Custer can be called up simultaneously. As a result, Custer's value as a commodity in a "future shock" world might exceed the wildest dreams of all the filmmakers and television moguls who did so much to keep him in the public mind.

Conversely, the prevailing trend toward displacing Custer as folk hero and recasting him as villain, along with the pantheon of Custers who have been summoned up over generations, thereby sending diametrically opposing signals when he is evoked, raises certain questions. If a large segment of society no longer identifies with Custer, or ceases to grasp the clear-cut symbolism he has evoked in the past, his star, like that of the Western in general, ultimately might be eclipsed. Should he become as hackneyed as the cardboard standee of *Man of the House*, will he finally be laid to rest? In a post-Holocaust society, might Custer's now-dominant incarnation as an allegorical whipping boy for the past sins of racism and genocide not be displaced by other, more recent demons, or will he continue to be the dominant American Satan that he has become through many media forms? As technology and science increasingly overshadow ceremony and religion, will he not be discarded as a relic of an irrelevant bygone time?

But if Custer, as Bruce Rosenberg suggests, embodies a sort of American antagonism against smothering authority "in modern, urban society," the name, if not the facts associated with him and his life, ought to find a continued niche in popular culture.[39] This particularly seems the case if the contention is correct that Americans tend to view the past "in their own image."[40]

Should that premise ring true, only widespread radical change in deep-seated thinking and behavior will erase Custer's pivotal place as part of the lore of both the West and the nation as a whole. In fact, if Custer's configuration in media is shaped by the times, during an era when presidential impeachment heightened the discussion about moral relativism, might he not even be due for reinvestiture as a hero?[41] Conversely, with frequent references in the late 1990s to ethnic cleansing, Washita's chief architect might be trotted out as an example of genocide.

It is the very dynamism of the myth that has kept Custer animated long after the final shot was fired at Little Bighorn. The multiple personalities that have been assigned to Custer by generations of yarn spinners have fashioned him into a valuable resource. He is an instantly recognizable icon who can take on many guises to convey a particular message to the audience. While these depictions tell little or nothing about Custer the man, they do reveal much about the point of view of those who invoke the myth. Indeed, if, as Joseph Campbell says, myths inform a society, so they also inform the careful observer about a society.

So it is that, whether in a tragedy or comedy, as leading man or bit player, protagonist or antagonist, Custer has moved from the realm of mortal man to immortal myth. Much of this has to do with the fact that his film and television repertoire is virtually unequaled. With Custer's impressive list of credits, the seasoned trouper seems destined to make more curtain calls before taking his final bow.

Chronology of Custer Films, Serials, and Television Programs

TITLE	RELEASE DATE*	PRODUCTION COMPANY	ACTOR (ROLE)
1. *On the Little Big Horn; or, Custer's Last Stand*	1909	Selig Polyscope Co.	Paul McCormick, Jr.
2. *On the Little Big Horn*	1910	Nestor	?
3. *Custer's Last Stand* (Possibly same as 1 above and issued under different title)	1910	Chicago Film	?
4. *Custer's Last Fight* (Possibly a.k.a. *Custer's Last Raid,* 1913)	1912	Bison	Francis Ford
5. *The Big Horn Massacre*	1913	Kalem	?
6. *Campaigning with Custer* (Possibly the same film as 7)	1913	Bison	?
7. *Camping with Custer* (Possibly the same film as 6)	1913	?	?
8. *The Massacre*	1914	Biograph	Wilfred Lucas[†]
9. *Colonel Custard's Last Stand*	1914	Frontier	?[†] (Colonel Custard)

* Dates provided are years of release, not copyright dates.
† Character based on Custer.
†† Shooting title or titles.

TITLE	RELEASE DATE*	PRODUCTION COMPANY	ACTOR (ROLE)
10. *Custer's Last Scout* (2 parts)	1915	Bison	?
11. *In the Days of '75 and '76*	1915	Black Hills Feature Film Company	?
12. *Britton of the Seventh* (4 parts)	1916	Vitagraph	Ned Finley
13. *Bob Hampton of Placer*	1921	Associated First National Productions	Dwight Crittenden
14. *Wild Bill Hickok*	1923	Paramount Pictures	Charles Dudley
15. *Custer's Last Stand* (Reissue of 1912 production)	1925	Quality Amusement Corporation	Francis Ford
16. *The Scarlet West*	1925	First National Pictures	Robert Edeson
17. *The Flaming Frontier*	1926	Universal	Dustin Farnum
18. *General Custer at Little Big Horn*	1926	Sunset Productions	John Beck
19. *The Last Frontier*	1926	Metropolitan	?
20. *Spoilers of the West*	1927	MGM	Charles Thurston
21. *The Last Frontier*	1932	RKO	William Desmond
22. *The World Changes*	1933	First National Pictures	Clay Clement
23. *Custer's Last Stand* (Serial, 16 parts)	1936	Weiss Productions	Franklin McGlynn, Jr.
24. *The Plainsman*	1937	Paramount	John Miljan
25. *Goofs and Saddles*	1937	Columbia	Ted Lorch[†] (General Muster)
26. *Oregon Trail* (Serial, 16 parts)	1939	Universal	Roy Barcroft
27. *Wyoming (Bad Man from Wyoming)*[††]	1940	MGM	Paul Kelly
28. *Santa Fe Trail*	1940	Warner Bros.	Ronald Reagan
29. *Badlands of Dakota*	1941	Universal	Addison Richards
30. *They Died with Their Boots On*	1941	Warner Bros.	Errol Flynn
31. *Law of the Badlands*	1944	Warner Bros.	Warren Douglas
32. *Fort Apache (War Party)*[††]	1948	Argosy and RKO	Henry Fonda[†] (Lieutenant Colonel Thursday)

TITLE	RELEASE DATE*	PRODUCTION COMPANY	ACTOR (ROLE)
33. *She Wore a Yellow Ribbon*	1949	Argosy and RKO	Custer not depicted
34. *Winchester '73*	1950	Universal Pictures	Custer not depicted
35. *Oh! Susanna (The Golden Tide)*††	1951	Republic	Forrest Tucker† (Lieutenant Colonel Unger)
36. *Little Big Horn*	1951	Screenguild	Custer not depicted
37. *Warpath*	1951	Paramount	James Millican
38. *Bugles in the Afternoon*	1952	Warner Bros.	Sheb Wooley
39. *Sitting Bull*	1954	United Artists	Douglas Kennedy
40. *Chief Crazy Horse*	1955	United International	?
41. *The Seventh Cavalry (The Return of General Custer)*††	1956	Columbia	Custer not depicted
42. *Gunsmoke* "Custer"	1956	CBS	Custer not depicted
43. *The Life and Legend of Wyatt Earp* "The Man Who Rode with Custer"	1957	ABC	Custer not depicted
44. *Cheyenne* "The Broken Pledge"	1957	ABC/Warner Bros.	Whit Bissell
45. *Tonka* (Later reissued as *Comanche*)	1958	Walt Disney Studios	Britt Lomond
46. *The Life and Legend of Wyatt Earp* "The General's Lady"	1958	ABC	Custer not depicted (Dorothy Green as Elizabeth Custer)
47. *Yancy Derringer* "Longhair"	1958	CBS	Grant Williams
48. *Bronco* "Payroll of the Dead"	1959	ABC/Warner Bros.	Custer not depicted
49. *Have Gun Will Travel*	1959	CBS	Custer not depicted
50. *Cheyenne* "Gold, Glory and Custer—Prelude" and "Gold, Glory and Custer Requiem" (2 parts)	1959	ABC/Warner Bros.	Barry Atwater
51. *Yellowstone Kelly*	1959	Warner Bros.	Custer not depicted

TITLE	RELEASE DATE*	PRODUCTION COMPANY	ACTOR (ROLE)
52. *Death Valley Days.* "The Great Lounsberry Scoop"	1960	?	Custer not depicted
53. *The Canadians*	1961	20th Century Fox	Custer not depicted
54. *The Twilight Zone* "The 7th Is Made Up of Phantoms"	1963	CBS	Custer not depicted
55. *La Carica del 7 Cavalleggeri* (English titles *Assault on Fort Texan* and *Heroes of Fort Worth*; French title *L'Assault du Fort Texan*)	1964	Fenix Film	Custer not depicted
56. *The Glory Guys (The Dice of God)*††	1965	United Artists	Andrew Duggan† (General McCabe)
57. *The Great Sioux Massacre*	1965	Columbia	Philip Carey
58. *The Plainsman*	1965	Universal	Leslie Neilsen
59. *Branded* "Call to Glory" (2 parts)	1966	NBC	Robert Lansing
60. *Time Tunnel* "Massacre"	1966	ABC	Joe Morros
61. *F Troop* "Old Iron Pants"	1967	ABC	John Stephenson
62. *Due Sergenti del General Custer* (English title *Two Idiots at Fort Alamo*)	1967	Fida Film/Balcazar	Custer not depicted
63. *Red Tomahawk*	1967	Paramount	Custer not depicted
64. *Legend of Custer* (Composite from ABC "Custer" TV series of Sept.–Dec.)	1967	?	Wayne Maunder
65. *Custer of the West* (*Custer's West* and *A Good Day for Fighting*)††	1968	Security Pictures	Robert Shaw
66. *Soldier Blue*	1970	Avco-Embassy	Custer not depicted
67. *Little Big Man*	1970	National General	Richard Mulligan
68. *Dirty Dingus Magee*	1970	MGM	John Dehner† "General"
69. *The Cowboys*	1972	Warner Bros.	Custer not depicted
70. *Touche pas la femme blanche* (English titles include *Don't Touch White Women; The Real Life of General Custer; The True Life of General Custer; Custer*)	1974	Mara Films/Les Films 66 /Laser CFDC	Marcello Mastroianni

TITLE	RELEASE DATE*	PRODUCTION COMPANY	ACTOR (ROLE)
71. *Won Ton Ton, the Dog Who Saved Hollywood*	1976	Paramount	Ron Liebman† (a.k.a. silent film star Rudy Montague as Custer)
72. *The Court-Martial of General George Armstrong Custer*	1977	NBC TV/Warner Bros.	James Olson
73. *The White Buffalo*†† (1983 telecast on NBC as *Hunt to Kill*)	1977	United Artists	Custer not depicted (Ed Lauter as Tom Custer)
74. *The Legend of the Golden Gun*	1979	NBC	Keir Dullea
75. *The Legend of the Lone Ranger*	1981	Universal Pictures	Lincoln Tate
76. *The Legend of Walks Far Woman*	1982	NBC	Custer not depicted
77. *Teachers*	1984	MGM/United Artists	Richard Mulligan† (Herbert)
78. *Quick and the Dead*	1987	HBO	Custer not depicted
79. "North and South, Book II"	1986	CBS	?
80. *Son of the Morning Star*	1991	Mount Productions/ Republic/ABC TV/ Preston Fisher Productions	Gary Cole
81. *Dr. Quinn, Medicine Woman* "The Epidemic"	1993	CBS	Taylor Nichols
82. *Dr. Quinn, Medicine Woman* "The Prisoner"	1993	CBS	Darren Dalton
83. "Class of '61"	1993	NBC	Joshua Lucas
84. *Dr. Quinn, Medicine Woman* "The Abduction" (2 parts)	1994	CBS	Jason Leland Adams
85. *Wagons East*	1994	Carlco Productions	Charles Rocket† (Major General Larchmont)
86. *Legends of the Fall*	1994	Tristar Pictures	Custer not depicted
87. *Dr. Quinn, Medicine Woman* "Washita" (2 parts)	1995	CBS	Jason Leland Adams
88. *Dr. Quinn, Medicine Woman* "For Better or Worse"	1995	CBS	Jason Leland Adams

	TITLE	RELEASE DATE*	PRODUCTION COMPANY	ACTOR (ROLE)
89.	*Buffalo Girls*	1995	CBS	John Diehl
90.	*Legend* . . . . "Custer's Almost Last Stand"	1995	TL Productions/UPN	Allen Hyde-White
91.	*The Lazarus Man* . . . . "Boy General"	1996	CBC	Maxwell Caulfield
92.	*Crazy Horse*	1996	TNT	Peter Horton
93.	*Stolen Women, Captured Hearts*	1997	CBS	William Shockley
94.	*Horse Whisperer*	1998	Wildwood Enterprises/ Touchstone Pictures	. . . . . . Custer not depicted (Little Bighorn battlefield shown)

Chronology of
Nationally Televised Documentaries*

SERIES or PROGRAM TITLE	EPISODE	NETWORK	BROADCAST
1. *You Are There*	"Grant and Lee at Appomatox"	CBS	1953
2. "The Real West"		?	1961
3. *The Western Way*	"The Persistent Myth"	PBS	1964
4. "Discovery"		ABC	1964
5. *Saga of Western Man*	"Custer to the Little Big Horn"	ABC	1965
6. *This Proud Land*	"The Big Sky Country"	?	1965
7. *Project 20 Special*	"End of the Trail"	NBC	1967
8. "Red Sunday"		PBS	1976
9. *Smithsonian World*	"Heroes and the Test of Time: A Look at George A. Custer and Painter Thomas Eakins"	PBS	1985
10. "Dreams along the Little Big Horn"		PBS	1988
11. "The Spirit of Crazy Horse"		?	1990

* Major treatment of Custer/Little Bighorn or significant coverage as part of a broader treatment.
† Compilation of various previously broadcast episodes on A&E.

SERIES OR PROGRAM TITLE	EPISODE	NETWORK	BROADCAST
12. *Time Machine*	"Custer's Last Trooper"	A&E	1990
13. "The Making of *Son of the Morning Star*"		ABC	1991
14. *The American Experience*	"Last Stand at Little Bighorn"	PBS	1992
15. *Archeology*	"Secrets of the Little Big Horn"	Learning Channel	1992
16. *Time Machine*	"Bloody Shenandoah"	A&E	1992*
17. *Time Machine*	"The Horse Soldier"	A&E	1992*
18. *Time Machine*	"Legends of the American West"	A&E	1992*
19. *Legends of the American West*	"The Real Story of Custer's Last Stand"	Trimark Pictures	1992
20. *Real West*	"Custer and the Seventh Cavalry"	A&E	1992
21. *Civil War Journal*	"Boy Generals"	A&E	1993*
22. *Civil War Journal*	"John S. Mosby"	A&E	1993*
23. *Civil War Journal*	"The Union Cavalry and Philip Sheridan"	A&E	1993*
24. *Civil War Journal*	"West Point Classmates"	A&E	1993*
25. *Wild West*	"Indians"		1993*
26. *Wild West*	"Soldiers"		1993*
27. *Real West*	"Crazy Horse"	A&E	1993*
28. *Real West*	"The Indian Wars" (2 Parts)	A&E	1993*
29. *Real West*	"Libbie Custer"	A&E	1993
30. *Real West*	"Sitting Bull and the Great Sioux Nation"	A&E	1993
31. *How the West Was Lost*	"A Good Day to Die"	Discovery Channel	1993
32. *The American Experience*	"The Way West" (parts 1 & 2)	PBS	1995
33. *Biography*	"George Custer: Showdown at Little Big Horn"	A&E	1995
34. *Biography*	"Crazy Horse The Last Warrior"	A&E	1995

SERIES OR PROGRAM TITLE	EPISODE	NETWORK	BROADCAST
35. *Biography*	"Sitting Bull"	A&E	1995*
36. *The West*	"Death Runs Riot" and "I Will Fight No More Forever"	PBS	1997*
37. *Biography*	"George Armstrong Custer: America's Golden Cavalier"	A&E	1997
38. *New Explorers*	"Betrayal at Little Big Horn"	A&E	1997
39. "Custer's Last Stand"†		History Channel	1998
40. "Haunted History: The Battle of Little Bighorn"		History Channel	1998
41. "Little Bighorn: The Untold Story"		History Channel	1999

Episodic Synopses of 1930s Custer Serials

THE LAST FRONTIER

RKO/Van Beuren • September 1932 • Sound, black and white • Twelve episodes

Credits

Director: Spencer Gordon Bennet and Thomas L. Storey
Story: Courtney Ryley Cooper with Creighton Chaney
Continuity and dialogue: George Plympton and Robert F. Hill
Photography: Edward Snyder and Gilbert Warrenton
Film editor: Thomas Malloy
Associate producer: Fred J. McConnell

Cast

Tom Kirby: Lon Chaney, Jr. (billed as Creighton Chaney)
General Custer: William Desmond
Wild Bill: Yakima Canutt

Lige Morris: Richard Neill
Jeff Maitland: Francis X. Bushman, Jr.
Rose Maitland: Judith Barrie
Buck: Leroy Mason
Indian Chief (Pawnee Blood): Frank Lackteen
Indian Girl: Fritzi Fern
Betty Halliday: Dorothy Gulliver
Colonel Halliday: Claude Payton
Aggie: Mary Jo Desmond
Happy: King Cole
Hank: Peter Morrison
Kit Gordon: Joe Bonomo
Bad Ben: Benny Corbett

EPISODE 1: "THE BLACK GHOST"

General Custer makes a cameo appearance to tell Colonel Halliday that gun smuggling to the Indians must be stopped. The local newspaper editor, Tom Kirby, takes the military to task, asserting that "the Indians are equipped with better guns than the soldiers." Custer thinks this is a disgrace and tells Halliday to halt the weapon trade or he will take care of the matter himself. Even as the cavalry officer speaks, wagons loaded with firearms are on the move. Bad Ben speaks to Jeff Maitland and his "sister" (actually his wife) Rose. The Black Ghost observes them from afar. The gang follows the mysterious rider, but he gets away, although not before hurtling a rock through the window of Halliday's quarters with a clue attached about the illegal rifle shipment.

The troopers fail to halt the weapon exchange as the Indians stage a mock attack and carry away the firearms before Custer arrives. Tom and Rose join Colonel Halliday's daughter Betty at a nearby ranch once the "raid" has ended. The war party returns and nearly captures Betty. They ride after her as she starts over a cliff. The Black Ghost comes to her aid, as both tumble into the river far below.

EPISODE 2: "THE THUNDERING HERD"

The Black Ghost saves Betty, who is startled by his mask. He responds in a Hispanic accent à la Zorro that he is a friend whom she can call upon at any time. Then he rides off, while Jeff speaks to the ringleader of the gang, Lige Morris, about continuing their clandestine trade with the Indians, a scheme that will require keeping the region a rough-and-tumble frontier.

The scene switches to Wild Bill, who presents Colonel Halliday with a new Sharps carbine he has taken from a dead brave. The conversation gets around to Jeff, whom Tom suspects as an outlaw, but Morris defuses this talk. Not convinced, Tom heads off to investigate. He finds a canoe loaded with arms and ammo. Later, he captures another shipment, this time in a wagon. Right after, he links up with Betty, who agrees to drive the confiscated shipment, but the Indians attack. As Betty attempts to avoid them, she falls off the driver's seat and lands between the horses on the wagon tongue. Tom reaches down to pull her up as the wagon overturns, rolling in front of a buffalo stampede.

EPISODE 3: "THE BLACK GHOST STRIKES"

Tom fires a shot and turns the stampede. Betty is captured by Indians, however, and Tom goes back to town with Wild Bill's help. Soon the Black Ghost reappears to find Betty. He makes his way to the Indian village where she is held captive. While there, he overhears a plan to steal more weapons so that the warriors will have ample arms while Custer will be left with no reserves. Securing Betty, the Black Ghost takes her with him as they head toward the gang's hideout. There they recover the wagon of ordnance and attempt to flee. They are discovered, and during the ensuing fight, the gunpowder in the wagon is set afire. An explosion follows.

EPISODE 4: "THE FATAL SHOT"

Betty and the Black Ghost escape the explosion by riding off on the wagon tongue pulled by the team of horses. Betty is knocked clear and found by soldiers, led by her father. The colonel launches a counterattack. The situation calms momentarily, allowing Tom, his sidekick, Happy, and his ward, Aggie, an orphan whom he had rescued from an Indian attack ten years earlier, to observe Jeff's poor treatment of Rose. This heightens Kirby's distrust of the pair.

Later, the bandits dress as Indians and recapture Betty. Tom, also disguised in Indian garb, slips into the gang's hideout, where Betty is located. She spots Tom and recognizes him but now thinks he is part of the plot.

EPISODE 5: "CLUTCHING SANDS"

In her dazed condition, Betty now believes Tom Kirby is a gang member. After Betty gets away, she informs her father of what she has seen. Word spreads quickly that Kirby is in league with the gunrunners. Happy attempts to calm the locals and defend his friend, but a gang member overcomes him. Aggie stops the fight with a gun. Betty sets out in search of Tom and on the way falls into quicksand. Tom hears her cries for help, but because he has been wounded, he cannot respond.

EPISODE 6: "TERROR TRAIL"

Tom manages to revive and make his way from the cave where he has passed out from his wound, after being taken to this safe place by Rose. He leaves the cave and arrives just in time to throw Betty a rope before she is swallowed by the quicksand. After this rescue, Tom falls into the hands of the gang.

EPISODE 7: "DOOMED"

Betty finds Tom aboard a raft, having been captured by the gang and trussed up with ropes. She manages to push Tom's guard overboard, then unties his bonds just in time for the two to jump free as the raft heads toward a waterfall. Tom makes it ashore safely but is apprehended by troopers who think he is at the bottom of all the Indian troubles. While the cavalry escorts him to jail, Betty falls into the hands of the gang once again.

All is not well for Lige Morris, however, who learns that he has lost a gun shipment because of Kirby. Things are not going well, and Morris vows that no one else will have the rich mines if he cannot own them.

As Morris hatches his newest plot, Tom escapes from his cell with the help of Happy. He dons his Black Ghost garb to set out in search of Betty. Tom finds her in a cabin guarded by two Indians. He enters. A fight erupts. The cabin catches fire as Tom's foes escape. Trapped by the flames, Tom and Betty struggle to open the window, but to no avail. It seems as if they are facing a horrible death.

EPISODE 8: "FACING DEATH"

At the last minute, the hero and heroine spy a trapdoor in the floor of the cabin. They cheat death again and ride off separately. Betty goes back to her father and informs him that Tom is not an outlaw. Meanwhile, Tom returns to his cabin to find that Aggie and Happy have headed to the goldfields. They will be in harm's way when Jeff's men attempt to take over the claims of the miners by force.

Learning of this, the colonel readies his troops for the field. In the meantime, Kirby has entered Morris's office in search of evidence against the villain. Lige discovers him, and four of the gang members seize the hero. Although outnumbered, he manages to escape, arriving at the mines just in time to discover Rose unconscious in a smoke-filled shaft that has been abandoned by the miners in their flight from Jeff's gang. While Tom kneels beside Rose to revive her, he does not realize that a keg of blasting powder is about to be ignited. There is an explosion.

EPISODE 9: "THUNDERING DOOM"
Somehow Tom and Rose have managed to avoid injury. Tom carries the dazed young woman out and turns her over to Jeff. He then draws his revolver and begins to exchange rounds with Lige's gang, which has now come onto the scene. The fight stops when a bugle signals that the cavalry is on its way. The outlaws flee. Tom goes back to town with Happy and Aggie.

Tom stops to check on Rose and tells her he will do everything he can to assist Jeff, who has agreed to reform. Lige will not let his former partner in crime go, because Jeff knows too much. The cavalry arrives at this point to save Placer City from capture by Morris's gang. Even as they drive off the ruffians, Lige goes to the Indians to turn them against the whites. One of the first objects of their rage is a stagecoach, with none other than Betty aboard. The warriors attack the coach, killing the driver and the guard. Betty attempts to take over the reins, but the stage races out of control and strikes a boulder. Betty screams. She seems doomed.

EPISODE 10: "THE LIFE LINE"
Tom speeds to Betty. Before he can get close, the coach crashes over a hill. Betty is thrown from the stage, but Tom finds her and whisks her away on his horse. The Indians try to reach the two, but Happy comes on the scene with deadly aim to kill the members of the raiding party.

Tom thanks Happy then leaves in the guise of the Black Ghost to apprehend Jeff and Morris. By now the two are beginning to argue. Jeff tells Rose that he will cease his lawless activities. Quitting the gang proves to be difficult, however. The townspeople think Jeff is the leader of the gang, a belief that Lige encourages. A mob sets out to find Jeff. Tom volunteers to draw them away by dressing up in Jeff's clothes. He instructs Happy to lead Rose and Jeff out of danger, then rides off with the vigilantes in pursuit. Betty joins him. Betty and Tom look as if they are going to escape when a large lasso yanks them off their horses. They fall over a cliff. As they are being pulled up, the rope frays and breaks.

EPISODE 11: "DRIVING DANGER"
Betty and Tom have made it to the top of the cliff. The posse is puzzled. Why did the two lead them astray? Tom replies that it was to save the pursuers from making a mistake they would regret. It is Morris, not Maitland, that they should be chasing. The posse is unconvinced. They want evidence to support this accusation. Tom says he will provide the proof, and sets out to find Jeff, who has been wounded by one of Lige's minions.

By this time the situation has deteriorated to the point that Colonel Halliday has been forced to declare martial law. He rounds up the settlers and orders them to form a wagon train and leave Placer City, which is Indian land. Disgruntled, they pack up and head out in their wagons.

Lige is desperate now. Kirby knows that Morris is the mastermind behind all the trouble in the area. He must get to Jeff before he is discovered in order to eliminate the star witness against him. He also has been informed by one of his men that Tom is the Black Ghost.

Lige has to act quickly. He must convince Pawnee Blood to attack the wagon train, which he does, but not before Tom, as the Black Ghost, discovers the plot. He rides to the fort for help.

As Tom leads the cavalry, Indians surround the wagon train. Morris's henchmen locate the wagon with Jeff, Rose, Happy, and Betty. They give chase, and in the heat of pursuit Betty is thrown from the wagon. She falls between the horses, but grabs on to the wagon tongue. It looks as if she will be killed.

EPISODE 12: "THE BLACK GHOST'S LAST RIDE"
Betty can hold on no longer and she drops from the wagon. The Black Ghost rides onto the scene, scoops Betty off the ground, and brings her back to safety. As he does, the Indians and Morris's cronies surround the wagon and take Rose and Jeff captive. They bring the two back to Lige's headquarters, but Betty finds the couple and almost frees them but is thwarted. Then Lige arrives on the scene.

Tom enters. He scuffles with one of Morris's men, while the outlaw leader beats a hasty retreat with Betty as hostage. Tom defeats his foe and rushes after Betty. He soon overtakes Lige and Betty, grabbing her from the villain's saddle. In the process Lige falls from his horse. Before he can get up, a herd of buffalo thunders down on him. He receives his just punishment.

Tom and Betty return to town, where he reveals himself as the Black Ghost. The two embrace and kiss, as the last episode comes to its conclusion.

CUSTER'S LAST STAND

Weiss Productions, Inc. • 1936 • Sound, black and white • Fifteen episodes,
also issued in edited version as a feature

Credits

Director: Elmer Clifton
Screenplay: George Arthur, Eddy Graneman, and Bob Lively
Film editors: Holbrook Todd and George M. Merrick
Assistant director: Adrian Weiss
Photography: Bert Longenecker
Musical director: Hal Chasnoff

Cast

Kit Cardigan: Rex Lease
Gen. George A. Custer: Frank McGlynn, Jr.
Mrs. Elizabeth Custer: Ruth Mix
Barbara Trent: Nancy Caswell
Wild Bill Hickok: Allen Greer
Fitzpatrick: William Farnum
Calamity Jane: Helen Gibson
Tom "Keen" Blade: Reed Howes
Buffalo Bill and Barney: Ted Adams
Sitting Bull: Howling Wolf
Rain-in-the-Face: Chick Davis
Crazy Horse: High Eagle
Blue Crow: Ed Winthrow
Marcus Reno: Franklyn Farm
Striker Martin: Carter Wayne

Frederick Benteen: Lafe McKee
Lieutenant Weir: Cactus Mack
Belle Meade: Lona Andre
Young Wolf: Chief Thundercloud
Buckskin: Milburn Moranti
Sergeant Flannigan: George Morrell
Lieutenant Cook: Jack Mulhall
Lieutenant Roberts: George Cheseboro
Red Fawn: Dorothy Guliver
Crow Scout: Patter Poe
Bobby: Bobby Nelson
Wagon Boss: Bill Desmond
Major Trent: Josef Swickard
Pete: Robert Walker
Judge Hooker: Walter James
Mabel: Mabel Strickland
Buzz: Marty Joyce
Spike: Ken Cooper
Hank: Creighton Hale
"Sunday": Sunday
Major Ware: Bud Buster
Sergeant Peters: Barney Fury
Brown Fox: Iron Eyes [Cody]
Curley and True Eagle: Carl Matthews
Renegades: Lone Star, Humming Bird, Swift Eagle, Tall
Tree, Little Eagle, Lone Pine, Herb Jackson, and J. Spencer

EPISODE 1: "PERILS OF THE PLAINS"

Under the leadership of Young Wolf, a band of Dakota Indians attacks a wagon train and slays the emigrants. During the battle, Young Wolf loses his magic arrow, which holds the key to the location of Medicine Cave, a place sacred to the Indians and rich in gold. Tom "Keen" Blade, wanting the arrow for himself, promises to help Young Wolf recover the item. The Indians attack another wagon train under Major Trent, but scout Kit Cardigan saves the caravan. At the end of the episode, he is hurled off a cliff in a runaway covered wagon, facing certain death.

EPISODE 2: "THUNDERING HOOFS"

Kit miraculously escapes. Young Wolf, believing that Major Trent has the magic arrow, takes his daughter Barbara as prisoner. Blade promises to arrange for the return of the arrow in exchange for Barbara's release. Cardigan, after a fight with the Indians, rescues Barbara. Belle Meade, owner of the saloon at Fort Henry, fears discipline by General Custer, the new commander at the post, and decides to move to nearby Black Pool. She meets Kit, and

they ride together. A herd of stampeding buffalo charges down on them.

EPISODE 3: "FIRES OF VENGEANCE"

Kit saves Belle's life, and they return to Fort Henry. Belle suggests that Major Trent, a doctor, would find a welcome in Black Pool. Trent's caravan leaves for Black Pool with Kit and a guard of soldiers. Indians attack the town. The fighting is vicious, and the losses are heavy on both sides. Kit attacks Lieutenant Roberts, a Custer subaltern who had tried to kill his commanding officer. As they fight in a barn, it catches fire from flaming arrows. The building crashes down upon them.

EPISODE 4: "GHOST DANCERS"

Cardigan and Roberts escape from the building. Troops from Fort Henry arrive in time to repel the Indians. They then turn to fight the fire, which is raging in the town. Blade captures Trent and demands the magic arrow, but Trent insists that it has disappeared in the Indian fight. Kit and Barbara set out to rescue her father. Barbara is roped by an Indian and drawn to the top of a cliff. As Kit tries to save her, he is captured. Blindfolded, the hero is forced to run the gauntlet. He topples over a high cliff.

EPISODE 5: "TRAPPED"

Kit lands safely in soft earth. He finds Buckskin, a scout, and orders him to go to Belle Meade for information about Trent, for Kit suspects Blade and knows that Belle is in his confidence. Sitting Bull threatens to torture Barbara to make her tell where the magic arrow is hidden. Barbara escapes, and Red Fawn, accused of helping her, is lashed to a wild mustang that is then turned loose. Bobby sneaks into Blade's headquarters. Blade throws a lever, and Bobby falls through a trapdoor.

EPISODE 6: "HUMAN WOLVES"

Bobby falls into a pit, where Buckskin is held prisoner. Together, they plan to escape. Kit and Barbara are attacked by a band of Indians under Young Wolf. Calamity Jane, hearing shots, rides in to help them, but they are no match for the Indians. Kit is captured. Young Wolf attacks him with a tomahawk. The other Indians close in on the two brave women.

EPISODE 7: "DEMONS OF DISASTER"

Buffalo Bill saves the women. A troop from Fort Henry rescues Kit. Red Fawn recovers the magic arrow. The battle continues, and the Indians are repelled. Buckskin and Bobby escape and release Major Trent. Sitting Bull calls his tribes together to prepare for war. Wild Bill Hickok becomes sheriff of Black Pool and is determined to clean up the town. He plans to start at Belle's saloon, which is the source of the Indian's liquor and Blade's headquarters. Blade's men await him there.

EPISODE 8: "WHITE TREACHERY"

Bill's quick draw saves him. Cardigan joins Hickok, and they drive back Blade's henchmen. Kit and Buckskin ride out to escort the pay wagon that is coming to Fort Henry. Two of Blade's men distract Kit, and the others capture the wagon after a fierce fight. Kit discovers their ruse and sets out to save the wagon. When the scout reaches the scene of the battle, the pay wagon is gone. Bobby comes upon Young Wolf and Roberts as they are planning an assault on Major Trent. Bobby is captured.

EPISODE 9: "CIRCLE OF DEATH"

Bobby escapes when Roberts and Young Wolf come to blows over their plans. Kit returns to Black Pool, convinced that Blade was responsible for the attack on the

pay train. He recovers the money from one of Blade's henchmen and starts out alone to take it to Fort Henry. Cardigan temporarily escapes Blade's clutches, but he is ambushed by a band of Young Wolf's Indians, who have taken to the warpath again. Kit rides on, unsuspecting, and the Indians swoop down upon him.

EPISODE 10: "FLAMING ARROW"

Lieutenant Cook and a troop of cavalry arrive in time to save Kit. After a hot skirmish, the Indians are forced to retreat. The magic arrow has been stolen again, and the Indians are determined to recover it. They attack at various points but are driven back. Finally, hearing that the arrow is at Fort Henry, Young Wolf leads an attack against the post. He gets inside the fort. Custer is kneeling over Mrs. Custer, who has been wounded, and Young Wolf attacks with his tomahawk.

EPISODE 11: "WARPATH"

Kit arrives in time to save Custer. Young Wolf flees. The battle rages, until the Indians finally are driven back in disorderly retreat. Sitting Bull, planning a new strategy for his war against the settlers, decides to assemble all the allied tribes at the Little Bighorn. Red Fawn has learned the location of the medicine cave and its gold, and Blade captures her. He tries to force the secret from her. Kit comes to the rescue. He is fighting one of Blade's men, when the floor collapses beneath them.

EPISODE 12: "FIRING SQUAD"

Kit overcomes his adversary, but Blade manages to escape. The hero then frees Bobby and Buzz by using a fake medicine arrow. Young Wolf carries this information to Blade, and they decide that Trent must once more be in possession of the real arrow. With the help of the corrupt Judge Hooker in Black Pool, Trent and Barbara are arrested. Tried and found guilty of trumped-up charges, they are sentenced to be shot within an hour. Bravely, Barbara and the major face the firing squad.

EPISODE 13: "RED PANTHERS"

The Trents drop at the first shots of the squad, and the men, believing them dead, go off for a drink. The Trents are placed in a covered wagon and driven off in the direction of Fort Henry. Bobby stays in Black Pool. Kit learns that the Trents have escaped death, and he searches for Bobby. Bobby has found the medicine arrow and gives it to Red Fawn. They are caught in Trent's cellar by Blade's gang and Young Wolf, however, who seizes Bobby and raises his tomahawk to scalp him.

EPISODE 14: "CUSTER'S LAST RIDE"

Kit rushes in to save Bobby. Red Fawn escapes with the medicine arrow. Kit reports to Custer at Fort Henry, and Custer gives his troops and scouts their final instructions. They march on to Little Bighorn. There the war with the Indians begins. No minor skirmish this, but a fight to the finish. Cardigan and Major Weir, in command of one squad of men, lead a charge. They press forward in the hope of joining Custer, but Kit is attacked by two Indians and falls to the ground, helpless.

EPISODE 15: "THE LAST STAND"

Craftily maneuvering his gun, Kit manages to kill his attackers. But the battle is over. Custer lies dead, surrounded by his brave troopers. Kit gets back to Black Pool, bent on making short work of Keen Blade. The men meet, and Kit gives Blade a sporting chance for his life. Blade loses. Saddened by the carnage of Little Bighorn, Kit and Barbara manage to find a ray of hope in their love for each other and the new West.

OREGON TRAIL

Universal Studios/Commonwealth Pictures • April 1939 • Sound, black and white • Fifteen episodes

Credits

Directors: Ford Beebe and Saul A. Goodkind
Photography: Jerry Ash and William Sickner
Original screenplay: George Plympton, Basil Dickey, Edmund Kelse, and W. W. Watson

Cast

Jeff Scott: John Mack Brown
Idaho Ike: Jim Toney
Deadwood: Fuzzy Knight
Bull Bragg: Jack C. Smith
Margaret Mason: Louise Stanley
Daggett: Forest Taylor
John Mason: Edward J. LeSaint
Colonel Custer: Roy Barcroft
Jimmie Clark: Bill Cody, Jr.
Dirk: Charles King
Morgan: James Blaine
Tompkins: Charles Murphy
Breed: Charles Stevens
Slade: Colin Kenny
General Sherman: Warner Richmond

General Terry: Kenneth Harlan
Indian Chief: Chief Thunderbird
Townsman: Horace Murphy
Beaver Dan: Michael Slade
Citizen: James Farley
Shafer: Frank LaRue
Pete: Tom London
Yellow Snake: Dick Botiller
Marshall: Dick Rush
Corporal: Lane Chandler
Crow Foot: Iron Eyes Cody
Indian: Shooting Star
Indian: Lucien Y. Maxwell
Indian: George Sky Eagle
Indian: Joe Molina
Indian: Bill Wikerson
Rider: Jack Shannon
Rider: George Sowards
Rider: Frank Strawbringer
Rider: Jack Casey
Rider: Bud McClure
Rider: Bob Clark
Rider: George Plues

CHAPTER 1: "RENEGADE REVENGE"

Custer, Terry, and Sherman confer at the fort about the increased problem with Indians and the 2,000 miles of road that have to be protected. The biggest challenge is the safety of wagon trains bound for Oregon. White renegades, led by a man named Morgan, are intent on maintaining a fur monopoly in the region and do not want settlers. To break this stranglehold, the officers solicit the aid of Jeff Scott and Deadwood Hawkins, "the best scouts in the West and the most trustworthy." The pair do not like working for the military but agree to assist. Custer pretends to arrest them as a cover so they can join the outlaw band.

The first encounter with the heavies takes place as a group of emigrants, including Jimmie Clark and Margaret Mason, attempt to cross a flooded river. Jimmie's father drowns in the process, while Jeff saves the heroine from a similar fate. The frontiersman then assumes the leadership of the group of pioneers as they press onward, so the gang members abandon the party and arrange for an Indian attack under Red Fox.

The raiders try to capture a wagon of firearms. Miss Mason is aboard. Scott goes after the vehicle as it lunges off a cliff and heads into the water below.

CHAPTER 2: "FLAMING FOREST"
The Indians do not press their pursuit. Again, Jeff rescues Margaret. Custer arrives on the scene to drive off the Indians. Then the former trail boss, Bull Bragg, returns to resume his role. Later, Jimmie trails Bragg and his fellow renegades. They hatch another plot, arranging for the prairie to be set afire. Jeff and Deadwood find Jimmie. A raging inferno awaits the unsuspecting settlers in a box canyon where Bragg has headed them. The heroes intercede. Many wagons are lost. Margaret is thrown from one of them and is about to be blown up by a keg of gunpowder.

CHAPTER 3: "THE BRINK OF DISASTER"
Jeff succeeds in whisking his lady fair from the clutches of certain death. Bragg goes into town with a charred wagon to report to Morgan that he has done away with another group. Even as Bull reports his supposed triumph, the wagon train enters town. Jeff seeks out the thug and fights him hand-to-hand in a saloon. The scout beats Bragg, who is taken away to jail by the crooked sheriff. There, Morgan sets up a plot to have his former flunky killed by Indians as Bragg is being taken to Fort Laramie for trial. The warriors attack the stage as planned. Everyone on board but Bragg dies. In the fray, Jeff manages to jump onto the coach and exchanges blows with Bull, who goes over the side as the scout and the stage plunge over a cliff, even as the Indians seize Bull and take him away.

CHAPTER 4: "THUNDERING DOOM"
One of Deadwood's old partners witnesses all this and reports what he saw, but not before Bragg gets away. Undaunted, Margaret's father decides they will hire a new wagon master and press on to Oregon. Morgan obliges and provides another member of his gang, while Bull returns to take his revenge. He plans to blast Jeff, Margaret, Jimmie, and Deadwood into eternity with a keg of powder when he finds the foursome together in a cabin just right for the purpose. It appears that he succeeds, as the blast goes off.

CHAPTER 5: "THE MENACING HERD"
The would-be victims are spared by hiding in a storeroom just as Custer rides onto the scene. With this, they go after Bull, who eludes them by holing up in a secret cave. When they get back to town, a party celebrates the safe return of the group. During the festivities, Bragg slips back into town for a meeting with Morgan about disposing of Scott once and for all. As the men speak, Jeff gets the drop on them, but soon the pair of desperadoes

reverse the situation. This momentarily frustrates the hero, but he is back in action just in time to find a cattle stampede, which Morgan's men have instigated to destroy the wagon train, rushing through town. Margaret is caught in the midst of the rampaging steers.

CHAPTER 6: "INDIAN VENGEANCE"
Jeff plucks Margaret away just in time. In the wake of the stampede, Morgan rouses the townspeople and manipulates them so that they will demand the wagon train's cattle herd in exchange for all the damage caused to the stores, as well as the death of the marshal and two citizens. Jeff stops this and works out an agreement. Even though bloodshed is avoided, several members of the wagon train think it is time to turn back to avoid any future trouble. Nevertheless, Mason and some of his followers are determined to continue. Morgan calls upon Yellow Snake to stop the pioneers from moving too far. He bribes the Indian leader into running off the wagon train's horses. In the process, the raiders capture Jimmie.

Jeff goes after the lad and agrees to be taken in exchange for the boy. The Indians tie the scout to the stake and prepare to burn him alive. Deadwood rushes to Idaho Ike and the fainthearted group of settlers, who have decided to go back to the East. He asks that they help him free Jeff, even as the flames begin to engulf the hero in the Indian village.

CHAPTER 7: "TRAIL OF TREACHERY"
Jeff's comrades save him from being burned alive. Yellow Snake is killed, and the whites make their way to town without a casualty. With Scott safe, Morgan must figure out another means to stop the wagon train. He also learns that some trappers are on their way to Fort Wallace. For the moment, he turns his attention to obtaining their pelts. He sends Bragg to seize the pelts. The scheme works but allows Jeff to trail the robbers. He nearly succeeds in apprehending Bragg, but the situation is reversed when some of the Indians enter the picture. Jeff barely escapes as a war party chases him and shoots him from his saddle. He rolls downhill into the river and is presumed drowned.

CHAPTER 8: "REDSKIN'S REVENGE"
Just when it appears that all is lost, Custer leads a patrol that scares the Indians away. Jeff tells Yellow Hair that he believes they can catch Bragg. While the troops join Custer and Scott, Mason decides to roll his wagons in order to avoid the snows that will soon fall. The timing is bad, because Morgan encourages the Indians to attack

the train as it continues its journey. Jeff tries to alert the pioneers of the danger, but he arrives on the scene at nearly the same time as the war party. He rallies the settlers and heads them back to town, with the warriors closing in as they reach the settlement. One of the Indians jumps on board the Mason wagon, and Jeff follows to engage in hand-to-hand combat. Morgan looks out his window and sees this struggle. He takes aim and shoots Jeff in the back. It seems that he has finally killed the meddling hero, even as Custer and his troops come galloping into the town to drive off the warriors.

CHAPTER 9: "THE AVALANCHE OF DOOM"

The war party escapes with Mason's fur-laden wagon. Inside, they find another unsuspected prize—Margaret. Morgan decides to deliver a ransom note from the gang, telling Mason to halt his move to Oregon if he wants to see his daughter alive. This is too much. Mason agrees to stop his quest, but the other members of the wagon train say they will continue their migration. Jeff, with Jimmie's help, finds Margaret. Jeff, Jimmie, and Deadwood rescue the heroine and almost capture Bragg and Breed, too. The heavies avoid this fate and ride to Morgan, who gives them further instructions to blow up the gorge through which the wagon train must pass the following day. Jeff, riding ahead, narrowly misses discovering this plot when a band of Indians sees him and gives chase. He must dive over a cliff into the water to avoid being taken.

CHAPTER 10: "THE PLUNGE OF PERIL"

The death fall does not injure Jeff or his mount. They both come ashore but too late to stop the explosion. It causes an avalanche, which blocks the pass. Jimmie goes to see what has happened. He spots some more Indians. Frantically, he rides back with a warning, only to learn that this is a peaceful trading party led by the friendly Crow Foot. Mason and his people make a fair exchange with Crow Foot for the furs he brings. Morgan does not want this news to reach other Indians. He arranges for Crow Foot and his party to be ambushed. It appears as if he also will be able to have his men murder Jeff. But the plan only works in part. While Crow Foot and his followers are killed, the scout escapes and manages to take Bragg prisoner at the same time. However, Bragg will not confess about who is in charge of the plot to prevent settlers from entering Oregon. He says he will reveal this information only after arriving safely in Paradise Valley, where he will have the protection of the law. Before they can reach that destination, the settlers are attacked by Morgan's men in force. The wagon carrying Bragg is their prime target. Jeff must jump aboard to fend off the would-be rescue. In the fight, the vehicle flies off a steep embankment.

CHAPTER 11: "TRAPPED IN THE FLAMES"

Bull Bragg slips away after the crash. Jeff Scott chases him and brings back his prisoner to the wagon train, which has been rescued with the help of some of Crow Foot's people. Morgan begins to fear that he will be exposed and orders that Bragg must not talk. As soon as the wagon train reaches Paradise Valley, Morgan gets word to Bragg to remain silent. He will be freed by the gang. The scheme seems as if it will be successful. Several of the outlaws attack the jail. During the fight, Bull knocks Jeff out by hurling a boot at his head. In the process, he likewise strikes a kerosene lamp. This starts a raging fire.

CHAPTER 12: "THE BAITED TRAP"

Miraculously, Jeff and Bull are pulled from the burning building by the pioneers. Afterward, Bragg kills his guard and dashes away. Morgan must find him before Scott does. The two heavies meet at the hideout, but instead of facing off, they rejoin forces and set out to dispose of Jeff Scott, who rides up. Morgan pretends to have been kidnapped by the gang and sends Jeff off in pursuit of Bull. The scout runs after the fleeing bandit and reaches him atop a large rock overlooking a lake below. As the pair fight, Breed fires. Both Scott and Bull plunge into the water.

CHAPTER 13: "CRASHING TIMBERS"

Jeff's horse senses that his master is in trouble and goes into the water. Scott grabs a stirrup, and the faithful mount drags the hero to shore. Deadwood rides up and finds his partner shaken but unharmed. Jeff tells his sidekick that he believes Bull has drowned. The two comrades head back to the cave where they held Morgan. As they prepare to leave, Deadwood stumbles upon the stash of pelts. Jeff says he will come back with a wagon for these later. In the meantime, he wants to find Bragg's body to assure that the villain has died. Failing to find any sign of the culprit, Jeff returns to the cave to pick up the furs. He finds Bragg there and once more takes the man prisoner. With this cargo, he drives his wagon to Mason's camp, but on the way, Bull slips his ropes. Scott and Bragg fight as the wagon runs away. It heads pellmell into a large, low branch that takes off the cover and knocks Bragg unconscious.

CHAPTER 14: " DEATH IN THE NIGHT"

Bragg is injured in the scuffle and brought back to the settlers' camp. Morgan does not want Bull to survive and sends Breed to ensure that he dies. Breed double-crosses his boss and makes a deal with Bragg in order for the two outlaws to take over the illegal operations for themselves. Breed frees Bragg. Scott must trail the bandit one more time. He finds Bragg in an Indian village where Jimmie, Margaret, and her father also are located, having been captured while going back to Fort Wallace to sell furs so that they can pay Morgan for land in Paradise Valley. Jeff liberates his three friends, then remains behind to destroy the ammunition that Morgan has provided the Indians so that they can make war on the whites. Just after lighting the fuse to the gunpowder, Breed jumps Scott. The two wrestle, and the ordnance explodes with terrific force.

CHAPTER 15: "TRAIL'S END"

Thrown clear from the blast, Jeff grabs Bull and carries him off. Bragg, who was mortally wounded in the explosion, can go no farther. Dying, he confesses that Morgan is the head of the gang. Breed overhears this conversation and rushes to Morgan to report that the game is over. Custer tells Scott that Morgan is a powerful man and it will require more evidence to convict him. The scout goes back into town and sets a trap to expose the crook. He succeeds, but Morgan's men come to their boss's aid. The big showdown takes place between Morgan's gang and Jeff's allies from the wagon train. With guidons waving in the breeze, Custer arrives on the scene to halt the fighting and subdue the bandits. Peace comes to Paradise Valley, while Jeff and Margaret embrace.

Custer *Television Series Episodic Synopses*

Credits

Creator: Samuel A. Peeples and David Weisbart
Executive consultant: Samuel A. Peeples
In charge of production: William Self
Producer: Frank Glickman
Series suggested by: Larry Cohen
Music sequence: Lionel Newman
Director of photography: William W. Spencer
Supervising music editor: Leonard Engel
Theme: Leith Stevens
Art directors: Jack Martin Smith and Russell Menzer
Unit production manager: Wes McAfee
Film Editor: Ronald J. Fagan
Production supervisor: Jack Sonntag

Music editor: Sam Levin
Sound effects editor: Ronald Ashcroft
Associate producer: Jacob Bernie
Post production coordinator: Robert Mintz
Set decorators: Walter M. Scott and Glen L. Daniels

Cast

Lt Col. George Custer: Wayne Maunder
Crazy Horse: Michael Dante
Gen. Alfred Terry: Robert F. Simon
California Joe: Slim Pickens
Capt. Myles Keogh: Grant Woods
Sgt. James Bustard: Peter Palmer

DATE FIRST AIRED
September 6, 1967

EPISODE TITLE
(WHEN LISTED)
"Sabers in the Sun"

Director: Sam Wanamaker Writer: Samuel A. Peeples
Producer: Robert Jacks

GUEST STARS
Anne L'Andry: Mary Ann Mobley
Capt. Marcus Reno: Alex Davian
Satanta: Rodolfo Acosta
Ezra Tyman: William Mims

Riding into Fort Hays, Kansas, during a torrential rain, Custer finds the sentry asleep, the enlisted men gambling in the stables, and the ringleader a tough, muscular ex-Confederate private who has no love for Yankees or officers. Custer removes his shoulder straps and challenges the man, James Bustard, to a fight. He bests the trouble-maker. Rather than making him go to the guardhouse, Custer promotes the private to sergeant. With new stripes, Bustard becomes a Custer man. Meanwhile, Capt. Myles Keogh has witnessed the fight. He says nothing and departs. Bustard tells Custer that the cigar-chomping soldier of fortune "doesn't carry any tales."

Custer soon joins forces with Keogh, Bustard, and an old friend, California Joe, a civilian scout. He also begins a stormy relationship with Gen. Alfred Terry. Soon Custer crosses swords with the jealous Marcus Reno, an officer who thinks that he, and not the Boy General, should command the 7th.

Custer pays no heed to his subordinate. Instead, he rides out in search of Terry. In the process, he finds a band of Kiowa waiting in ambush for the general. Yellow Hair springs the trap. He joins Terry's column as it returns to the fort. On the way, they meet Ezra Tyman, the post sutler, who secretly plans to supply Satanta and Crazy Horse's people with breech-loading shotguns. The rag-tag 7th needs to be whipped into shape to face this formidable, well-armed foe.

As the raw recruits struggle to become horse soldiers, they try the patience of Sergeant Bustard, who attempts to teach the men to ride. Custer sets the tone by jumping on his mount and running the saber course. Progress is slow. Terry restricts the regiment to work details and drill. Unhappy, Custer continues to oversee the training of his men, even while white miners enter Indian territory in search of gold. Raiding parties attack the sourdoughs for the yellow metal they require to buy firearms from Tyman.

All this frustrates Custer, who makes his way to the enlisted barracks, where he finds Keogh playing a harmonica. He suggests that the Irish-born officer should provide something besides dirges. Keogh responds with what he thinks would be a "smashing song" for the regiment. He then breaks into "Garry Owen." This lifts the spirits but does not help the 7th as it continues its menial duties. The 5th Cavalry, with Terry at the head, takes to the field, unknowingly to face the firepower of the crooked sutler's shotguns.

Crazy Horse sets his trap. He cuts off Terry. Now Custer has his chance to show that the 7th "is prepared to fight." Against orders, he and his troopers gallop to the rescue of the besieged general and his command. Despite this daring feat, Terry continues to assign the 7th mundane woodcutting and garrison police tasks. Nevertheless, Custer's men have achieved a new esprit after their taste of glory in battle.

DATE FIRST AIRED
September 13, 1967

GUEST STARS
John Rudford: James Daly
Lt. Tim Rudford: Chris Robinson
Sergeant Mason: Jack Hogan

Custer defies General Terry and rides into hostile Sioux territory where Crazy Horse holds sway. Custer's mission: to rescue Lieutenant Rudford, the headstrong son of an influential publisher whose paper attacks Yellow Hair, painting him as a vainglorious murderer.

DATE FIRST AIRED
September 20, 1967

GUEST STARS
Kermit Teller: Ralph Meeker

Custer's men join Kermit Teller's cattle drive as an escort through Sioux country. Teller holds all cavalrymen in contempt, while Custer's men resent being assigned as nursemaids to a herd of cattle.

DATE FIRST AIRED
September 27, 1967

GUEST STARS
Yellow Hawk: Larry Pennell
Sgt. John Tuvey: Art Lund

A Cheyenne, Yellow Hawk, escapes from the army's custody. Custer must find and stop the man in order to prevent an uprising.

DATE FIRST AIRED   EPISODE TITLE
October 4, 1967   **"Massacre"**

Director: Hershel Daugherty Writer: Daniel Mainwaring

GUEST STARS
Benton Conant: Philip Carey
Grey Fox/Bledsoe: Arthur Franz
Jake Halsey: Jan Arvan
Trooper Cassidy: Chase Cordell
Private Morgan: Richard Alden
Lieutenant: Eric Mathews
Driver: Bill Walker

Custer leads a detail with a secret shipment through Sioux territory under the direct control of arrogant State Department official Benton Conant. Gray Fox, a white man who has married a Lakota woman, informs Crazy Horse about the wagon train and its destination. Crazy

Horse wants to seize the prize. Gray Fox is all too willing to resume his white identity as Bledsoe to make the plan work. Assuming the guise of a miner, Bledsoe rides to Custer's column, pretending that he is escaping from Indians. He joins the detail and eventually makes contact with his undercover partner, none other than Conant. The State Department man has become a turncoat because the stakes are high. This mysterious shipment contains $2 million in gold, partial payment to the Russians for the purchase of Alaska. The plotters have agreed to split the loot with Crazy Horse, but the plan fails. In the end, Custer thwarts the scheme and drives off Crazy Horse's superior force. As the Sioux leader rides away, he vows, "There will be other days Yellow Hair."

DATE FIRST AIRED   EPISODE TITLE
October 11, 1967   **"War Lance and Saber"**

California Joe, Keogh, and Custer obtain permission from General Terry to go on a bear hunt. Keogh spots one of the animals but overloads his cartridge. The recoil knocks him over, although the slug manages to wound the creature. Custer pursues the injured animal. The bear causes a rockslide that traps Custer. At just that time, a band of Blackfeet appears on the scene with a prisoner, Crazy Horse. Seeing this, Joe and Keogh head back to Fort Hays because they assume Custer has been killed.

Keogh wants permission to take the regiment on maneuvers so he can search for Custer's body. Terry says that that effort possibly would stir up the Blackfeet and perhaps even cause them to ally themselves with their enemy, the Sioux, because so many soldiers in their area would be taken as a sign of hostility. Keogh is not content with this situation.

Eventually he is allowed to go on patrol with a few men. Keogh tells California Joe that he thinks the general would not be too surprised if the detachment got "accidentally lost" in the area where they last saw Custer. Keogh, Bustard, Joe, and a few men set out, eventually coming upon some Blackfeet trackers. This makes Keogh reflect that the Indians might be looking for Custer, too, and that the colonel could still be alive. They press on, but with no success. Finally, Keogh concedes that they will not find their comrade. The group turns back the next day rather then "stir up a hornet's nest," as Terry had warned.

Soon Custer finds his way into their camp, which is just across the Rosebud. He startles Keogh and orders the detachment to get saddled and mounted. Custer hopes to capture Crazy Horse and his small group of followers, who have only about a twenty-minute lead. Keogh gladly responds. The patrol closes in on the enemy. With drawn sabers, Custer, Keogh, and the cavalrymen charge. They kill a number of Sioux, but Crazy Horse eludes capture. Keogh asks Custer if he is disappointed, then indicates that he is certain the two men will meet again.

DATE FIRST AIRED
October 17, 1967

GUEST STARS
Rio: Hick Hill
Lieutenant Moreno: Robert Loggia
Auguste Grulé: Pierre Jalbert
Lieutenant Cox: Paul Peterson

Lt. Carlos Moreno is a Kiowa who has received a commission in the cavalry. The men of his command suspect him and believe that because his people are friendly to the Sioux, he is a spy. They presume Moreno is bent on thwarting efforts to woo yet a third tribe, the Arapaho, from their Sioux allies. All this proves unfounded in the end.

DATE FIRST AIRED   EPISODE TITLE
November 1, 1967   **"Breakout"**

GUEST STARS
Ned Quimbo: Ray Walston
Nora Moffett: Kathleen Nolan
Uvalde: Burr DeBenning
Deedricko: Gene Evans

At a remote stage stop, Custer and other passengers withstand a siege by Indians. The danger is not only from without but also from within, because two members of the trapped party are cold-blooded killers.

DATE FIRST AIRED   EPISODE TITLE
November 8, 1967   **"Desperate Mission"**

GUEST STARS
James Stanhope: Lloyd Bochner
Jeb Powell: Darin McGavin
Matt Ryker: Charles Dierkop
Billy Nixon: Bill Gray
Red Wolf: X Brands
Pete Bishop: John J. Fox

Rod Tolby: Jon Locke
Trooper "Rio": Hick Hill
Standing Bear: Hal Jon Norman
lst Trooper: Mike Farrell
Aged Pawnee: Phil Donate
Indian Woman: Frances Spanier

Smallpox strikes a Pawnee village, and Custer and his men burn it in hopes of stopping the spread of the disease. All the men of the band are absent but return at the very time the cavalrymen conclude their duties. Red Wolf, believing that the troopers have attacked his people, leads the warriors into the camp, killing everyone but Custer, who is knocked out in the fray.

When Yellow Hair awakens, he returns to General Terry and obtains permission to find Red Wolf, who by now has taken contaminated blankets from his stricken village and set out to the land of the Pawnee. This could mean that Red Wolf will carry death to his entire nation. Also, Terry fears that he will persuade the Pawnee to join with the Sioux out of revenge for the supposed slaughter that the 7th Cavalry carried out on helpless women and children. Custer wants to contact Red Wolf and tell him the true story.

Custer raids the guardhouse and puts together an unlikely mercy mission made up of thieves, swindlers, and murderers, all of whom join for various personal reasons. Custer then sets out with his ragtag detail.

Along the way, Custer is stricken with smallpox. He survives, but three of the men are killed by Sioux and the fourth by Custer, who shoots a man who tries to murder the patrol's acting noncommissioned officer. The three survivors eventually reach Standing Bear's village, just minutes after Red Wolf's band has appeared. Custer attempts to tell the enraged warrior that his men were not responsible for attacking the camp, and after hand-to-hand combat, he finally succeeds in relaying his important message about the dread illness in time to provide a vaccine to save the Pawnee.

DATE FIRST AIRED
November 15, 1967

EPISODE TITLE
"Under Fire"

GUEST STARS
Samson: William Windom
Trooper Johnny Trimble: John Nealson
Jason Talbert: James McCallion
Charley Miller: John Cliff

Crazy Horse makes a deal with a renegade scout. He will divulge the source of gold in the Black Hills in exchange for the white man's pledge to lead Custer into a Sioux ambush.

DATE FIRST AIRED
November 22, 1967 (color)

EPISODE TITLE
"Death Hunt"

Director: Leo Penn
Assistant director: Donald Gold
Writers: Steve McNeil and Richard Barlett

GUEST STARS
Mrs. Peverly: Patricia Harty
Chief Tall Knife: William Smith
Melinda Terry: Barbara Hale
Running Feet: Ned Romero

A crusading woman journalist, who is a niece of President U. S. Grant, and a Cheyenne leader share one thing in common: They want Custer's scalp, one in a literary sense and the other in a literal sense. The reason for their ire is that Custer's men inadvertently killed the brother of the Cheyenne, Tall Knife. The reform-minded Mrs. Peverly intends to have the secretary of war launch a full investigation into the matter. She sees Custer as a murderer based on his actions at the Washita, where she claims he massacred innocent women and children. Yellow Hair retorts that his men killed over a hundred warriors on orders from Gen. Phil Sheridan. Black Kettle's people had left a trail of rapine and murder in Kansas and Colorado that could not go unpunished, says Custer.

In the meantime, Tall Knife swears revenge. He dares Custer, his old friend, to meet him on a "death hunt." When the 7th's field commander does not oblige, the Cheyenne attack the fort. General Terry sends his sister Melinda and Mrs. Peverly away in the event that the garrison is overrun. On the way to presumed safety, the two women are abducted by the war party. Sergeant Bustard makes his way back to the post and reports this event. With the hostages in hand, Custer now must accept Tall Knife's challenge in exchange for the women's freedom.

Despite Terry's orders to the contrary, Custer sneaks out to do battle. Tall Knife allows all three of the white captives a short head start before he rides in pursuit à la *The Most Dangerous Game.* They manage to lead the hunters on a merry chase. Custer dispatches the war party one by one, until only Tall Knife remains. The men pair off in mortal combat. Custer spares Tall Knife's life. In return, peace is restored. Mrs. Peverly adopts a better opinion of Custer. They, too, make a truce.

DATE FIRST AIRED
November 29, 1967

GUEST STARS
Zebediah Jackson: Rory Calhoun
Sergeant Carhew: Adam Williams
John Glixton: Stacy Harris
Brave Dog: Rod Redwing
Cpl. Thomas Hagen: Hal Lynch
Annie Jackson: Ellen Clark

Former Confederates head West through Crow country. Custer must maintain a balancing act in order to avoid resuming the Civil War on one hand or inciting the Crow on the other.

DATE FIRST AIRED   EPISODE TITLE
December 6, 1967   **"Dangerous Prey"**

Director: Leo Penn
Writer: Richard Sale

GUEST STARS
Colonel Charrington: Albert Salmi
War Cloud: Donnely Rhodes
Lieutenant Lamey: Robert Doyle
Bent Arm: George Kemas
Grey Wolf: Mike Adler
Brave Bull: John Cardos

Custer and two other officers survive an attack at a remote way station. One of the men, Colonel Charrington, is under arrest and on his way to a court-martial for a ruthless attack on a friendly village that was flying a flag truce (based loosely on Col. John Chivington's attack on Black Kettle). War Cloud, who was the leader of this ill-fated band, has turned belligerent. Once he learns that Custer has escaped with two other soldiers, he vows to hunt them down.

Custer and two other officers must use strategy to escape their pursuers. They don moccasins to disguise the fact that they are white men. Custer leads them toward the Black Hills, in a direction that he hopes will confuse his enemy. The ploy works in part. The three manage to slay several of

War Cloud's warriors, but one of their own, Lieutenant Lamey, is killed. Custer likewise sustains a wound.

It finally comes down to two Sioux versus two soldiers, but reinforcements soon flesh out War Cloud's group. Armed with only basic weapons, Custer and Charrington take refuge in a cave to wait out a torrential rainstorm. The colonel lets Custer know that he wanted to gain glory by attacking War Cloud's village and that Washita had been an inspiration. Custer is repulsed by this thought. He calls the colonel a murderer. The Boy General claims he respects the Plains Indians, despite years of making war on them.

In the end, Custer outwits the Indian trackers. Although he avoids a final encounter with them, he must face the colonel. Charrington tries to kill his rival officer and take credit for the daring escape from the Sioux. Custer vanquishes the deranged man and brings him back for court-martial.

DATE FIRST AIRED   EPISODE TITLE
December 13, 1967   **"Spirit Woman"**

GUEST STARS
Watoma: Agnes Moorehead
Eldo: James Whitmore

Agnes Moorehead casts off her "Bewitched" role to assume the part of a Sioux mystic and associate of Sitting Bull who wants to bring peace to her people with the whites. She is beset by some of her own people as she attempts to reach General Terry, with whom she wishes to parley, a situation that puts her in jeopardy with Indian and whites alike. Custer must protect her from both sides.

DATE FIRST AIRED
December 20, 1967

GUEST STARS
Col. Sean Redmond: Edward Mulhare
Brigid O'Rourke: Barbara Rush
Finn MacDiarmuid: Dennis Patrick

Irishmen intent on raiding Canada draw the attention of a pompous British officer, who intends to stop them. Custer must deal with the factions and the Indians as well.

DATE FIRST AIRED
December 27, 1967

EPISODE TITLE
"The Raiders"

GUEST STARS
Venessa Ravenhill: Yvonne DeCarlo
Major Benteen: Peter Adams
Blue Antelope: Jeff Scott

Convinced that Kiowas are being blamed for raids on wagon trains they did not make, Custer asks the help of the tribe to find out who really is responsible for the attacks.

DATE FIRST AIRED
Never aired (series canceled)

EPISODE TITLE
"Pursued"

Director: Leo Penn
Writer: John Dunkel

GUEST STARS
Dan Samuels: Earl Holliman
Red Moon Woman: Pilar Seurat
Trader: Dub Taylor
Trapper: Hank Patterson
Roan Horse: Felice Orlandi

Dan Samuels, a former government scout, has stolen food from the army to help feed his wife's people. She is a Cheyenne and comes to visit the man before he is taken away to stand trial. Custer allows Samuels to speak to Red Moon Woman because the frontiersman is an old friend. The husband and wife speak for a few moments, then Dan knocks down one of the guards and kills the other one in the scuffle. It was his life or that of the soldier's. He flees.

Custer receives permission from Terry to track down his old comrade. He catches up with Samuels, and they exchange words, then fight hand-to-hand. Custer vows to bring the man in because he must uphold the law.

Just as he is about to take charge of his prisoner, a Sioux war party rides into the picture. One of their advance guards chances upon Custer and Samuels. Custer saves the life of a trapper named Hank Patterson, but in the process is knocked out. Believing the colonel dead, Samuels again makes good his escape.

When Custer revives, he stalks the runaway, soon finding Samuels with his expectant wife. Red Moon Woman offers to go in her spouse's place, but Custer tells her this is not the white man's way. Soon after they conclude this conversation, the woman goes into labor. It is a breach birth, but Custer manages to deliver the baby, a girl, and save the mother as well. This still does not change his mind about taking back the child's father to face justice. Once more, the Sioux appear, which means Custer must set aside his mission in order to survive.

Samuels takes his family and attempts to bluff his way past the warriors. They do not believe him. A fight takes place, and Custer rushes into the fray. All the Sioux are killed, but not before their leader, Roan Horse, fatally wounds Samuels. Custer buries his fallen friend. Red Moon Woman returns to her people with the new Cheyenne Princess, as the baby's father called her.

Notes

INTRODUCTION

1. George N. Fenin and William K. Everson, *The Western from Silents to Cinerama* (New York: Orion Press, 1962), 12.

2. Some of the more important publications that influenced my continued research included three articles by Paul Andrew Hutton: "From Little Big Horn to Little Big Man: The Changing Image of a Western Hero in Popular Culture," *Western Historical Quarterly* 7 (January 1976): 19–45, "Hollywood's General Custer: The Changing Image of a Military Hero in Film," *Greasy Grass* 2 (May 1986): 15–21, and "'Correct in Every Detail': General Custer in Hollywood," *Montana: The Magazine of Western History* 41 (Winter 1991): 28–57, as well as Hutton's work with Brian Dippie, "Custer in Pop Culture: An Update," in Gregory J. W. Urwin and Roberta E. Fagan, eds., *Custer and His Times* (Conway: University of Central Arkansas, 1987). In addition, Kent Ladd Steckmesser, *The Western Hero in History and Legend* (Norman: University of Oklahoma Press, 1965), and Edward Tabor, *Changing Images of the Warrior Hero in America: A History of Popular Symbolism* (New York: Edwin Mellen Press, 1982), provided context for considering a broader conception of Custer and the Little Bighorn.

3. Bruce Rosenberg, *Custer and the Epic of Defeat* (University Park: Pennsylvania State University Press, 1974), 86.

4. Brian Dippie, *Custer's Last Stand: The Anatomy of an American Myth* (Lincoln: University of Nebraska Press, 1994), 3.

5. Joseph Campbell, *The Hero with a Thousand Faces* (New York: Pantheon Books, 1948), remains an important study comparing hero myths. In turn, Campbell drew some of his analysis from Otto Rank, whose main discourses were translated and appear in Philip Freund, ed., *The Myth of Birth of the Hero and Other Writings* (New York: Vintage, 1956). Robert A. Segal, *Joseph Campbell: An Introduction* (New York: Garland Publishing, 1987), provides a brief overview of Campbell's studies.

6. For instance, William J. Fetterman, who, during 1866, rode into history near Fort Phil Kearny in today's Wyoming against Red Cloud, Crazy Horse, and many others, would be all but forgotten in fiction and by the public, with but a few exceptions. Fiction related to Fetterman and Fort Phil Kearny includes Michael Whitney Straight, *Carrington: A Novel of the West* (New York: Alfred Knopf, 1960); Lewis B. Patten, *Massacre Ridge* (New York: Signet, 1971); and Terry Johnston, *Sioux Dawn* (New York: St. Martin's Press, 1990). In the realm of film, only Universal-International's 1951 *Tomahawk*, with Preston Foster as Col. Henry Carrington and Arthur Space as Capt. William Fetterman, came to the silver screen. Robert Fuller played Fetterman in a made-for-television production. *Chief Crazy Horse*, with Victor Mature, also covered the clash with Carrington's troops to a great extent. Both *Son of the Morning Star* and TNT's *Crazy Horse* likewise had scenes related to the Fetterman fight. These works are few in number, however, in comparison with the numerous publications, films, and television shows concerning Custer and the Little Bighorn.

7. Rosenberg, *Custer and the Epic of Defeat*, 112–13.

8. Richard Slotkin, *Gunfighter Nation: The Myth of the Frontier in Twentieth-Century America* (New York: Atheneum, 1992), 18. This is an underlying theme in another volume by Slotkin, *The Fatal Environment: The Myth of the Frontier in the Age of Industrialization, 1800–1890* (Middletown, CT: Wesleyan University Press, 1986).

9. Slotkin, *Gunfighter Nation*, 374.

10. For a provocative look at this subject, consult Shirley A. Leckie, *Elizabeth Custer and the Making of a Myth* (Norman: University of Oklahoma Press, 1993).

11. Dippie, *Custer's Last Stand*, 7.

12. Brian W. Dippie, "Of Bullets, Blunders, and Custer Buffs," *Montana: The Magazine of Western History* 41 (Winter 1991): 78.

13. Brian W. Dippie and Edward T. LaBlanc, "Bibliography of Custer Dime Novels," *Dime Novel Roundup* 28 (July 15, 1969): 66–70, provides a listing of the over twenty-four dime novel titles that were produced between 1876 and 1929. This is only a fraction of the number of comic books that contain references to Custer, as indicated in Brian W. Dippie and Paul A. Hutton, *The Comic Book Custer: A Bibliography of Custeriana in Comic Books and Comic Strips* (n.p.: Brazos Corral of the Westerners, n.d.). Between the dime novel and the comic book and comic strip, Custer has reached an immense audience, particularly juvenile readers, for the last 115 years.

14. Austin and Alta Fife, "Ballads of the Little Big Horn," *American West* 4 (February 1967): 46–49, 86–89, offers an introductory essay in the field of music. A much more satisfactory treatment is found in Brian Dippie and John Carroll, *Bards of the Little Big Horn* (Bryan, TX: Guidon Press, 1978), and an updated listing of poetry by Dippie and Hutton, "Custer and Pop Culture."

15. Don Russell, *Custer's Last* (Fort Worth, TX: Amon Carter Museum, 1968), provides an overview of pictorial renditions of the event.

16. In 1876 both J. V. Arlington's *The Red Right Hand* and *Sitting Bull; or, Custer's Last Charge* had appeared on stage, with the latter title opening "at the Wood's Museum in New York City to a 'good audience.'" Dippie, *Custer's Last Stand*, 90–91. Decades later, a play was published by a white clergyman who purportedly had gained his information from American Indian sources and as such took their point of view. See A. McGaffey Beede, *Sitting Bull and Custer* (Bismarck, ND: Bismarck Tribune Co., 1913).

17. Micheal D. Easton, *Rare Americana*, catalog 23, item 365, program for July 19, 1887, Adam Forepaugh's Wild West show performance held in Harrisburg, Pennsylvania (research center of the Autry Museum of Western Heritage, Los Angeles).

18. Supposedly, Custer's Last Stand, or "The Cavalry and Indian Story," was one of seven themes in Westerns, the other six being "The Union Pacific Story" (railroads and stagecoaches); "The Ranch Story" (including trail drives); "The Empire Story" (any of the other story lines, but on a grand or epic scale); "The Revenge Story" (sometimes combined with one of the other themes); "The Outlaw Story"; and "The Marshal Story." Frank Gruber, "The Ways to Plot a TV Western," *TV Guide* (August 30, 1959): 5–7.

19. Joseph W. Reed, *American Scenarios: The Uses of Film Genre* (Middletown, CT: Wesleyan University Press, 1989), 18, 60. Reed's book uses an image of John Miljan as Custer from *The Plainsman* as his cover graphic, as well as a variation on this motif for the end papers and opposite the title page, thereby underscoring the readily identifiable nature of the historic figure turned popular culture celebrity. Other works that look at American cinema's depiction of history also are recommended to provide context to the study of Custer in film. These include George F. Custen, *Bio/Pics: How Hollywood Constructed Public History* (New Brunswick, NJ: Rutgers University Press, 1992); Robert Brent Toplin, *History by Hollywood: The Use and Abuse of the American Past* (Urbana: University of Illinois Press, 1996); and Michael R. Pitts, comp., *American History: A Filmography of Over 250 Motion Pictures Depicting U.S. History* (Jefferson, NC: McFarland & Company, 1984). Of note, the last-named work has a segment devoted to Custer (pages 98–101).

20. Slotkin, *Gunfighter Nation*, 101. Slotkin questions whether such a public ever really existed.

21. Edward Buscombe, ed., *The BFI Companion to the Western* (New York: Atheneum, 1988), 37, notes that B movies were the bottom half of a double feature, whereas the more expensive opening picture was the A film.

22. Ibid., 252.

23. Ibid., 13, 256, 278, 347–48. According to Buscombe, more than 7,000 Westerns had been produced in the United States since the beginning of the film industry, making them "the major genre of the world's major national cinema." In addition, some statistics aid in understanding the potential weight of Westerns from 1930 through the 1960s. For instance, in 1930, A Westerns represented but 2.6 percent of film productions made by the seven major studios and 21.4 percent of all Westerns. The next year, these numbers went down to 1.6 percent and 16.7 percent, respectively, although taken together, the genre still represented 16 or 17 percent of all films produced in 1931. For the next several years, the numbers fluctuated, yet by the end of the 1930s, "the Western was the most consistently popular and most widely produced form of action film and a significant field for the active fabrication and revision of public myth and ideology." Additional figures through the early 1960s are also discussed. Television is factored into the equation, with the further explanation that "for the most part of the 1950–1970 period movies remained the most important source of mythmaking."

Interestingly, not until *Little Big Man* (1970) did a production hinging on the Custer and Little Bighorn story make a major return. During the early 1970s, that picture was ranked number two, at $15 million. (Number one that year was *Love Story*, at $50 million.) "Big Rental Films of 1970," *Variety* (January 5, 1973): 9. This put *Little Big Man* as number forty-four in the history of film top domestic money makers to that time, with *Gone with the Wind*, at $74.2 million being the reigning champion. "All-Time Box Office Champs," *Variety* (January 5, 1973): 11.

24. Rosenberg, *Custer and the Epic of Defeat*, 254.

25. Slotkin, *Gunfighter Nation*, 257.

26. Ibid., 8, 258.

27. Ibid., 8. Also see Herbert J. Gans, *Popular Culture and High Culture: An Analysis and Evaluation of Taste* (New York: Basic Books, 1974).

28. Not all early movies took a negative view of Indians, including ones related to the Custer saga, a point Roberta E. Pearson makes in "The Revenge of Rain in the Face? or, Custers and Indians on the Silent Screen," Daniel Bernardi, ed., *The Birth of Whiteness: Race and the Emergence of U.S. Cinema* (New Brunswick: Rutgers University Press, 1996), 273–99. As to the propensity after World War II to cast American Indians in a favorable role, see Steve Neale, "Vanishing Americans: Racial and Ethnic Issues in the Interpretation and Context of Post War 'Pro-Indian' Westerns," in Edward Buscombe and Roberta E. Pearson, eds., *Back in the Saddle Again: New Essays on the Western* (London: British Film Institute, 1996), 8–28.

For more on the changing image of American Indians on the silver screen, consult Gretchen M. Bataille and Charles L. P. Silet, eds., *The Pretend Indians: Images of Native Americans in the Movies* (Ames: Iowa State University Press, 1980); Ralph and Natasha Friar, *The Only Good Indian* (New York: Drama Book, 1972); Ezra Goodman, *The Fifty-Year Decline and Fall of Hollywood* (New York: Simon and Schuster, 1961), 430–31; Michael Hilger, *The American Indian in Films* (Metuchen, NJ: The Scarecrow Press, 1986); John E. O'Connor, *The Hollywood Indian: Stereotypes of Native Americans in Film* (Trenton: New Jersey State Museum, 1980); Paul Rotha, *Film Till Now: A Survey of World Cinema* (London: Spring Books, 1967), 440–41; Richard Slotkin, *Regeneration through Violence* (Middletown, CT: Wesleyan University Press, c. 1973); Raymond William Stedman, *Shadows of the Indian* (Norman: University of Oklahoma Press, 1982); and John Tuska, *The American West in Film* (Westport, CT: Greenwood Press, 1985).

29. Dippie, *Custer's Last Stand*, xi.

30. "Custer had come to be part of Sioux culture," wrote one historian, "just as Sitting Bull had become part of American culture. " As such, "in a complex process of cross-fertilization in the early twentieth century, Lakota stories and American stories were merging." Richard White, "Frederick Jackson Turner and Buffalo Bill," in *The Frontier and American Culture*, James R. Grossman, ed. (Berkeley: University of California Press, 1994), 43. To some degree, this same statement could be made about other American Indian groups.

31. This is somewhat akin to the observation that "many ideas that pass for Indian thinking are in reality theories originally advanced by anthropologists and echoed by Indian

people in an attempt to communicate the real situation." Vine Deloria, Jr., *Custer Died for Your Sins: An Indian Manifesto* (New York: Avon Books, 1972), 87.

Another commentator even went so far as to note that white tourists who already are "aware of past sins against the Indians are actually more comfortable visiting" the Little Bighorn than they would be traveling to a site such as Wounded Knee. Wayne Michael Scharf, "Sabers and Tomahawks," *Custer/Little Bighorn Battlefield Advocate* 2 (Spring 1995): 2.

The same situation exists relative to the tragic events of 1890 at the Pine Ridge Reservation in South Dakota. Wounded Knee, unlike the Little Bighorn, evidently did not appeal to a mass audience, which producers sought as their target. Nonetheless, as pointed out in Kevin Brownlow, *The War, the West, and the Wilderness* (New York: Alfred A. Knopf, 1979), 235, William F. Cody did concentrate on this event in his 1913 epic, known variously as *The Indian Wars Refought; The Last Indian Battle, or, From the Warpath to the Peacepipe; The Wars for Civilization in America, Buffalo Bill's Indian Wars; Indian Wars Pictures*; and *The Adventures of Buffalo Bill*. See pages 224–35 of that book for additional details about this silent feature. The only other productions to portray this story were CBS's *Great Adventures* television series, which ran two parts in 1963 titled "The Death of Sitting Bull" and "Massacre at Wounded Knee," and a very loose interpretation of the Ghost Dance and death of Sitting Bull in *Kenny Rogers as the Gambler III: The Legend Continues* (1987).

Fictional titles related to Wounded Knee and the Ghost Dance include Milton Lott, *Dance Back the Buffalo* (New York: Pockett Books, 1968), and Douglas Jones, *Arrest Sitting Bull* (New York: Scribner, 1977). The conclusion of Terry C. Johnston's *Whisper of the Wolf* (New York: Bantam Books, 1991) also focuses on the Ghost Dance.

32. This explains why the made-for-television *Class of '61* (1993) could offer a devil-may-care Cadet Custer in the mold of *Santa Fe Trail* or *They Died with Their Boots On*, while at the same time, the series *Dr. Quinn, Medicine Woman* drew upon the Custer of *Little Big Man* as the quintessential white militarist bent on destruction of those who oppose him and ready to do the bidding of the power brokers who could further his career.

Also in the spirit of changing times, *Son of the Morning Star* was narrated by two women characters, Kate Bighead and Elizabeth Custer, rather than from the male point of view of Custer, Crazy Horse, or the like. Additionally, Isaiah Dorman, the only African American with the Custer column, was depicted in a cameo despite the fact that the character is not introduced in any way during the miniseries to provide a clue to who the black being killed onscreen at the Little Bighorn was. Nevertheless, the presence of an actor representing this slain civilian indicates the changing sensitivities of productions in the post civil-rights era.

33. As one means of comparison, Custer, or fictional characters derived from Custer, figured into no less than seventy motion pictures, film serials, and television episodes (see appendix A). Such contemporaries as William F. Cody appeared in nine movies himself and was a character in a minimum of forty-five movie and TV productions. William

Butler "Wild Bill" Hickok has been portrayed no less than forty-six times on the big and small screens combined. Sitting Bull was depicted at least twenty-one times, and Crazy Horse thirteen times. Grant and Sheridan tied, at twelve Westerns, and William Sherman was a character in five. These figures do not include television documentaries. Based on Buscombe, *The BFI Companion to the Western*, 92–3, 104, 130, 147–48, 218, and 220–21, along with additional research assembled by the author.

34. Dippie, *Custer's Last Stand*, xxi.

35. Patricia Nelson Limerick, "The Adventures of the Frontier in the Twentieth Century," in *The Frontier in American Culture*, 93.

36. According to one analysis, Custer has been altered "from a symbol of courage and sacrifice in the winning of the West . . . into a symbol of the arrogance and brutality displayed in the white exploitation." Throughout the process, "the only constant factor in this reversed legend is a remarkable disregard for historical fact." Hutton, "From the Little Bighorn to Little Big Man," 45.

On a related topic, Roberta E. Pearson, "'Custer Still the Hero': Textual Stability and Transformation," *Journal of Film and Video* (Spring/Fall 1995): 82–97, debates a single-cause explanation that shifts in beliefs determine the content of film and television productions. While this argument is sound, there still is merit in examination of movies and TV productions within the context of the times in which they were made, just as in other forms of creative expression. Another factor that often is overlooked is personal perspectives of the writer, director, and other key personnel who produce programming.

CHAPTER ONE

1. As one historian observed, "Estimations of Custer today usually turn on estimations of his performance at the Little Bighorn, and these have been as varied as the epithets applied to him—the Darling of the Gods, the Last of the Cavaliers, the Napoleon of the Plains, the Murat of the American Army, the Chief of Thieves, Glory-hunter." Brian W. Dippie, ed., *Nomad: George A. Custer in Turf, Field and Farm* (Austin: University of Texas Press, 1980), xi.

2. Between 1867 and 1875 Custer wrote under the pseudonym Nomad for *Turf, Field and Farm*, a sportsmen's magazine published in New York. Over these years, fifteen of his letters appeared in that periodical. Most of the articles have to do with hunting, but three treat Indian campaigns and differ from the versions given in *My Life on the Plains; or, Personal Experiences with Indians* (New York: Sheldon, 1875). As such, researchers should beware of accepting Custer's words as accurate statements of fact. Indeed, materials authored by Custer were produced as "*literary* works, meant to entertain."

They reflected his own fondness for "works of history and . . . a real love of poetry." In this, Benteen's quip dubbing one of Custer's titles as "My Lie on the Plains" seems to have been aptly put, as were the white-haired captain's comments that *My Life on the Plains* "was readable enough, but to one who was along through the whole series of years which it covers, the falsity of much of it is as glaring as the sun at noonday." Dippie, *Nomad*, xiv–xvi. Hereinafter, references citing this autobiography will be taken from Milo Milton Quaife, ed., *My Life on the Plains by George Armstrong Custer* (New York: Carol Publishing Group, 1993).

3. Robert M. Utley, *Cavalier in Buckskin: George Armstrong Custer and the Western Military Frontier* (Norman: University of Oklahoma Press, 1988), 12.

4. Ibid., 16.

5. George B. McClellan, *McClellan's Own Story* (New York: C. L. Webster & Co., 1887), 364–65.

6. As quoted in Utley, *Cavalier*, 20.

7. As quoted in Leckie, *Elizabeth Bacon Custer and the Making of a Myth*, 25.

8. Ibid., 72.

9. Ibid., 31.

10. Utley, *Cavalier*, 25.

11. Leckie, *Elizabeth Bacon Custer*, 32.

12. For a useful chronology of Custer's life see D. Mark Katz, *Custer in Photographs: A Visual Portrait of One of America's Most Intriguing Civil War Heroes* (New York: Bonanza Books, 1985), 143–53.

13. For more on the period from 1861 to 1865, read Gregory J. W. Urwin, *Custer Victorious: The Civil War Battles of General George Armstrong Custer* (East Brunswick, NJ: Associated University Press, 1983).

14. As quoted in Utley, *Cavalier*, 38.

15. John M. Carroll, *Custer in Texas: An Interrupted Narrative* (New York: Sol Lewis, 1975), provides additional details on this immediate post–Civil War period in Texas.

16. Utley, *Cavalier*, 39.

17. Ibid.

18. Marguerite Merington, ed., *The Custer Story: The Life and Intimate Letters of General George A. Custer and His Wife Elizabeth* (New York: The Devin-Adair Company, 1950), 188. The letters in this volume, although useful, must be reviewed with care because they often were reworked by the editor, whose papers are in the New York Public Library.

19. As quoted in Evan S. Connell, *Son of the Morning Star: Custer and The Little Bighorn* (New York: Harper and Row, 1985), 276.

20. Theodore Davis, "With Generals in Their Camp Homes: General George A. Custer," *Chicago Brand Book* (Chicago: Chicago Corral of the Westerners, 1945–46), 118–19.

21. Robert M. Utley, ed., *Life in Custer's Cavalry: Diaries and Letters of Albert and Jennie Barnitz, 1867–1868* (New Haven: Yale University Press, 1977), 46.

22. Ibid., 49–50.

23. Ibid.

24. Letter from Autie to Libbie, May 10, 1867, as quoted in Leckie, *Elizabeth Bacon Custer*, 96.

25. Ibid., 97.

26. Quaife, *My Life on the Plains*, 204.

27. Lawrence A. Frost, *The Court-Martial of General George Armstrong Custer* (Norman: University of Oklahoma Press, 1968), provides detailed information relative to this series of incidents and their consequence.

28. Slotkin, *Gunfighter Nation*, 12, defined savage war as "both a mythic trope and an operative category of military doctrine." As such, "the premise . . . is that ineluctable political and social differences—rooted in some combination of 'blood' and culture—make coexistence between primitive natives and civilized Europeans impossible on any other basis than that of subjugation." In this light, "native resistance to European settlement therefore takes the form of a fight for survival." Because of the alleged "'savage' and bloodthirsty propensity of the natives, such struggles inevitably become 'wars of extermination' in which one side or the other attempts to destroy its enemy root and branch."

29. Quaife, *My Life on the Plains*, 216.

30. Utley, *Life in Custer's Cavalry*, 198.

31. Slotkin, *Gunfighter Nation*, 16, defines the "'man who knows Indians'" in terms of one who was "the frontier hero [who] stands between the opposed worlds of savagery and civilization, acting sometimes as mediator or interpreter between races and cultures but more often as civilization's most effective instrument against savagery."

32. Ibid., 35. In point of fact, "journalists who began the process of mythologizing Custer were initially attracted to his story by recognition that the man and the event were realizations of the myths in which they believed." Slotkin, *The Fatal Environment*, 373. Moreover, Custer might be seen as "an early type of organization man, hiding in the costumes of the cavalier trooper and the Frontier buckskin." Ibid., 375.

33. Stan Hoig, *The Sand Creek Massacre* (Norman: University of Oklahoma Press, 1961), was the standard reference on this tragic event, although David Svaldi, *Sand Creek and the Rhetoric of Extermination: A Case Study in Indian-White Relations* (Lanham, MD: University Press of America, c. 1989), and Bruce Cutler, *The Massacre at Sand Creek: Narrative Voices* (Norman: University of Oklahoma Press, 1995), offer additional perspectives.

34. As quoted in Charles K. Mills, *Harvest of Barren Regrets: The Army Career of Frederick William Benteen* (Glendale, CA: Arthur H. Clark Company, 1985), 169.

35. Connell, *Son of the Morning Star*, 197.

36. Merington, *The Custer Story*, 239.

37. Ibid., 258.

38. Herman Krause and Gary D. Olsen, comps., *Prelude to Glory: A Newspaper Accounting of Custer's 1874 Expedition to the Black Hills* (Sioux Falls, SD: Brevet Press, 1974), 101–2, quoting William E. Curtis, *Chicago Interocean*, July 9, 1874.

39. Donald E. Danker, ed., *Man of the Plains: Recollections of Luther North, 1856–1882* (Lincoln: University of Nebraska Press, 1961), 185.

40. Francis Paul Prucha, *American Indian Treaties: The History of a Political Anomaly* (Berkeley: University of California Press, 1994), 283. This study should be read in its entirety to gain an insight into the concept of treaties and efforts to execute them. Additionally, even today there are those who agree with Black Elk's views that the whites had no right to be in the Black Hills, as Donald Worster discusses in his *Under Western Skies: Nature and History in the American West* (Oxford: Oxford University Press, 1992), 106–53, in a chapter titled, "The Black Hills: Sacred or Profane?"

41. Robert M. Utley, *The Lance and the Shield: The Life and Times of Sitting Bull* (New York: Henry Holt, 1993), 76–164, places Sitting Bull in the context of many Plains Indians who rejected the call to reservations and saw the incursion of whites in the "Hills of Black" as a "thieves road" that must be blocked to preserve their culture and source of food.

42. Slotkin, *The Fatal Environment,* 325–70, discusses the ramifications of the Black Hills gold discovery and its broader implications, not only for Custer but also for the nation at that time.

43. Utley, *Cavalier,* 153.

44. William Belknap to Alfred Terry, April 13, 1876, Glen Swanson Collection.

45. For primary sources on this topic, see *Trial of William W. Belknap in the Senate of the United States, 1876* (Washington, DC: U.S. Government Printing Office, 1876), and *Report of Committee on Sale of Post Traderships,* House Report no. 799, 44th cong., 1st sess.

46. Frederick Whittaker, *The Life of General George A. Custer* (New York: Sheldon & Company, 1876), reprinted this letter. The original was sold as lot number 7250 at an auction held on November 9, 1988, by Butterfield & Butterfield in San Francisco.

47. Connell, *Son of the Morning Star,* 259.

48. Utley, *Cavalier,* 164, postulates that Custer was not looking to gain the presidency or even a civilian office, such as commissioner of Indian affairs, but instead hoped to secure promotion to brigadier general.

49. Richard Upton, ed. and comp., *The Custer Adventure* (Fort Collins, CO: The Old Army Press, 1975), 13.

50. Ibid., 15.

51. Capt. E. S. Godfrey, "Custer's Last Battle," *Century Magazine* (January 1892): 358–84, served as a source for this and the quotations that immediately precede it. The article was one of the first in-depth accounts by a participant of the Little Bighorn battle and contained both firsthand information and speculation about Custer's actions after he left the remainder of the regiment behind.

52. E. C. Bailly, "Echoes from Custer's Last Fight," *Military Affairs* (1953): 170–73, reprinted portions of a letter from Lt. Winfield S. Edgerly recounting the activities of the evening of June 23.

53. Earl A. Brininstool, *Troopers with Custer: Historical Incidences of the Battle of Little Big Horn* (Harrisburg, PA: Stackpole, Co., 1952), 71–72, and Francis M. Gibson, microfilm roll 6, frame 6201 (unpublished manuscript, Elizabeth Custer Collection, Little Bighorn Battlefield National Monument).

54. *Annual Report of the Secretary of War, 1876,* vol. 1 (Washington, DC: Government Printing Office, 1876), 32. This source was an official report made by Reno shortly after the battle. Three years later, the major provided a more extensive account when he called for and received a review of his actions in answer to allegations that he had been responsible for the debacle. His expanded testimony is found in W. A. Graham, *The Official Record of a Court of Inquiry Convened at Chicago, Illinois, January 13, 1879, by the President of the United States Upon the Request of Major A. Reno . . .* (Pacific Palisades, CA: W. A. Graham, 1951), 499–542.

55. *Annual Report of the Secretary of War, 1876,* 32–33.

56. Brininstool, *Troopers with Custer,* 92.

57. Peter Thompson, *Narrative of the Little Bighorn Campaign,* ed. by Daniel O. Magnussen (Glendale, CA: Arthur Clark Company, 1974), 145–46.

58. George Custer to Elizabeth Custer, April 10, 1867, published in Elizabeth Custer, *Tenting on the Plains,* vol. 3 (Norman: University of Oklahoma Press, 1971), 552–53.

CHAPTER TWO

1. Original telegram from Terry at Camp on Little Big Horn River to Assistant Adjutant General of Military Division of Missouri, Chicago (Library of Congress).

2. Telegram from R. C. Dunn to H. T. Crosby, July 6, 1876, reprinted as a facsimile in *The Custer Battle Papers: A March into Immortality* (n.p.: Frontier Press, 1969). The next day, Sheridan communicated by telegram with Sherman, dispatching reinforcements for Alfred Terry and George Crook and stating, "There is nothing to be regretted but the loss of poor Custer & the officers & men with him." Sheridan went on to assert that "Terry's column was sufficient" to have met the enemy "if Custer had waited for the junction." Telegram from Philip Sheridan to William Sherman, July 7, 1876, Glen Swanson Collection.

3. Paul Andrew Hutton, *Phil Sheridan and His Army* (Lincoln: University of Nebraska Press, 1985), 315.

4. Some attempted to lay the blame for the Custer debacle on the Republicans, a particularly attractive proposition in the South, where Reconstruction was coming to an end and Southern Democrats were making a bid to return to national prominence. The July 18, 1876, headline of the *Atlanta Weekly Commonwealth* read: "Grant, the Murderer of Custer."

   Grant's own take on the matter was very different. He concluded, "I regard Custer's Massacre as a sacrifice of troops brought on by Custer himself, that was wholly unnecessary—wholly unnecessary." As quoted in Utley, *Cavalier,* 6.

5. For details, see Frederick Whittaker, "General George A. Custer," *Galaxy* (September 1876): 362–71.

6. Whittaker, *The Complete Life of Gen. George A. Custer,* 609–10.

7. Ibid., 606–8. For the official investigation, which convened on January 13, 1879, at Chicago's Palmer House, read W. A. Graham, ed., *Abstract of the Official Proceedings of the Reno Court of Inquiry* (Harrisburg, PA: Stackpole, 1954).

8. "Miscellany and Advertiser," *Galaxy* (December 1876).

9. Leckie, *Elizabeth Bacon Custer,* 230. *My Life on the Plains* was reprinted in a much expanded form as early as 1885, the year Mrs. Custer's first book was released. The new version was titled *Wild Life on the Plains and Horrors of Indian Warfare, by General G. A. Custer, U.S.A. with a Graphic Account of the Last Fight on the Little Big Horn, as Told by His Wily Foe Sitting Bull* (St. Louis: Sun Publishing Co., 1885). The subtitle indicated the pro-Custer approach to the revised volume, which contained among other things, Reno's report about the battle, a supposed translation of Sitting Bull's accounts of that day, and a number of illustrations, not the least of which were images of the Last Stand and William F. Cody's "first scalp for Custer."

10. Ibid., 237.

11. F. S. Dellenbaugh, *George Armstrong Custer* (New York: The Macmillan Company, 1917), v.

12. Other biographies include Frazier Hunt, *Custer: The Last of the Cavaliers* (1928); Milton Ronsheim, *The Life of General Custer* (1929); Shannon Garst, *Custer: Fighter of the Plains* (1944); Fred Dustin, "George Armstrong Custer," *Michigan History Magazine* (1946); Marguerite Merington, ed., *The Custer Story: The Life and Intimate Letters of George A. Custer and His Wife Elizabeth* (1950); Quentin Reynolds, *Custer's Last Stand* (1951); Margaret Leighton, *The Story of General*

Custer (1954); Nelle Deex, *Glory Trek: The Story of General Custer's Last Stand* (1959); Jay Monaghan, *Custer: The Life of General George Armstrong Custer* (1959); Lauran Paine, *The General Custer Story: The True Story of the Battle of the Little Big Horn* (1960); Augusta Stevenson, *George Custer: Boy of Action* (1963); Lawrence A. Frost, *The Custer Album: A Pictorial Biography of General George A. Custer* (1964); D. A. Kinsley, *Favor the Bold,* vol. 1, *Custer the Civil War Years* (1967) and vol. 2, *Custer the Indian Fighter* (1968); William Heuman, *Custer Man and Legend* (1968); Stephen Ambrose, *Crazy Horse and Custer: The Parallel Lives of Two American Warriors* (1975); Evan S. Connell, *Son of the Morning Star: Custer and the Little Bighorn* (1984); Eddie Dieber, *General George Custer's Biography in Pictures* (n.d.); Brian W. Dippie, "George A. Custer," in Paul Hutton, ed., *Soldiers West: Biographies from the Military Frontiers;* Robert M. Utley, *Cavalier in Buckskin* (1988); Jeffery D. Wert, *Custer: The Controversial Life of George Armstrong Custer* (1996); and Louise Barnett, *Touched by Fire: The Life, Death, and Mythic Afterlife of George Armstrong Custer* (1996); and Brice C. Custer, *Sacrificial Lion: George Armstrong Custer* (1999). Two other works concentrate on Custer's Civil War years but contain considerable biographical background: Gregory I. W. Urwin, *Custer Victorious: The Civil War Battles of George Armstrong Custer* (1983), and Edward G. Longacre, *Custer and His Wolverines: The Michigan Cavalry Brigade 1861–1865* (1997). Many of these publications were written for a juvenile market. For a brief summation of most of these titles, consult Dippie, *Custer's Last Stand,* 181–84.

13. Leckie, *Elizabeth Bacon Custer,* 292–93, provides a synopsis of this revision and how it came about. Another response, one that took the Godfrey articles to task, is found in Fred Dustin, *The Custer Fights: Some Criticisms of Gen. E. S. Godfrey's "Custer's Last Battle," in Century Magazine for January 1892, and of Mrs. Elizabeth Custer's Pamphlet of 1921* (Hollywood, CA: E. A. Brininstool, 1936).

Decades earlier, Elizabeth Custer began correspondence with Edward Godfrey and shared her views with him on a number of matters. For instance, on at least one occasion, she asked him to serve as a watchdog for a major project depicting Little Bighorn, the massive cyclorama of the 1880s. As such, the former 7th Cavalry officer was an early champion in Mrs. Custer's camp. Brian W. Dippie, "'What Valor Is': Artists and the Mythic Movement," in Charles E. Rankin, ed., *Legacy: New Perspectives of the Battle of the Little Bighorn* (Helena: Montana Historical Society, 1996), 224.

14. Fredric F. Van de Water, *Glory-Hunter: A Life of General Custer* (New York: The Bobbs-Merrill Company, 1934), 18.
15. Ibid., 17–19.
16. Ibid.
17. Ibid., 24–43.
18. Brininstool to William J. Ghent, January 18, 1923.
19. Brininstool to William J. Ghent, May 27, 1926.
20. Fred Dustin, *The Custer Tragedy: Events Leading Up to and Following the Little Big Horn Campaign of 1876* (Ann Arbor: Edwards Brothers, 1939), xv.
21. *The Custer Tragedy by Fred Dustin,* advertisement sheet, 1939, in the research center of the Autry Museum of Western Heritage, Los Angeles. The opening statement exclaimed,

"This authoritative book is based upon more than thirty years' quest for the truth about this great Indian battle."
22. Ibid.
23. Dippie, *Custer's Last Stand,* 183.
24. From Brian Pohanka's introduction to the reprint of W. A. Graham's *The Custer Myth* (Mechanicsburg, PA: Stackpole Books, 1995), xxiv. Stackpole also published the original edition of this book in 1953. With the exception of the Pohanka introduction, the 1995 edition is a reprint and will be used here as the source for Graham's findings.
25. Ibid., xxv.
26. Ibid., 122.
27. Ibid., 217.
28. As quoted on page xxvi of Graham's *The Custer Myth,* from the original November 12, 1953, letter in the collection of Frank Mercantante. Indeed, Graham wholly followed this course when he released his *Abstract of the Official Proceedings of the Reno Court of Inquiry.* In this case, Kuhlman did concede to Graham, "The announcement that you are to publish the Official Record of the Reno Court of Inquiry is the best news that has come to Custer students since the day of the battle." Similar praise was given by Brininstool and Dustin in an undated form letter advertising subscriptions for purchase of the limited edition (125 were to be printed) self-publication of the Reno Court document (original in the research center of the Autry Museum of Western Heritage, Los Angeles).
29. Amazingly, Graham never visited the battlefield, while Dustin went there only once, with Kuhlman and Brininstool. Because the terrain provides certain keys to understanding the engagement, it would seem imperative to have an in-depth grasp of the ground to place other evidence in context. This was Kuhlman's line of reasoning, and his painstaking fieldwork at the site itself "gave him an intimate knowledge of every fold and crevice in the battlefield." Letter from Robert Utley to Brian Pohanka, August 4, 1993, courtesy Brian Pohanka.

Additional information about Kuhlman's background was taken from letters sent by Kuhlman to Hugh W. Shick, March 25, 1955; November 29, 1958; and December 9, 1958, Glen Swanson Collection. In the first letter, Kuhlman mentioned that since he was six years old, he had walked through many fields that had conjured up images in his mind. In the December letter, he wrote that he was "pretty fed up on the Custer subject and have turned to another subject."
30. Kuhlman indicated that he sometimes received information about the battle through psychic powers or from visions after he had smoked the "sacred pipe." See representative letters from Kuhlman to Hugh Shick, January 27, 1954, and October 20, 1954, Glen Swanson Collection.
31. See the Bibliography for this and other key Kuhlman publications.
32. W. A. Graham to Hugh Shick, January 3, 1951, Glen Swanson Collection.
33. Don Rickey, *History of Custer Battlefield* (Billings, MT: Custer Battlefield Historical Museum Association, 1967), 89.
34. Edward S. Luce, *Keogh, Comanche and Custer* (St. Louis: n.p., 1939). He also coauthored *Custer Battlefield National Monument, Montana* (Washington, DC: National Park Service, 1952) with his wife, Evelyn.

35. Representative correspondence indicating the extent of friction, jealousy, and disagreement among certain of the Little Bighorn's most notable students can be found in exchanges between Kuhlman and Graham, July 7, 1948; April 2, 1949; March 5, 1950; and May 30, 1951, Glen Swanson Collection.

36. W. A. Graham to E. S. Luce, January 4, 1940, Glen Swanson Collection.

37. Three bibliographies provide some appreciation as to the extensive writings concentrating on Little Bighorn as history: Tal Luther, *Custer High Spots* (Fort Collins, CO: Old Army Press, 1972); James Patrick Dowd, *Custer Lives* (Fairfield, WA: Ye Galleon Press, 1982); and T. A. Swinford, *Custeriana: A Field Guide to Custer Literature by T. A. Swinford and Tal Luther* (Tempe, AZ: Old Army Press, 1999).

38. The segment on fiction draws extensively on Vincent A. Heier's "Fiction Stranger than Truth: A 'Novel' Approach to Custer in Literature" (3rd Annual Symposium, Custer Battlefield Historical & Museum Association, held at Hardin, Montana, on June 23, 1989). Reverend Heier has graciously allowed much of his work in this field to be reproduced here.

39. Ibid., 501–2.

40. Kent Steckmesser, "Custer in Fiction," *The American West* 1 (Fall 1964): 47–52; 63–64.

41. Slotkin, *The Fatal Environment*, 510.

42. Dippie and LaBlanc, "Bibliography of Custer Dime Novels," 67.

43. Steckmesser, "Custer in Fiction," 8.

44. Slotkin, *The Fatal Environment*, 511.

45. Steckmesser, "Custer in Fiction," 51.

46. As one example of the continuing youth-oriented fiction, read Brian Burke, *Soldier Boy* (San Diego: Harcourt Brace & Company, 1997), a novel that centers on a troubled adolescent from the slums of Chicago who, although underage, enlists in the 7th Cavalry and dies at the Little Bighorn.

47. Enid Meadowcraft's *Crazy Horse* (New York: Garrard, 1965), written for the second- through third-grade level, is a prime example.

48. Paul Goble, *Red Hawk's Account of Custer's Last Battle* (New York: Pantheon Books, 1969). Similarly, in Chief D. Eagle, *Winter Count* (Denver: Golden Bell, 1960), a work intended for an older audience, Lakota Turtleneck and his white wife, Evensigh, are the focal point of the story, rather than Custer and his command.

49. Nathaniel Benchley, *Only Earth and Sky Last Forever* (New York: Harper, 1972), and James Foreman, *The Life and Death of Yellow Bird* (New York: Farrar, 1973).

50. Steckmesser, "Custer in Fiction," 52.

51. Ibid., 53.

52. Dippie, *Custer's Last Stand*, 68.

53. Steckmesser, "Custer in Fiction," 63.

54. Dippie, *Custer's Last Stand*, 71.

55. Steckmesser, "Custer in Fiction," 63.

56. Ibid.

57. Deloria, *Custer Died for Your Sins*, 23.

58. Dippie, *Custer's Last Stand*, 72.

59. Ibid., 73.

60. Walter B. Gibson, adapter, *Rod Serling's Twilight Zone Revisited* (New York: Grossett & Dunlap, 1964), includes a short story, "Two Live Ghosts," that is representative of this genre.

61. Steven Utley and Howard Waldrop, "Custer's Last Jump," in Terry Carr, ed., *Universe 6* (Garden City, NY: Doubleday & Co., 1976), 84–85.

62. Other "alternate history" works include Philip Jose Farmer, *Quest to Riverworld* (New York: Warner Books, 1993); Mark Summer, *Devil's Tower* (New York: Ballantine, 1996); Brian M. Thomsen, "Blood-stained Ground," in Harry Turtledove, ed., *Alternate Generals* (Riverdale, NY: Bean Publishing, 1998); Harry Turtledove, *How Few Remain* (New York: Ballantine Books, 1997); and Turtledove's sequel, *The Great War: American Front* (New York: Ballantine Publishing Group, 1998).

63. In the iconoclastic, antimilitary atmosphere of the Cold War era, science-fiction writer Harlan Ellison took this point of view to its logical conclusion when he placed Custer, Hitler, Jack the Ripper, and other sordid historical characters in hell for his short story "And Hitler Painted Roses," in Harlan Ellison, *Strange Wine: Fifteen Stories from the Nightside of the World* (New York: Harper & Row, 1978). Mark Summer's *Devil's Tower* takes this one step further and turns Custer into a demon.

64. For additional fictional references, consult Dippie, *Custer's Last Stand*, 193–201, and Hutton, *The Custer Reader*, 393. Several works of fiction not covered in the foregoing texts are included in the Bibliography, courtesy of Reverend Heier. It is notable that a number of these works either served as the basis for film and television productions or were spinoffs from such productions, again indicating the symbiotic relationship among various popular media forms related to Custer and the Little Bighorn.

65. Paula Fairman, *The Tender and the Savage* (Los Angeles: Pinnacle Books, 1980), back cover.

66. Rebecca Drury, *Savage Beauty* (Wayne, PA: Banbury Books, 1982), front cover.

67. E. J. Hunter, *White Squaw* (New York: Kensington Publishing Corp., 1985), back cover.

68. Terry C. Johnston, *Long Winter Gone* (New York: Bantam Books, 1990). For a related reference as a means of providing context, read Barbara Zimmerman, "Mo-nah-se-tah: Fact or Fiction" (4th Annual Symposium, Custer Battlefield Historical & Museum Association, held in Hardin, Montana, on June 22, 1990).

69. Terry C. Johnston, *Seize the Sky* (New York: Bantam Books, 1991).

70. James Foreman, *Life and Death of Yellow Bird* (New York: Farrar, 1973).

71. Michael Blake, *Marching to Valhalla: The Last Testimony of George Armstrong Custer* (New York: Vallard, 1996).

72. See Richard Mattheson, *The Memoirs of Wild Bill Hickok* (New York: Jove Books, 1996), for a typical example of how Custer became part of a stock company of characters in fiction, film, and television as proto Westerners.

73. The subject of poetry related to Custer and the Little Bighorn is beyond the scope of this volume, as are the lyrics to many songs. For more on this aspect of shaping the Custer myth, consult Dippie and Carroll, *Bards of the Little Big Horn;* Dippie and Hutton, "Custer and Pop Culture"; and Dippie, *Custer's Last Stand*, 12–31; 185–91.

74. Neihardt, *Black Elk Speaks*, 108–9.

75. Connell, *Son of the Morning Star*, 308, pointed out one of the pitfalls of this approach: "It should be kept in mind that years afterwards these Indians told white journalists and politicians what they thought the whites wanted to hear. They believed, correctly or not, that if they said the wrong thing they would be punished."

76. Jerome A. Greene, comp. and ed., *Lakota and Cheyenne Indian Views of the Great Sioux War, 1876–1877* (Norman: University of Oklahoma Press, 1994), xxi–xxii; xviii. As one example of skepticism, Graham pointed to "discrepancies and contradictions and inconsistencies" he found in Indian statements. He raised an interesting point when deliberating over such testimony in that the differences between the Plains Indian culture and the white culture were so profound that it was extremely difficult for either side to really understand the other or "to reach a common ground." Graham, *The Custer Myth*, 3–4. As if taking up Graham's challenge, Herman J. Viola, *Little Bighorn Remembered: The Untold Indian Story of Custer's Last Stand* (New York: Times Books, 1999), attempts to illuminate American Indian interpretations of the battle.

77. As artist E. Lisle Reedstrom has pondered, the time has come perhaps to "walk in the Indian moccasins for a few miles to learn a bit more of the truth." "Custer Paintings and Historical Accuracy," *Roundup Magazine* 2 (September–October 1994): 19. Consult Leslie Tillett, ed. and comp., *Wind on the Buffalo Grass: The Indians' Own Account of the Battle of Little Big Horn River, the Death of Their Life on the Plains* (New York: Thomas Y. Yoseloff, 1976), for pictorial representations of the Little Bighorn by Indian participants. For context relative to traditional Indian pictorial presentations, read Joyce M. Szabo, *Howling Wolf and the History of Ledger Art* (Albuquerque: University of New Mexico, 1994).

78. Dippie, "'What Valor Is,'" 210.

79. Reedstrom, "Custer Paintings," 19. For further information, see Don Russell, *Custer's List: A Checklist of Pictures Relating to the Battle of the Little Big Horn* (Fort Worth: Amon Carter Museum, 1969), and "Custer's List—Continued," in Paul A. Hutton, ed., *Garry Owen 1976: Annual of the Little Big Horn Associates* (Seattle: Little Big Horn Associates, 1997). As with all popular culture elements related to this topic, such a list is outdated the moment it reaches the press.

80. The qualitative issue is a main point for Reedstrom in "Custer Paintings," 16–19.

81. Russell, *Custer's Last*, 55–56, discusses the idea of accurate rendition of details and succinctly asks, "Who, among the hundreds of artists, has shown The Last Stand as it really happened?" He might have asked an additional question: Was there really a Last Stand at all, at least in the sense that it has been conceived of by white illustrators, writers, and various film and television productions?

82. Dippie, "'What Valor Is,'" 215.

83. Dippie, *Custer's Last Stand*, 33, 36.

84. Ibid., 33.

85. For more on this famous "Barroom Custer," see "Editions of the *Custer's Last Fight* Lithograph and Print," (Photostatic copy, September 20, 1991, Corporate Archives, Anheuser Busch Corporation, St. Louis, MO).

86. Russell, *Custer's Last*, 21–39, offers additional information about some of the first mass-produced color images and traveling pictorial versions of the Little Bighorn.

87. Dippie, *Custer's Last Stand*, 33.

88. Alex Nemerov, "Doing the 'Old America,'" in William H. Truettner, *The West as America: Reinterpreting Images of the Frontier, 1820–1920* (Washington, DC: The Smithsonian Institution Press, 1991), 291.

CHAPTER THREE

1. Henry Blackman Sell and Victor Weybright, *Buffalo Bill and the Wild West* (Basin, WY: Big Horn Books, 1979), 129. At the Battle of Warbonnet Creek, an encounter that took place shortly after the fight on the Greasy Grass, Buffalo Bill allegedly killed a Cheyenne war leader, Yellow Hair (known as Yellow Hand in earlier times due to an error in translation), in single combat. This histrionic tableau found its way into the Wild West show repertoire amidst the cheers from the crowd. For the most recent publication related to this encounter, read Paul L. Hedren, *First Scalp for Custer: The Skirmish at Warbonnet Creek, Nebraska, July 17, 1876* (Glendale, CA: Arthur H. Clark Co., 1980).

2. For details, see Joseph Rosa and Robin May, *Buffalo Bill and His Wild West: A Pictorial Biography* (Lawrence: University of Kansas Press, 1989), 83–90. Sitting Bull signed a contract with Cody's Wild West on June 6, 1885, for "a four-month stay with the show at $50 a week, two weeks' pay in advance, a $125 bonus, and the concession to sell photographs and autographs of himself. . . . In the United States, Sitting Bull was liable to be booed when he appeared in the arena, though not in Canada, where the crowds cheered him and the government and other officials honored him." Ibid., 90–91.

3. Dippie, "'What Valor Is,'" 217–18.

4. Sell and Weybright, *Buffalo Bill*, 148, 156.

5. Slotkin, *Gunfighter Nation*, 76.

6. Don Russell, *The Wild West; or, A History of the Wild West Shows* (Fort Worth: Amon Carter Museum of Western Art, 1972), 27.

7. Slotkin, *Gunfighter Nation*, 76–77.

8. Custer, *Tenting on the Plains*, 46–47.

9. Undated clipping from c. 1895 San Francisco Bay–area newspaper, with accompanying photograph of Crawford and his troupe (research center Autry Museum of Western Heritage Museum, Los Angeles).

10. Russell, *The Wild West*, 31–32, 68. During 1911 and 1912, this last-mentioned show was known as Thompkins Real Wild West and Frontier Exhibition. From 1913 through 1914, it went under the name Thompkins Wild West and Cooper-Whitby Circus. Ibid., 126–127.

11. Ibid., 52.

12. Ibid., 62. One source contended that the San Juan Hill presentation "was not as dramatic a spectacle as his [Buffalo Bill's] rendition of Custer's Last Stand—but gradually even General Custer was being forgotten as a new, very lively national hero, a personal friend of Colonel Cody's rode into prominence" in the person of Theodore Roosevelt. Sell and Weybright, *Buffalo Bill and the Wild West*, 208.

13. Russell, *The Wild West,* 72.

14. Charles Ulrich's *On the Little Big Horn: A Comedy-Drama of the West in Four Acts* was published by T. S. Denison in 1907. Given its subtitle, the work provided little material for Selig's 1909 motion picture, because the main figure in this melodrama is a fictional character, Maj. Paul Ludlow. In fact, Custer never appears in the play, but in the final act, word arrives of his "massacre." Ulrich did have contact with Selig later, however, as evidenced by an advance he received for story rights to *The Queen of the Harem.* Charles Ulrich to William Selig, November 2, 1914(?), folder 522, Selig Collection (Margaret Herrick Library, Motion Picture Academy of Arts and Sciences, Beverly Hills, California). Ulrich also wrote other Western-based stage productions, including *The Honor of a Cowboy* and *The Man from Nevada.*

15. George N. Fenin and William K. Everson, *The Western from Silents to the Seventies* (New York: Grossman Publishers, 1973), 52–53. Charles A. Jahant, "Chicago: Center of Silent Film Industry," *Chicago History* 3, no. 1 (Spring–Summer 1974): 45–53, offers more background on that city's place in early film production.

16. Dan Gagliasso, "Custer's Last Stand on Celluloid," *Persimmon Hill* 10, no. 1 (Spring 1991): 5.

17. In fact, as early as 1902, a Sheridan, Wyoming, dentist had come up with the concept of Crows taking the part of the Indians while national guardsmen and other locals were to play the troopers at a county fair held in the area. The event ended in a fistfight between whites and Indians at the conclusion of the reenactment. Dippie, *Custer's Last Stand,* 95–96.

The 1990 feature *War Party* revolved around the idea of a historical reenactment as the catalyst for a more dramatic exchange. During the sham battle, one of the Indian participants in the pageant accidentally kills a white, leading to a massive manhunt by government authorities to capture the two young men involved in the incident.

18. Dippie, *Custer's Last Stand,* 94. The Last Stand also had been restaged the previous year, as part of the 1908 Fourth of July Crow Fair. The event was held at the battlefield, with the Crow taking the part of the Lakota and Cheyenne, and perhaps national guardsmen stood in for the 7th Cavalry. Remarkably, this Reenactment was filmed as part of over 30,000 feet of motion-picture footage taken during that time under Joseph Dixon, a Princeton graduate who led an expedition to the Crow reservation under the sponsorship of department store mogul Rodman Wanamaker. Besides the mock battle, the camera recorded Curly and three other surviving Crow scouts posed in front of the Custer Hill monument, a parade, an arts and crafts display, a horse race, and a cinematic rendition of *The Song of Hiawatha.* Thomas A. Britten, *American Indians in World War I: At Home and at War* (Albuquerque: University of New Mexico Press, 1997), 32. Much of the film survived, including the Last Stand scene, thereby making this the oldest known surviving footage of a recreation of the Little Bighorn fight.

19. Olin D. Wheeler, "The Custer Battlefield," in *Wonderland: 1901* (St. Paul: Northern Pacific Railroad, 1901), 27.

20. Ibid., 40.

21. Dippie, *Custer's Last Stand,* 93. Numbers remained impressive, albeit lower than in the past. For instance, 233,222 visitors made their way to the battlefield, according to 1990 National Park Service figures, then 295,252 came in 1991, and the count went up to 331,404 in 1992. *Custer/Little Bighorn Battlefield Advocate* (Spring 1995), 6.

22. For more on early automobile tourism to the area, read Nora B. Kinsey, "Custer Memorial Highway," *American Review of Reviews* 64 (August 1921), 184–86.

23. Division of Publicity, *Carrying On for Fifty Years the Courage of Custer, 1876–1926,* 5. Another 1926 pamphlet provided by the Hardin Chamber of Commerce likewise offered information about "the resources and location of Big Horn, Montana, in the Crow Indian Country, made habitable and famous by General George A. Custer and his immortal band of brave soldiers." Inside, "The Custer Fight Anniversary Program" appeared for the June 24–26 semicentential. Research Center Autry Museum of Western Heritage, Los Angeles.

Between 1965 and 1974, even the Crow people, on whose reservation the battle site is located, staged "their recreation of the Last Stand 'from the Indian point of view.'" Dippie, *Custer's Last Stand,* 95, and Joseph Medicine Crow, panel discussion, 1994 Little Bighorn Legacy Symposium, Hardin, Montana. The annual Crow production ceased when it no longer proved economically feasible or rewarding. "Custer's Last Last Stand," *Newsweek* 83 (March 11, 1974): 15. Some years later, however, the event was resurrected and again became a tourist attraction. As a further indication of the importance of the battlefield to local economics, the Crows imposed a 4 percent resort tax on "motels, gift shops, trout fishing guides and dude ranches within their reservation" to obtain revenue from the visitors drawn to the battlefield area. Barry Schlachter, "120 Years Later, Battle Rages On at Little Bighorn," *San Francisco Chronicle* (December 4, 1995).

24. Fred J. Balshofer and Arthur Miller, *One Reel a Week* (Berkeley: University of California Press, 1967), 45–47, and Rotha, *The Film Till Now,* 201–2.

25. Fenin and Everson, *The Western,* 56–57. The next year, 1910, the Chicago Film Company released a two-reel production titled *Custer's Last Stand,* while another production company, Nestor, put out a one-reel picture called *On the Little Big Horn.* Larry Langman, *A Guide to Silent Westerns* (Westport, CT: Greenwood Press, 1992), 99, 311. These pictures evidently were not Selig's films but titles that possibly drew upon the 1909 production's release.

26. The film was Tom Mix's first Western, according to the filmography presented in John H. Nicolas, *Tom Mix: Riding Up to Glory* (Oklahoma City: National Cowboy Hall of Fame, 1980), 90, and Paul E. Mix, *Tom Mix: A Heavily Illustrated Biography with a Filmography* (Jefferson, NC: McFarland & Company, 1995), 241. Other cast members included Hobart Bosworth, Betty Harte, and Frank Maish. In 1910, Mix actively assisted in locating American Indians, cattle, and bucking horses for Selig's use. Tom Mix, November 1, 1910, Charles Gallaway Clarke, Letters and Telegrams for Early Stars, 1910–1912," (Margaret Herrick Library, Motion

Picture Academy of Arts and Sciences, Beverly Hills, California), thereby demonstrating his continued association with Selig at this introductory stage of his movie career.

27. "Great Custer Massacre Graphically Repeated," *Billings Daily Gazette* (September 26, 1909): 2. Dippie, *Custer's Last Stand*, 98–99, provides additional excerpts from newspaper accounts of the filming. This source indicates that some of the battle sequences were taken from reenactments at the site with Crows and national guardsmen, while others were made in Chicago. Then the two elements were edited together for the final version.

28. The actual incident was the arrest of Rain-in-the-Face by Capt. Tom Custer for the murder of a veterinarian and a settler who accompanied the 7th Cavalry into the Black Hills. Utley, *Custer and the Great Controversy*, 126–31. Connell's *Son of the Morning Star*, 380–91, looks at the Rain-in-the-Face story in light of Longfellow's poem, among other considerations.

29. The information in the forgoing text related to *On the Little Big Horn* was taken from "Selig Polyscope," *Film Index* (November 27, 1909), 16–17, and *Moving Picture World* (November 27, 1909), 773.

30. "On the Little Big Horn; or, Custer's Last Fight," Release Supplements, folder 501, Selig Collection (Margaret Herrick Library, Motion Picture Academy of Arts and Sciences, Beverly Hills, California).

31. Born in 1882, Thomas H. Ince entered the motion-picture industry as a young man and was one of the pioneer directors of note. From 1910 through 1920, he made a number of Westerns as part of the 150 releases credited to him. These included *The Indian Massacre* (1912) and *The Heart of an Indian* (1913), both examples of his usually sympathetic view of the American Indian, not unlike later productions such as *Broken Arrow*, made decades later and praised as being innovative in this regard. Ince used working cowboys and American Indians in his films and thus worked well with William S. Hart when he became a producer with this notable figure. Allen Eyles, *The Western: An Illustrated Guide* (New York: A. S. Barnes and Company, 1967), 69.

Ince was not unique, however, because the silent films were not monolithic or always negative when it came to depictions of American Indians. In fact, "the silent screen reflected and refracted the contradictory position and representation of Native Americans within contemporary U.S. society and culture," or so argues Pearson, "Custers and Indians," 275.

32. Independents were film companies that did not belong to the powerful Motion Picture Patents Company, holder of all rights to the various cinematic equipment of the time. In effect, the Patents Company possessed a legal monopoly on the entire industry. Gerald Mast, *A Short History of the Movies* (New York: Pegasus, 1971), 57–59.

33. According to Brownlow, *The War, the West, and the Wilderness*, 259–60, Francis Ford starred in and actually directed this picture, which bore an "astonishing resemblance in its treatment to D. W. Griffith's *The Massacre*. Yet the films were in production at the same time and finished on the same day. Additionally, Brownlow asserted, *"The Massacre* was an attempt to outdo Ince on his own ground." For more infor-

mation on this production, consult Vincent A. Heier, Jr., "Thomas Ince's *Custer's Last Fight:* Reflections on the Making of the Custer Legend in Film," [St. Louis Westerners] *Westward,* 5 (May 1976): 21–26

34. Reed, *American Scenarios*, 26, 29, 36–38. It should be remembered, however, that for such films, "history was its vehicle, not its purpose." George MacDonald Fraser, *The Hollywood History of the World from One Million B.C. to Apocalypse Now* (New York: Fawcett Columbine, 1988), 19. Fraser wrote this book in response to the "popular belief that where history is concerned, Hollywood [meaning the film industries of the English-speaking world] always gets it wrong. . . . What is overlooked is the astonishing amount of history Hollywood has got right, and the immense unacknowledged debt which we owe the commercial cinema as an illuminator of the story of mankind." Ibid., xi–xii. Given the author's work on such notable fiction efforts as "The Flashman Papers," his thesis may be interesting but is difficult to support if carefully reviewed.

35. A rather detailed and lengthy article about the film, "The Final Battle of a Famous Indian Fighter in Two Reels by Bison," was written by Louis Reeves Harrison. *The Moving Picture World* (June 22, 1912): 1116–18. The 1925 reissue of this picture was lengthened, chiefly by adding longer title cards. A video version of this reissue is now available from Old Army Press of Fort Collins, Colorado.

36. Connell, *Son of the Morning Star,* 383–84, points out that allegedly two sabers were carried at the battle by officers, but all the remaining edged weapons of this sort were packed away. Custer's hair was worn short at the time because of the nature of campaigning in hot weather. Nevertheless, fictional depictions of him often overlook this fact.

37. Reed, *American Scenarios*, 26, 29, 36–38.

38. D. W. Griffith was a member of Bison, a production company that followed Selig's lead and came to California in 1909. The original production unit included Mary Pickford and a group of New York actors called the "101 Bisons." They filmed their first Westerns in Griffith Park (the name was coincidental), but after 1911, they fled to the isolation of Big Bear Valley to escape the detection of the Patents Company. Balshofer and Miller, *One Reel a Week,* 55.

A comparison of Griffith with his fellow Bison director, Ince, can be found in William K. Everson, *A Pictorial History of the Western Film* (Secaucus, NJ: Citadel Press, 1969), 23–36. This information is of interest not only to those studying early Westerns, but also to researchers on the growth of the film industry in California.

39. *The Massacre* featured many techniques that Griffith had perfected and that would make him noteworthy, including "rapid cutting and cross-cutting, double and parallel action, detail close-ups, and analytical montage." With the addition of the first known use of the moving camera, this film heralded later aspects that Griffith used in *Birth of a Nation*. Seymour Stern, comp., *An Index to the Creative Work of David Wark Griffith*. Part 1, The Birth of an Art, 1908–1915 (Hollywood, CA: Sight and Sound Series, 1944), 16.

40. Griffith did make many films that "had something of a cultural and social importance to say." Everson, *A Pictorial History of the Western Film,* 23–36. Good triumphing over evil,

sobriety, the sanctity of the family, and other virtues formed part of the positive themes espoused by Griffith's work. Conversely, his productions also carried many racist overtones that tended to negate some of his supposed impact as an uplifting force.

41. Kenneth MacGowan, *Behind the Screen: The History and Techniques of the Motion Picture* (New York: Dell Publishing Co., 1965), 151.
42. Hutton, "From Little Big Horn to Little Big Man," 28.
43. Jon Tuska, *The American West in Film: Critical Approaches to the Western* (Westport, CT: Greenwood Press, 1985), 204.
44. *Custer's Last Scout* was produced by Bison and starred William Clifford and Marie Walcamp. The director was Henry MacRae. Langman, *A Guide to Silent Westerns*, 100.
45. The real Alfred Chapman was "the self-proclaimed chief scout and interpreter with the Seventh Cavalry as well as an eyewitness to the Last Stand." This two-reel picture was based on Chapman's declaration that he was "'the only living witness of the Custer massacre!'" Dippie, *Custer's Last Stand* , 82–83.
46. A synopsis of this picture can be found in "Independent Film Stories," *The Moving Picture World* (January 2, 1915): 126.
47. A rare nitrate print of this picture, filmed in the vicinity of the northwestern Nebraska community of Chadron, is available on VHS tape from the Nebraska Historical Society, Lincoln. Troops from nearby Fort Robinson portrayed Custer's cavalry, but no credit is given the individual who played Custer.
48. In addition to Cyrus Townsend Brady, *Britton of the Seventh* (1914), the industry has used many other novels as the basis for films on the subject. These include Randall Parrish's *Bob Hampton of Placer;* Courtney Ryley Cooper's *The Last Frontier,* for the picture of the same name; David Appel's *Comanche* (1951), for *Tonka;* Frank Gruber's *Broken Lance,* for *Warpath;* Ernest Haycox's *Bugles in the Afternoon;* Glendon F. Swarthout's *A Horse for Mrs. Custer,* the inspiration for *The Seventh Cavalry,* 1956; Hoffman Birney's *Dice of God,* the source for *The Glory Guys,* 1965; and Thomas Berger's *Little Big Man* and Douglas C. Jones's *The Court-Martial of General George Armstrong Custer,* for television.

Other literary endeavors that were made into films included selections from Courtney Ryley Cooper and Frank J. Wilstach, for *The Plainsman* (1937), and James Warner Bellah's short story "Massacre" for *Fort Apache* (1948). Connell's *Son of the Morning Star* served as the inspiration for a television miniseries of the same name, although, it could be argued that the script seemed even more influenced by Stephen Ambrose's *Crazy Horse and Custer.* Though not a work of fiction, the fact that the book was a bestseller accounted for its conversion into a screenplay. For more insight into the use of literature as movie material, consult George Bluestone, *Novels into Film* (Berkeley: University of California Press, 1961). Also of interest in relation to this study is Jim Hitt, *The American West from Fiction (1823–1976) into Film (1909–1986)* (Jefferson, NC: McFarland & Company, 1990).
49. Ned Finley, "Stories of the Movies," *The Moving Picture World* (January 15, 1916): 470, provides a synopsis of the film plot.
50. George Blaisdell, "Vitagraph Shows Two Good Dramas," *The Moving Picture World* (January 15, 1916): 439, lists Darwin Kahr as Britton and Eleanor Woodruff as his leading lady, Barbara. Ned Finley played Custer, and troops from Fort Clark, Texas, served as the cavalry in the film.
51. Patricia King Hanson, exec. ed., *The American Film Institute Catalog of Motion Pictures Produced in the United States Feature Films, 1911–1920* (Berkeley: University of California Press, 1988), 101.
52. The synopsis of the picture was taken from Kenneth W. Munden, ed., *The American Film Institute Catalog of Motion Pictures Produced in the United States, 1921–1930* (New York: R. R. Bowker, 1971), 72–73.
53. Reed, *American Scenarios*, 17–20, 41.
54. Munden, *American Film Institute Catalog*, 902, and Diane Kaiser Koszarski, *The Complete Films of William S. Hart: A Pictorial Record* (New York: Dover Publications, 1980), 143.
55. Munden, *American Film Institute Catalog*, 487.
56. This was the same fate that Alfred Chapman faced in *Custer's Last Scout,* and it was a verdict that would be rendered for many other characters in future Westerns. For more discussion of this topic, consult Henry Nash Smith, *Virgin Land: The American West as Symbol and Myth* (New York: Vintage Books, 1950), 52–137.
57. According to "Checkup," *Motion Picture News* (December 11, 1926), 2241, exhibitors rated *The Flaming Frontier* as follows in terms of response at the box office: poor, 1; fair, 3; good, 11; big, 7. Overall, the picture received an average rating of 76 percent. The 8,829-foot feature was long by standards of the day.
58. Munden, *American Film Institute Catalog*, 159.
59. Frank Thompson, *Lost Films: Important Movies That Disappeared* (New York: Citadel Press, 1996), 135.
60. The program also indicated that General Godfrey was the special guest of honor for this premiere. "Moss' Colony Theater New York City World Premier: Carl Laemmle Presents Flaming Frontier," Original Opening Night Program (research center, Autry Museum of Western Heritage, Los Angeles).
61. Ibid., 5–10.
62. One such example exists in the research center of the Autry Museum of Western Heritage, Los Angeles.
63. Thompson, *Lost Films,* 142.
64. Munden, *American Film Institute Catalog*, 284.
65. Alan Gevinson, ed., *Within Our Gates: Ethnicity in American Feature Films, 1911–1960* (Berkeley: University of California Press, 1997), 374, adds that the film's alternate title was *Custer at Little Big Horn.*
66. Pearson, "Custers and Indians," 281–82.
67. Ibid., 283–84.
68. *Photoplay* (June 1926), 53, and Munden, *The American Film Institute Catalog,* 420.
69. Munden, *American Film Institute Catalog*, 757–58.
70. Buscombe, *BFI Companion,* 34–35.
71. Founded in March 1922, the Motion Picture Producers and Distributors of America (MPPDA) became better known as the Hays Office after the head of that organization, former Postmaster General of the United States Will Hays. All the major studios voluntarily formed this self-regulatory body in response to charges of immorality within the industry and

complaints that onscreen depictions were equally profane. Under Hays, studios submitted materials in advance to determine whether the topic was suitably virtuous. The MPPDA even provided lists of plays and books that were deemed inappropriate for transformation to film. This process, which came to be institutionalized as the Productions Code, was voluntary, but by the early 1930s, the Roman Catholic Church's National Legion of Decency increased pressure on producers to maintain strict standards. Macgowan, *Behind the Screen*, 352–59.

72. Phil Hardy, *The Western: The Complete Source Book* (New York: William Morrow and Company, 1983), 20.

73. Westerns had experienced difficult times toward the end of the silent movie era. From a peak of more than 227 titles in 1925, the genre declined for a period. Buscombe, *BFI Companion*, 34.

74. Hardy, *The Western*, xv.

75. One historian wrote that a search for stability among the public at large led to Hollywood's "sudden revival of interest in history and legend, and the ransacking of the literary archives for simple tales of the wholesome virtues" as one response to the Depression. Rotha, *The Film Till Now*, 446.

76. Jay Robert Nash and Stanley Ralph Ross, *The Motion Picture Guide*, vol.2 (Chicago: Cinebooks, 1985), 3924–25.

77. Jeremy Pascall, *50 Years of the Movies* (Middlesex, England: Hamlyn Publishing Group, 1981), 7–59.

78. Several sources provide background on this cinematic form, including Roy Kinnard, *Fifty Years of Serial Thrills* (Metuchen, NJ: Scarecrow Press, 1983); Kalton C. Lahue, *Continued Next Week: A History of the Moving Picture Serial* (Norman: University of Oklahoma Press, 1964); Raymond William Stedman, *The Serials: Suspense and Drama by Installment* (Norman: University of Oklahoma Press, 1971); and Ken Weiss and Ed Goodgold, *To Be Continued . . .* (New York: Crown Publishers, 1972).

79. *The Last Frontier* Files (Margaret Herrick Library, Academy of Motion Picture Arts and Sciences, Beverly Hills, California).

80. Microfilm Collections, Motion Picture Copyrights (University of Southern California Cinema and Television Library, Los Angeles).

81. *"Custer's Last Stand": Based on Historical Events Leading Up to Custer's Last Fight*, A Weiss Production, original pressbook in Vincent A. Heier Collection.

82. Fenin and Everson, *The Western*, 231. Among other conventions were "the Indian princess hopelessly in love with the hero, the hero seeking a man who killed his brother, the cowardly Army officer who must redeem himself . . . and similar old chestnuts." Ibid., 232.

83. *The Oregon Trail* represented "the 'streamlined' but standardized 'B' Westerns of the late Thirties." Nonetheless, the authors pronounced this serial a "pedestrian affair, loosely constructed, and excessively reliant on stock footage." Ibid.

84. "Film Reviews," *Variety Weekly* (January 20, 1937): 14. The picture led at the Los Angeles box office during its opening week, with $22,000 in ticket sales, a great sum in its day. Shooting began on July 21, 1936, location work coinciding with other sequences being filmed at the Paramount ranch. Ibid., 8.

85. Howard Hawks was in the process of turning the script for *Seventh Cavalry*, by veteran writer Dudley Nichols (who, among his many credits, collaborated with John Ford on *Stagecoach*), into a film. The picture was envisioned as another vehicle for Gary Cooper as a Frederick Benteen–like character who would be set in opposition to his old adversary from *The Westerner*, Walter Brennan, as Custer. Hutton, "Correct in Every Detail: General Custer in Hollywood," in Rankin, *Legacy*, 242. The anti-Custer overtones of this Samuel Goldwyn production were strongly influenced by Van de Water's writings. Further, this was the first of at least two major proposed Little Bighorn features to be shelved and remained unrealized.

86. Robert Kurson, *The Official Three Stooges Encyclopedia* (Chicago: Contemporary Books, 1998), 86, 296–97.

87. *MGM Production Bulletin*, December 6, 1940 (Margaret Herrick Library, Academy of Motion Picture Arts and Sciences, Beverly Hills, California).

88. *The New York Times Film Reviews, 1913–1968*, vol. 3 (New York: Arno Press, 1970), vol. 3, 1809.

89. Tony Thomas, Rudy Behlmer, and Clifford McCarthy, *The Films of Errol Flynn* (New York: Citadel Press, 1969), 77–81, 87–90, discuss Flynn's earlier pair of Westerns, *Dodge City* (1939) and *Virginia City* (1940). Also see Tony Thomas, *The Films of Olivia de Havilland* (Secaucus, NJ: Citadel Press, 1983), 161–87, for more on this period in the lives of Flynn and de Havilland.

90. George Armstrong Custer, as is well known, was the "goat" of the class of 1861, graduating thirty-fourth out of thirty-four. John Bell Hood was forty-fourth of fifty-two in his class of 1853. He served on the frontier and received a wound in an Indian campaign before resigning in April 1861 to join the Confederacy. Hood was an infantryman, as was James ("Pete") Longstreet, class of 1842, having graduated fifty-fourth of sixty-two. He served in both Florida and the Mexican War, as well as on the frontier. Another infantryman, George Edward Pickett, also was at the bottom of his fifty-nine-man class of 1846. He fought in the Mexican War and on the frontier prior to leaving the U.S. Army for the Confederate States. Philip Henry ("Little Phil") Sheridan left West Point in 1853, a year later than originally planned due to "a serious breach of discipline—threatening Cadet Sgt. W. R. Terrill with a bayonet, and then attacking him with his fists after Terrill reported him for the first offense." Sheridan was in the infantry at first, but then transferred to the cavalry. Mark M. Boatner, III, *The Civil War Dictionary* (New York: David McKay Company, 1959), 216, 407, 490, 651, 746.

91. Reagan enjoyed taking the part and admired Custer, as he later noted. Ronald W. Reagan, "Looking Back at *Santa Fe Trail*," *Greasy Grass* 6 (May 1990): 2–4. The actor turned politician went on to make a half dozen more Western features, including another Civil War–related vehicle, *The Last Outpost* (1959). For additional information, consult Tony Thomas, *The Films of Ronald Reagan* (Secaucus, NJ: Citadel Press, 1980).

92. See John M. Cassidy, *Civil War Cinema* (Missoula, MT: Pictorial Histories Publishing Company, 1986), 133–48, for other examples of this genre.

93. At that time, no overall biography of substance existed, and one could stray from the facts without too much reaction from the public. Interestingly, Henry Ford had once con-

sidered a series of educational films about historic figures, including George A. Custer, but these pictures were never produced. Mayfield Bray, *Guide to the Ford Film Collection in the National Archives* (Washington, DC: National Archives, 1970), 37.

94. *The New York Times Film Reviews*, vol.3, 1825.

95. Tom O'Neil, "The Making of *They Died with Their Boots On*," *Research Review: The Journal of the Little Big Horn Associates* vol. 4, no. 2 (June 1990): 22–29.

96. William R. Meyer, *The Making of the Great Westerns* (New York: Arlington House, 1979), 114.

97. Hutton, "Hollywood's General Custer," 17. The influence of this cinematic venture can be illustrated by a c. 1950 educational filmstrip supplied for junior high school use, covering a lesson on Custer's life. The text draws heavily upon the story line of *They Died with Their Boots On*, and all the images are stills from the film, save the last one, which is of John Miljan as Custer in *The Plainsman*. Vincent A. Heier Collection.

CHAPTER FOUR

1. According to Dan Ford, *Pappy: The Life of John Ford* (New York: Prentice-Hall, 1979), 227, director Ford found Bellah's short story compelling because "it seemed to articulate all his wartime emotions, his fascination with the American military tradition, and the special nobility he felt was born of combat." Moreover, Ford found the legend of Custer more intriguing than the historic figure. Andrew Sinclair, *John Ford* (New York: Dial Press, 1979), 142.

2. Ford compared his character to Custer in an interview with Peter Bogdanovich, *John Ford* (Berkeley: University of California, 1968), 86, stating that it was "good for the country to have heroes to look up to. Like Custer—a great hero. Well, he wasn't. Not that he was a stupid man—but he did a stupid job that day." Also see Russell Campbell, "Fort Apache," *The Velvet Light Trap* no. 2 (August 1971): 10; William T. Pilkington, "Fort Apache," in William T. Pilkington and Don Graham, eds., *Western Movies* (Albuquerque: University of New Mexico Press, 1979); and Tony Thomas, *The West That Never Was* (Secaucus, NJ: Citadel Press, 1989), 104–11.

3. Meyer, *The Making of the Great Westerns*, 174.

4. Tuska, *The American West in Film*, 53. Also consult Slotkin, *Gunfighter Nation*, 318–19, for the concept of defeat and Last Stand symbolism.

5. Hutton, "Hollywood's General Custer," 19. In another summation of *Fort Apache*, Richard Slotkin viewed the film as "a seminal work of mythography" because, as he states, "it signals the completion of one cultural transformation and the beginning of another." In Ford's hands, "the Frontier is not only a way of coming to terms with memory; it also provides us with the mythic basis for a new ideology, designed to build national solidarity in the face of the threatening advance of Soviet Communism." Slotkin, *Gunfighter Nation*, 343.

6. Ford also incorporated Custer into later work, most notably *She Wore a Yellow Ribbon* (1949), which opens with voice-over narrator Carleton Young informing the audience, "Custer is dead." Young continues to tell how "around the bloody guidon of the Seventh Cavalry lie two hundred and twelve officers and men." Capt. Nathan Brittles (John Wayne), at

his dead wife's grave, also carries the news of Custer's defeat along with the death of many of his command, including that "happy go-lucky Irishman, Myles Keogh."

Seven years later, Ford originally filmed a scene for *The Searchers* in which Peter Ortiz appears in the guise of Custer. He is confronted by the film's main character, Ethan Edwards, as the strains of "Garry Owen" can be heard in the background. This not so thinly veiled reference to Washita ended up on the cutting-room floor. Hutton, "'Correct in Every Detail,'" 47, and Gagliasso, "Custer's Last Stand on Celluloid," 10. This editing might have been due in part to the incongruity of the scene, in which the Indian-hating Edwards essentially deplores Custer's methods. Ford also might have cut the scene because he believed that the public would not accept such a sympathetic angle toward the American Indians. In speaking about *The Searchers*, he stated, "The audience likes to see Indians get killed. They don't consider them human beings." Bogdanovich, *John Ford*, 94. For more on this influential director, read Ford, *Pappy: The Life of John Ford;* Tag Gallagher, *John Ford: The Man and His Films* (Berkeley: University of California Press, 1986); J. A. Place, *The Western Films of John Ford* (Secaucus, NJ: The Citadel Press, 1974); and Sinclair, *John Ford: A Biography.*

7. Michael R. Pitts, *Western Movies: A TV and Video Guide to 4200 Genre Films* (Jefferson, NC: McFarland & Company, 1986), 282. The film's director, Charles Marquis Warren, also wrote the screenplay for *Oh! Susanna.* He directed or wrote about seventeen Western motion pictures, including *Trooper Hook, Arrowhead,* and *Springfield Rifle,* all films with a frontier military tie. "Title Change," *Hollywood Reporter* (August 25, 1950): 13, mentioned the shooting title as *The Golden Tide.* The same publication reviewed the picture the following year. "'Susanna' Well Mounted Cavalry—Redskins Tale," *Hollywood Reporter* (March 9, 1951): 4.

8. "Little Big Horn," *Variety Weekly* (May 30, 1951), 6.

9. *The New York Times Film Reviews*, vol. 4, 2566–67.

10. Smith Darr, *Los Angeles Times* (October 13, 1950), and "Pictorial Synopsis of *Warpath*," undated typed sheet in Margaret Herrick Library, Academy of Motion Picture Arts and Sciences, Beverly Hills, California.

11. "New Film," *Newsweek* (March 10, 1952): 68. Also see "*Bugles in the Afternoon* Is Valid Action Western," *Hollywood Reporter* (January 31, 1952): 3, which pronounced the picture "a stirring action drama, short on strong story motivation but long on vivid outdoor pageantry."

12. Fenin and Everson, *The Western from Silents to Cinerama*, 11.

13. The 1954 picture was not the first film to deal with the subject. In 1914, American Rotograph Co. made *Sitting Bull—The Hostile Sioux Indian Chief.* Both Crazy Horse and Sitting Bull form part of the story, but the focus is on a white girl, Ruth Randall, and her suitor, U.S. Army officer Lieutenant Scott. Patricia King Hanson, exec. ed., *The American Film Institute Catalog of Motion Pictures Produced in the United States: Feature Films, 1911–1920, Film Entries* (Berkeley: University of California Press, 1988), 846.

To place this alternating set of views in context see Robert F. Berkhofer, Jr., *The White Man's Indian: Images of American Indians from Columbus to the Present* (New York: Alfred A. Knopf, 1978), and Roy Harvey Pearce, *Savagism and Civilization: A Study of the Indian and the American Mind* (Baltimore: Johns Hopkins Press, 1965). For more on American Indians in early cinema, consult Karen C. Lund, *American Indians in Silent Film: Motion Pictures in the Library of Congress* (Washington, DC: Library of Congress, 1992).

14. *The New York Times Film Reviews*, vol.4, 2827. In an effort to lend credibility, however, the picture listed "Iron Eyes Cody (Famous T.V. Star)" in the credits as being the technical advisor and in charge of Indian costume. Cody, an American Indian, had been involved with more Custer films than any other individual, beginning with Ince's 1912 feature. He also appeared in the original version of *The Plainsman, They Died with Their Boots On, Fort Apache,* and *The Great Sioux Massacre*, as well as two serials, *Custer's Last Stand* and *Oregon Trail*. Iron Eyes Cody and Collin Perry, *Iron Eyes Cody: My Life as a Hollywood Indian* (New York: Everest House, 1982), provides additional information on this longtime actor.

15. "1954 Boxoffice Champs," *Variety* (January 5, 1954): 59.

16. Jack Moffitt, "*Chief Crazy Horse* Okay Cavalry vs. Indians Yarn," *Hollywood Reporter* (February 22, 1955): 5.

17. "Three Up, Three Down," *Time* (May 30, 1955): 84.

18. Al Herwitz, "Synopsis: Seventh Cavalry" (unpublished, undated manuscript from Columbia Films' director of publicity), and "Columbia Pictures Corporation Presents Randolph Scott in *The Seventh Cavalry*," unpublished typescript, February 22, 1956, Margaret Herrick Library, Academy of Motion Picture Arts and Sciences, Beverly Hills, California.

   The aftermath of the Little Bighorn battle formed part of the plot for at least two other films of the 1950s. *Pony Soldier* (1952) has mountie Tyrone Power attempting to keep peace with the Cree, who have been attacked by U.S. troops after they slipped south across the border to hunt buffalo following the 1876 summer campaign. A similar storyline in *Saskatchewan* (1954) has mountie Alan Ladd persuading the Cree not to join the Sioux, who have fled northward in 1876. Pitts, *Western Movies*, 313, 372.

19. *The New York Times Film Reviews*, vol. 5, 3117. For additional information on the horse Comanche as symbol and historic figure, read Elizabeth Atwood Lawrence, *His Very Silence Speaks: Comanche—The Horse Who Survived Custer's Last Stand* (Detroit: Wayne State University, 1989).

20. Dippie, *Custer's Last Stand*, 112.

21. For additional critical reactions to this film, see "Injun Sal," *Newsweek* (January 5, 1959): 69; *Monthly Film Bulletin* (May 1959): 62; and "Tonka," *Screen Stories* (February 1959): 63.

22. In fact, Custer exited from the silver screen for a brief period, only being alluded to in 1961, when the aftermath of the Little Bighorn was the point of departure for another feature, not unlike *She Wore a Yellow Ribbon*. In the case of a later picture, *The Canadians*, however, the story focused on the plight of the 6,000 Indians who fled to Canada "after wiping out Custer" and the "three Canadian Mounties sent out to deal with them (and assorted baddies)." Brian Garfield, *Western Films: A Complete Guide* (New York: Rawson Associates, 1982), 132.

23. Tuska, *The American West in Film*, 206.

24. Benteen actually was a Southerner from Virginia who remained loyal to the Union; however, he was married throughout the period depicted in this film, whereas Reno, a Northerner from Carrollton, Illinois, was single. John M. Carroll, ed., *They Rode with Custer: A Biographical Directory of the Men That Rode with George A. Custer* (Mattituck, NY: John M. Carroll & Company, 1987).

25. "Great Sioux Massacre Custer's Last Stand Again Done Up in Excellent Action and Production Values," *Variety Weekly* (September 22, 1965): 18.

26. *Library of Congress Catalog of Motion Pictures and Film Strips, 1969* (Washington, DC: Library of Congress, 1970), 156. The picture also employed footage from *Sitting Bull*, both films being made by the same director, Sidney Salkow. Tuska, *The American West in Film*, 206.

27. James Powers, "*Glory Guys* Big Western with Spectacular Action," *Hollywood Reporter* (June 9, 1965): 3.

28. Bill Ornstein, "Four Companies Are after Fromkess' Custer Feature," *Hollywood Reporter* (December 3, 1964): 3, and "Big Year for General Custer," *Hollywood Reporter* (March 30, 1965): 4.

29. Wendell Mayes, *The Day Custer Fell* screenplay, final, April 2, 1965, (Vincent Heier Collection, St. Louis).

30. Hutton, "'Correct in Every Detail,'" 50.

31. Charlton Heston, *The Actor's Life: Journals 1956–1976* (New York: E. P. Dalton, 1976), 211.

32. "Slicing 'Custer' Pie Thin," *Hollywood Reporter* (March 11, 1965): 3.

33. In 1863, the 7th Cavalry (which was not formed until 1866) stands in the way of Robert E. Lee's efforts to bring Maxmillian's forces in Mexico as reinforcements for the Confederacy, or so the story goes in *The Charge of the Seventh Cavalry*. *Two Sergeants of General Custer* featured a pair of Union enlisted men going undercover to infiltrate the Confederate Army. Thomas Weisser, *Spaghetti Westerns—the Good, the Bad and the Violent: A Comprehensive, Illustrated Filmography of 558 Eurowesterns and Their Personnel, 1966–1971* (Jefferson, NC: McFarland & Company, 1992), 55, 337–38.

34. "The Plainsman," *Films and Filming* (April 1967): 7, and "Feature Reviews," *Boxoffice Bookin' Guide* (August 15, 1966): 3047, discuss the remake of *The Plainsman*.

35. Garfield, *Western Films*, 266. According to this source, the role of Dakota Lil had been written for Betty Hutton, with whom Keel had starred in *Annie Get Your Gun*, but "she'd had a feud with someone and walked off the movie." Joan Caulfield thus assumed the character.

36. *The New York Times Film Reviews*, vol. 5, 3770. Also see "Review of New Film 'Custer of the West,'" *The Film Daily* (January 24, 1968): 7–8, and "The Plainsman," *Films and Filming* (April 1967): 7, which observed that "by 1955 the Western had absorbed both [Sigmund] Freud and [Sen. Joe] McCarthy." This seems to be somewhat evident in *Custer of the West*.

37. During a real-life drama that ended in 1967, Major Reno's family succeeded in officially clearing their ancestor's name. This was just prior to the release of *Custer of the West*, and subsequently, Charles Reno, a grandnephew, attempted to sue Cinerama Releasing Corporation and Security Pictures for $25 million. The court found against the family, ruling that Major Reno was beyond injury and the present family was not defamed or injured. "He Loses Last Stand on Gen. Custer Film," *Los Angeles Times* (March 18, 1967).

38. A 1970 release, *Soldier Blue,* was even more open in its anti-military overtones, using the 1864 Sand Creek Massacre as a point of reference rather than the Little Bighorn incident, although the story is set in 1876 and the title character, Honus Gant, a private ("Soldier Blue") with the 11th Colorado Volunteers, has joined the unit in part to carry on where his father left off, the elder Gant having been killed with Custer at the Little Bighorn. S. K. Oberbeck, "U.S. Cav Go Home," *Newsweek* (August 26, 1970): 65, provides some useful conclusions about this picture in the context of the times in which it was made. Also see Dan Georgakas, "They Have Not Spoken: American Indians in Film," in Bataille and Silet, *The Pretend Indians: Images of Native Americans in the Movies,* 137–40, which provides a synopsis of both *Soldier Blue* and *Little Big Man,* including the opinion that "Arthur Penn takes a longer and more sophisticated road to dish out the same conclusions as in *Soldier Blue.*"

39. Mulligan appears in *Teachers* (1984) as a patient escaped from a mental institution who impersonates an American history instructor and appears in class wearing various period costumes to bring his lessons to life. In one scene, he shows up as Custer. Even before this, a 1976 spoof on Hollywood of the 1920s, *Won Ton Ton, the Dog Who Saved Hollywood,* included a cameo of Custer as one of the film characters seen in the picture.

40. "Little Big Man," *Motion Picture Exhibitor* (December 23, 1970): 21, also stated that this was "an epic western of great wit and style; should delight critics and audiences despite its virulent anti white man bias." Moreover, the reviewer indicated that it was "a 'message picture,' documenting the callous and systematic extermination of the American Indians by the white race. There is not a single decent white person in the film." The movie had its impact and characterized many subsequent portrayals at the theater and on television, including *Dances with Wolves* more than twenty years later.

41. Original makeup artist's script, (research center, Autry Museum of Western Heritage, Los Angeles).

42. By way of comparison, read Charles K. Hofling, M.D., "George Armstrong Custer: A Psychoanalytical Approach," *Montana: The Magazine of Western History* 21 (Spring 1971): 32–43.

43. "Touche Pas la Femme Blanche!," *Variety* (January 30, 1974).

44. Peter Bondanella, *Italian Cinema, from Neorealism to the Present,* 2nd ed. (New York: Continuum, 1990), 270.

45. Ibid., 230.

CHAPTER FIVE

1. Rick Marschall, *History of Television* (New York: Gallery Books, 1986), 28. The networks, a term from radio, were DuMont, CBS, NBC, and ABC, a newly established offshoot of NBC. Ibid., 21–22.

2. Richard West, *Television Westerns: Major and Minor Series, 1946–1978* (Jefferson, NC: McFarland & Company, 1987), lists the numerous versions of the genre on the small screen. The book provides some insight into the popularity of the Western through the late 1960s and its gradual decline to the point of demise late in the twentieth century. Gary A. Yoggy, *Riding the Video Range: The Rise and Fall of the Western on Television* (Jefferson, NC: McFarland & Company, 1995), also provides important background regarding the evolution of TV Westerns. There were thirty-two prime-time Westerns in 1959; the previous year, twelve of the top twenty-five Nielsen-rated shows were Westerns, which accounted for seven of the top ten. Ibid., 1.

3. SuzAnne Barabas and Gabor Barabas, *Gunsmoke: A Complete History* (Jefferson, NC: McFarland & Company, 1990), 459. Veteran film director Charles Marquis Warren produced this episode. He was no stranger to the topic, having written and directed *Little Big Horn* in 1951.

4. Ibid., 376.

5. Lynn Woolley, Robert W. Malsbary, and Robert G. Strange, Jr., *Warner Bros. Television* (Jefferson, NC: McFarland & Company, 1987), 26.

6. Ibid., 28.

7. Ibid., 54.

8. Credits for this 1964 episode included the script by Rod Serling, producer Bert Granet, and director of photography George T. Clemens. The cast was headed by Ron Foster as Connors, Randy Boone as McCluskey, and Warren Oates as Langsford. The other national guardsmen were Robert Bray as the captain, Greg Morris as the lieutenant, Wayne Mallory as the scout, Lew Brown as a sergeant, Jacques Shelton as a corporal, and Jeffrey Morris as a radio operator. Marc Scott Zicree, *The Twilight Zone Companion* (New York: Bantam Books, 1989), 369–70.

9. Vincent Terrance, *The Complete Encyclopedia of Television Programs, 1947–1976,* vol.1 (New York: A. S. Barnes and Company, 1976), 289–90, provides brief information about this series.

10. Taken from "Old Ironpants," by Arthur Julian *(F Troop* series). Script analyst, P. James. Synopsis dated January 17, 1966, based on final script dated August 20, 1965, University of Southern California, Warner Bros. Archives, Los Angeles.

11. Weisbart also noted that Shaw was to play Custer in his production, but his signing with Phil Yordan helped seal the doom of *The Day Custer Fell.* Dave Kaufman, "Custer Rides Again: On TV," *Variety* (May 23, 1967): 7.

12. Ibid., 7. See also P. M. Clepper, "He's Our George," *TV Guide* (September 23, 1967): 32–34; "Custer," *Variety* (September 7, 1967): 11, 15; "Custer," *Variety* (October 13, 1967): 16; *New York Times* (September 7, 1967); and *Newsweek* (August 7, 1967): 51. The *Newsweek* article "criticized the show, pointing out that Custer was not a suitable hero because he was 'court-martialed twice, left his men to die, discarded a son sired through Indian wenching, and had a reputation for cruelty.'" Hutton, "'Correct in Every Detain,'" 51. Regardless, several of the episodes were combined into a feature for release overseas as *The Legend of Custer* (1967), on the assumption that foreign audiences still viewed the former hero in a more favorable light. Roberta E. Pearson's "White Network/Red Power: ABC's *Custer,*" in Lynn Spigel and Michael Curtin, eds., *The Revolution That Wasn't: Sixties Television and Social Context* (New York: Routledge, 1996), goes into more detail on this series.

13. Bustard hailed from Ireland and was not a former Confederate. He seems to have ben one of the "wild geese," men from the Emerald Isle who served in foreign armies, as he listed his profession as soldier on his enlistment papers. He

was a sergeant with Keogh when killed at the Little Bighorn. Carroll, *They Rode with Custer,* n.p.

14. Maunder did play another Western role, Scott in "Lancer," the 1968–70 CBS series, where he joined another former Custer impersonator, Andrew Duggan of *The Glory Guys.* West, *Television Westerns,* 59.

15. Deloria, *Custer Died for Your Sins,* 31. According to another source, "The show created a minor furor at the outset when certain Indian's rights groups objected to the glorification of their favorite enemy," Custer, who "was typecast as a hero with minor blemishes resulting from an excess of zeal." Consequently, "given the climate of heightened ethnic awareness and prevailing opinion about the Boy General, *Custer* was a veritable masterpiece of mistiming." Dippie, *Custer's Last Stand,* 120. Put another way, "the series offered an outdated image of the Old West." J. Fred MacDonald, *Who Shot the Sheriff?* (New York: Preager, 1987), 118.

16. The show's "stress on military glory ran counter to a growing debate by 1967 over the military role of the United States in the Vietnam War." MacDonald, *Who Shot the Sheriff?,* 118.

17. According to Hutton, "'Correct in Every Detail,'" 51, "The overexposure caused by television, a loss of faith in old conventions, and the death or retirement of major stars all contributed to a stark decline in the Western in the 1960s."

18. Pitts, *Western Movies,* 84. In a 1977 feature film, George Custer's younger brother Tom appears alone. As depicted in *The White Buffalo,* this two-time Medal of Honor recipient is a bulky, balding bully who cannot hold his liquor. He confronts one of the picture's main characters, Wild Bill Hickok, but backs down. The film was telecast in 1983 on NBC under the title *Hunt to Kill.* James Robert Parish and Michael R. Pitts, *The Great Western Pictures,* vol. 2 (Metuchen, NJ: Scarecrow Press, 1988), 404–6.

19. This fact might best be illustrated by another theatrical form, a stage presentation from the 1970s, *Libbie: The Pleasure of Her Company,* which has Mrs. Custer responding to a 1930s radio program about her beloved Autie. A radio program did air a few years before Mrs. Custer's death. On March 9, 1930, the "Durant Heroes of the World" played its "General Custer" program, with George and Tom Custer being the main characters. (Script in the John Carroll Collection, Bryan, TX.)

Other radio portrayals included an abbreviated version of *They Died with Their Boots On* for CBS's *Cavalcade of America,* a half-hour broadcast that aired in 1941 with Errol Flynn as Custer to promote the movie. On August 5, 1949, *Fort Apache* played for NBC's *Screen Director's Playhouse,* with John Wayne reprising the role of Captain York and Ward Bond assuming the role of Lieutenant Colonel Thursday. There also was a cameo appearance of Custer in the November 7, 1948, "Lee and Grant at Appomattox" episode of CBS's "You Are There," a convention that was followed on TV years later for the same event in *North and South, Book 2,* where an extra plays Custer as he silently received the flag of surrender. Finally, a radio episode of "Gunsmoke" dealt with a deserter from the Little Bighorn.

20. Pitts, *Western Movies,* 229.

21. Praise was profuse, with *Time* magazine pronouncing this revisionist tome "a new American classic," while other reviews lauded Connell for bringing alive so many long gone characters to give a vivid eyewitness feeling to his "masterpiece." See Yoggy, *Riding the Video Range,* 387, for representative reactions by the press to this publication.

22. Ken Tucker, "'Morning Star': The Review," *Entertainment Weekly* (February 1, 1991): 27, contended that the pain in the voices of the two women narrators "dramatizes the agony of this period in our history as effectively as everything on the screen."

23. Telephone conversations with Evan S. Connell, author of *Son of the Morning Star,* April 7, 1988, and with John Carroll, technical consultant to *Son of the Morning Star,* April 11, 1988.

24. John J. O'Connor, "Custer, Call Your Spin Doctor," *New York Times Magazine* (February 3, 1991): 29.

25. The picture's chief technical consultant contended that although this was not "the perfect Custer movie," the production was "the best by far made, and may well become the standard by which all future Custer movies . . . will be measured." John M. Carroll, "Son of the Morning Star," *Sight & Sound* (Winter 1990): 29. Another writer remarked that "all the Indians in the miniseries are portrayed by American Indians and speak in native tongues" and that "all horses, tepees and weaponry were obtained from Indians." Susan King, "Dances with Custer," *TV Times* (February 3–9, 1991): 82.

26. Dan Gagliasso, "Too Much History? A Review of the ABC-Television Movie *Son of the Morning Star,*" *Montana: The Magazine of Western History* 41 (Winter 1991): 91.

27. Stephen Galloway, "115 years after Custer's Last Stand, Native Americans Are Back on the Warpath—over Hollywood's Portrayal of Them," *TV Guide* (February 2, 1991): 11–12, believed that *Son of the Morning Star,* though "not quite equal to the monumental Kevin Costner epic," still was "light-years from old-time Hollywood Westerns." The production went to "great pains . . . to ensure authenticity," although some American Indians in the TV movie felt that there could have been improvements in the depictions of the Indians, particularly Crazy Horse.

Another look at the presentation concurred that *Son of the Morning Star* was "by far the most accurate version [of the Custer story] every filmed." Nevertheless, Gary Cole's "teeth-gnashing intensity evinces none of the charm or elan that so marked the real Custer and will make it difficult for audiences to sympathize with his fate." Paul Andrew Hutton, "Custer Legend Rises Again in 'Son,'" *TV Guide* (February 2, 1991): 13.

28. Gagliasso, "Too Much History?," 91, maintained that *Son of the Morning Star* was "a professional attempt to dramatize western history." Republic Pictures hoped that others would reach the same conclusion and took out a two-page advertisement to encourage members of the Academy of Television Arts and Sciences to consider the production for an Emmy as best miniseries, using quotations from the *Los Angeles Times* calling it "first-class, grandly staged filmmaking," and the assessment of the *Chicago Tribune* that "the

script, acting and cinematography are above reproach." *Variety* (June 20, 1991): 18–19

29. David Seals, "The New Custerism," *The Nation* (May 13, 1991): 638. The critic also contended that the show demonstrated that "the celluloid residuals of Manifest Destiny, played out as emotional climax" had not died.

30. Jason Leland Adams settled in as Custer for the last several years of "Dr. Quinn," two other actors having played him earlier in the series. Even then, the actor was cast as another character in between his stints as Long Hair, playing Preston A. Lodge III in the premiere of the show's fourth season. Why they gave another role to Adams after establishing him as Custer is unknown.

31. This was a promotion for actor Diehl, who previously portrayed a private in another Turner production, *Gettysburg* (1993), and later assumed the role of another historic figure, Joe DiMaggio, in HBO's *Rat Pack* (1998).

32. During the same evening on which the "Legend" episode appeared, May 8, 1995, Rick Burns aired the second part of his program, featuring the Little Bighorn battle,"The Way West" for PBS's "American Experience" series. The previous night, the first episode covered Washita. The simultaneous historical and fictional treatments of Custer bespeak of the continued impact of the figure in both the real and imaginary spheres.

33. Jane Marie Gaines and Charlotte Cornelia Herzog, "The Fantasy of Authenticity in Western Costume," in Buscombe and Pearson, *Back in the Saddle Again*, 172–81, delves into the trend to present "costume realism" in order to deliver "a new version of the 'truth' about the way it was on the frontier."

34. This production was loosely based upon the actual capture of eighteen-year-old Sarah White from her family farm in Kansas, and the subsequent capture about a month later of nineteen-year-old Anna Morgan from her new husband's homestead. For details, see Quaife, *My Life on the Plains*, 401–20.

35. These are known as "alignments" and are broken down into the following categories by game rules: lawful good, lawful neutral, lawful evil, neutral good, true neutral, neutral evil, chaotic good, chaotic neutral, and chaotic evil. The definitions of these variants are somewhat self-explanatory but are spelled out in *Baldur's Gate Game Manual* (Irvine, CA: Interplay Productions, c. 1998), 88–90, 143. Custer has been cast in many of these categories during his long film and television history, ranging from the earliest silent depictions as lawful good (character "believing in an orderly, strong society") to chaotic good (character who believes "in all the virtues of goodness and right, but [has] little use for laws and regulations," as in *They Died with Their Boots On*) to Lt. Col. Owen Thursday's lawful neutral (character to whom "order and organization are of paramount importance" and "the benefits of organization and regimentation outweigh any moral questions raised by [his] actions") to chaotic evil (character "motivated by the desire for personal gain" and who sees "absolutely nothing wrong with taking whatever [he wants] by whatever means possible"). This has become the dominant portrayal, beginning with *Tonka* and carried on through post–Korean War productions.

36. Fraser, *The Hollywood History of the World*, 37.

37. Hutton, "Hollywood's General Custer": 21.

38. As just one indication of the intense requirement for recyclable or recognizable subjects, between 1990 and 1997, the booming passion for "edutainment" has spawned more than a dozen nationally broadcast television documentaries featuring Custer and the Little Bighorn as major elements.

    While purporting to be factual, these programs likewise draw upon Custer's legend and in many respects contribute to its perpetuation. For further insight into the subject, read the essay by one of these documentary makers, Paul Stekler, "Custer and Crazy Horse Ride Again . . . and Again, and Again" Filmmaking and History at the Little Big Horn," *Montana: The Magazine of Western History* 42 (Autumn 1992): 63–72, and Roberta A. Pearson, "The Twelve Custers, or, Video History," in Edward Buscombe and Roberta Pearson, eds., *Back in the Saddle Again: New Essays on the Western* (London: British Film Institute Publishing, 1998), 197–213.

39. Rosenberg, *Custer and the Epic of Defeat*, 282. Stated another way, the secret of Custer's long-standing myth is that "its symbols provide a unique American figuration of the perils and potentials of modernization." Richard S. Slotkin, "Signifying on the Little Bighorn," in Rankin, *Legacy*, 300.

40. Fraser, *The Hollywood History of the World*, 189.

41. In fact, even before Michael Blake had concluded his manuscript for *Marching to Valhalla*, the trades reported that New Line Cinema offered him "$3 million in a preemptive buy" for both the rights of the not yet completed book and his film adaptation of the publication. The idea was that Brad Pitt would be slated as the lead. Anita M. Busch and Michael Fleming, "Pitt to Play Custer for New Line," *Daily Variety* (December 11, 1995). Given that Pitt was *People* magazine's "sexiest man" selection in 1995, it seems that Custer had potential to be revived at the box office in kinder, gentler tones, or at least as a sex symbol, after being so long on the outs with the media.

    The film did not make it to the screen, however, at least not with Pitt in the starring role. The script was completed, but it differed from the novel in many ways. In fact, an early draft was more akin to the episodic *They Died with Their Boots On* than to Blake's novel. The property seemingly was given new life when director Oliver Stone showed an interest in it in 1998. Stone and Blake were to revise the script, but it appears that it will join Goldwyn's *Seventh Cavalry* and Mayes's *The Day Custer Fell* as a film that never was produced.

Bibliography

UNPUBLISHED MATERIALS

"Call Bureau Cast Service Association of Motion Picture Producers, Inc., for M.G.M." August 14, 1940. Margaret Herrick Library, Academy of Motion Picture Arts and Sciences, Beverly Hills, CA.

"Call Bureau Cast Service Association of Motion Picture Producers, Inc., for Universal Studios." April 12, 1939. Margaret Herrick Library, Academy of Motion Picture Arts and Sciences, Beverly Hills, CA.

"Call Bureau Cast Service Association of Motion Picture Producers, Inc., for Warner Bros." February 1952. Margaret Herrick Library, Academy of Motion Picture Arts and Sciences, Beverly Hills, CA.

Clarke, Charles Gallaway. Letters and Telegrams from Early Stars. Margaret Herrick Library, Academy of Motion Picture Arts and Sciences, Beverly Hills, CA.

"Columbia Pictures Corporation Presents Randolph Scott in *The Seventh Cavalry.*" February 1956. *The Seventh Cavalry* File. Margaret Herrick Library, Academy of Motion Picture Arts and Sciences, Beverly Hills, CA.

The Custer Tragedy by Fred Graham. Advertisement sheet, c. 1939, Autry Museum of Western Heritage, Los Angeles.

"Durant Heroes of the World." "General Custer" radio script, March 9, 1930. John M. Carroll Collection, Bryan, TX.

"Editions of Custer's Last Fight." Photostatic copy, September 20, 1991. Corporate Archives, Anheuser Busch Corporation, St. Louis.

Gibson, Francis. Unpublished manuscript. Microfilm roll 6. Elizabeth Custer Collection, Little Bighorn Battlefield National Monument.

"Here Come *The Glory Guys.*" Undated publicity release. Margaret Herrick Library, Academy of Motion Picture Arts and Sciences, Beverly Hills, CA.

Herwitz, Al. "Synopsis Seventh Cavalry." Unpublished and undated typescript, Columbia Films Director of Publicity. Margaret Herrick Library, Academy of Motion Picture Arts and Sciences, Beverly Hills, CA.

James, P. "Old Iron Pants." Synopsis, January 17, 1966. University of Southern California, Warner Brothers Archives.

Langellier, John P. Telephone interview with Evan S. Connell, April 7, 1988, Sausalito, CA.

Last Frontier Production File. Margaret Herrick Library, Academy of Motion Picture Arts and Sciences, Beverly Hills, CA.

"Little Big Man." Undated publicity release. Margaret Herrick Library, Academy of Motion Picture Arts and Sciences, Beverly Hills, CA.

Mayes, Wendell. "The Day Custer Fell." Screenplay, April 2, 1965. Vincent A. Heier, Jr., Collection, St. Louis.

M.G.M. Production Bulletin, December 6, 1940, and June 17, 1940. Margaret Herrick Library, Academy of Motion Picture Arts and Sciences, Beverly Hills, CA.

Motion Picture Copyrights. Microfilm Collection, University of Southern California Cinema and Television Library, Los Angeles.

"Pictorial Synopsis of *Warpath.*" Undated typed sheet. Margaret Herrick Library, Academy of Motion Picture Arts and Sciences, Beverly Hills, CA.

"Synopsis by Columbia Studios, Al Horwitz, Director of Publicity." Undated typed sheet. Margaret Herrick Library, Academy of Motion Picture Arts and Sciences, Beverly Hills, CA.

Telegram from Alfred Terry at Camp on Little Big Horn River to Assistant Adjutant General of Military Division of Missouri, Chicago. Library of Congress, Washington, DC.

Telegram from Philip Sheridan to William Sherman, July 7, 1876. Glen Swanson Collection.

Ulrich, Charles. Letter to William Selig, November 2, 1914(?). Folder 322, Selig Collection, Margaret Herrick Library, Academy of Motion Picture Arts and Sciences, Beverly Hills, CA.

BOOKS AND MONOGRAPHS

Ambrose, Stephen E. *Crazy Horse and Custer: The Parallel Lives of Two American Warriors.* Garden City, NY: Doubleday & Company, 1975.

Annual Report of the Secretary of War, 1876. Vol. 1. Washington, DC: Government Printing Office, 1876.

Balshofer, Fred J., and Arthur C. Miller. *One Reel a Week.* Berkeley: University of California Press, 1967.

Barabas, SuzAnne, and Gabor Barabas. *Gunsmoke: A Complete History.* Jefferson, NC: McFarland & Company, 1990.

Barnett, Louise. *Touched by Fire: The Life, Death, and Mythic Afterlife of George Armstrong Custer.* New York: Henry Holt, 1996.

Bataille, Gretchen M., and Charles L. P. Silet, eds. *The Pretend Indians: Images of Native Americans in the Movies.* Ames: Iowa State University Press, 1980.

Ben-Amon, Dan, and Liliane Weissberg, eds. *Cultural Memory and the Construction of Identity.* Detroit: Wayne State University Press, 1998.

Berkhofer, Robert F., Jr. *The White Man's Indian: Images of the American Indian from Columbus to the Present.* New York: Alfred A. Knopf, 1978.

Bernardi, Daniel, ed. *The Birth of Whiteness: Race and the Emergence of U.S. Cinema.* New Brunswick, NJ: Rutgers University Press, 1996.

Billington, Ray Allen. *America's Frontier Heritage.* New York: Holt, Rinehart and Winston, 1966.

Bluestone, George. *Novels into Film.* Berkeley: University of California Press, 1961.

Boatner, Mark M., III. *The Civil War Dictionary.* New York: David McKay Company, 1959.

Bogdanovich, Peter. *John Ford.* Berkeley: University of California Press, 1968.

Bondanella, Peter. *Italian Cinema, from Neorealism to the Present.* 2nd ed. New York: Continuum, 1990.

Bray, Mayfield. *Guide to the Ford Collection in the National Archives.* Washington, DC: National Archives, 1970.

Brininstool, E. A. *Major Reno Vindicated: From a Letter Written in 1925 by Col. W. W. Graham, U.S.A., with Comments by E. A. Brininstool.* Hollywood, CA: n.p., 1935.

———. *Troopers with Custer: Historic Incidents of the Battle of Little Big Horn.* Harrisburg, PA: Stackpole Company, 1952.

Britten, Thomas A. *American Indians in World War I at Home and at War.* Albuquerque: University of New Mexico Press, 1997.

Brownlow, Kevin. *The War, the West, and the Wilderness.* New York: Alfred A. Knopf, 1979.

Buel, J. W. *Heroes of the Plains; or, Lives and Wonderful Adventures of Wild Bill, Buffalo Bill, Kit Carson, Capt. Payne, Capt. Jack, Texas Jack, California Joe, and Other Celebrated Indian Fighters, Scouts, Hunters, and Guides: Including a True and Thrilling History of Gen. Custer's Famous "Last Stand" on the Little Big Horn, with Sitting Bull.* St. Louis: N. D. Thompson, 1883.

Burt, Mary E., ed. *The Boy General: Story of the Life of Major General George A. Custer as Told by Elizabeth Custer.* New York: Charles Scribner's Sons, 1901

Buscombe, Edward, ed. *The BFI Companion to the Western.* New York: Atheneum, 1988.

Buscombe, Edward, and Roberta E. Pearson, eds. *Back in the Saddle Again: New Essays on the Western.* London: British Film Institute, 1998.

Campbell, Joseph. *The Hero with a Thousand Faces.* New York: Pantheon Books, 1948.

Carnes, Mark C., ed. *Past Imperfect: History According to the Movies.* New York: Henry Holt and Company, 1995.

Carroll, John M. *Custer in Texas: An Interrupted Narrative.* New York: Sol Lewis, 1975.

———, ed. *They Rode with Custer: A Biographical Directory of the Men That Rode with George A. Custer.* Mattituck, NY: John M. Carroll & Company, 1987.

Cassidy, John M. *Civil War Cinema.* Missoula, MT: Pictorial Histories Publishing Company, 1986.

Clint-Irion, Mary. *The Spirit of the Plains.* Los Angeles: Paramount Pictures, 1936.

Cody, Iron Eyes, and Collin Perry. *Iron Eyes Cody: My Life as a Hollywood Indian.* New York: Everest House, 1982.

Connell, Evan S. *Son of the Morning Star: Custer and the Little Big Horn.* New York: Perennial Library, 1985.

Cullen, Jim. *The Civil War in Popular Culture: A Reusable Past.* Washington, DC: Smithsonian Institution Press, 1995.

Custen, George F. *Bio/Pics: How Hollywood Constructed Public History.* New Brunswick, NJ: Rutgers University Press, 1992.

The Custer Battle Papers: A March into Immortality. N.p.: Frontier Press, 1969.

Custer, Brice C. *Sacrificial Lion: George Armstrong Custer.* El Segundo, CA: Upton and Sons, 1999.

Custer, Elizabeth Bacon. *"Boots and Saddles"; or, Life in Dakota with General Custer.* New York: Harper and Brothers, 1885.

———. *Following the Guidon.* New York: Harper and Brothers, 1890.

———. *Tenting on the Plains; or, General Custer in Kansas and Texas.* New York: Charles L. Webster, 1887.

Custer, George Armstrong. *My Life on the Plains; or, Personal Experiences with Indians.* New York: Sheldon & Company, 1875.

Custer, George Armstrong, et al. *Wild Life on the Plains and Horrors of Indian Warfare, by General G. A. Custer, U.S.A. with a Graphic Account of the Last Fight on the Little Big Horn, as Told by His Wily Foe Sitting Bull.* St. Louis: Sun Publishing Co., 1885.

"Custer's Last Stand" Based on Historical Events Leading Up to Custer's Last Stand. Weiss Production Press Book. Original in the Collection of Vincent Heier, St. Louis, 1936.

Cutler, Bruce. *The Massacre at Sand Creek: Narrative Voices.* Norman: University of Oklahoma Press, 1995.

Daily, Edward. *From Custer to McArthur: The Seventh U.S. Cavalry (1866–1945).* Paducah, KY: Turner Publishing Co., 1997.

Danker, Donald E., ed. *Man of the Plains: Recollections of Luther North, 1856–1882.* Lincoln: University of Nebraska Press, 1961.

Deex, Nelle. *Glory Trek: The Story of General Custer's Last Stand.* New York: William-Frederick Press, 1959.

Dellenbaugh, Frederick S. *George Armstrong Custer.* New York: Macmillan Company, 1919.

Deloria, Vine, Jr. *Custer Died for Your Sins: An Indian Manifesto.* New York: Avon Books, 1969.

Dieber, Eddie. *General George Armstrong Custer's Biography in Pictures.* Grand Forks, ND: Washburn Printing Center, n.d.

Dippie, Brian. *Custer's Last Stand: The Anatomy of an American Myth.* Lincoln: University of Nebraska Press, 1994.

———, ed. *Nomad: George A. Custer in Turf, Field and Farm.* Austin: University of Texas Press, 1980.

———, ed. Garry Owen 1976: Annual of the Little Big Horn Associates. Seattle: Little Big Horn Associates, 1977.

Dippie, Brian, and John Carroll. *Bards of the Little Big Horn.* Bryan, TX: Guidon Press, 1978.

Dippie, Brian, and Paul A. Hutton. *The Comic Book Custer: A Bibliography of Custeriana in Comic Books and Comic Strips.* N.p.: Brazos Corral of the Westerners, n.d.

Division of Publicity. *Carrying On for Fifty Years with the Courage of Custer, 1876–1926.* Helena: Montana Department of Agriculture, Labor and Industry, 1926.

Dowd, James Patrick. *Custer Lives!* Fairfield, WA: Ye Galleon Press, 1982.

Dustin, Fred. *The Custer Fight: Some Criticisms of Gen. E. S. Godfrey's "Custer's Last Battle," in Century Magazine for January 1892, and of Mrs. Elizabeth Custer's Pamphlet of 1921.* Hollywood, CA: E. A. Brininstool, 1936.

———. *The Custer Tragedy: Events Leading Up to and Following the Little Big Horn Campaign of 1876.* Ann Arbor: Edward Brothers, 1939.

Everson, William K. *A Pictorial History of the Western Film.* New York: Citadel Press, 1969.

Eyles, Allen. *The Western: An Illustrated Guide.* New York: A. S. Barnes & Co., 1967.

Fenin, George N., and William K. Everson. *The Western from Silents to the Seventies.* New York: Orion Press, 1973.

Ford, Dan. *Pappy: The Life of John Ford.* New York: Prentice-Hall, 1979.

Fox, Richard Alan. *Archaeology, History, and Custer's Last Battle: The Little Bighorn Reexamined.* Norman: University of Oklahoma Press, 1993.

Fraser, George MacDonald. *The Hollywood History of the World From One Million B.C. to Apocalypse Now.* New York: Fawcett Columbine, 1988.

Friar, Ralph, and Natasha Friar. *The Only Good Indian.* New York: Drama Book, 1972.

Frost, Lawrence A. *The Custer Album: A Pictorial Biography of General George A. Custer.* Seattle: Superior Publishing Co., 1964.

———. *General Custer's Libbie.* Seattle: Superior Publishing Co., 1975.

Freund, Philip, ed. *The Myth of Birth of the Hero and Other Writings.* New York: Vintage, 1956.

Fulghum, Robert. *It Was on Fire When I Lay Down on it.* New York: Villard Books, 1989.

Gallagher, Tag. *John Ford: The Man and His Films.* Berkeley: University of California Press, 1986.

Gans, Herbert J. *Popular Culture and High Culture: An Analysis and Evaluation of Taste.* New York: Basic Books, 1974.

Garfield, Brian. *Western Films: A Complete Guide.* New York: Rawson Associates, 1982.

Garst, Shannon. *Custer: Fighter of the Plains.* New York: Julian Messner, 1944.

Gevinson, Alan, ed. *Within Our Gates: Ethnicity in American Feature Films, 1911–1960.* Berkeley: University of California Press, 1997.

Gibson, Walter B., adapter. *Rod Serling's Twilight Zone Revisited.* New York: Grossett & Dunlap, 1964.

Goodman, Ezra. *The Fifty-Year Decline and Fall of Hollywood.* New York: Simon and Schuster, 1961.

Graham, W. A., ed. *Abstract of the Official Proceedings of the Reno Court of Inquiry.* Harrisburg, PA: Stackpole, 1954.

———. *The Custer Myth: A Sourcebook of Custeriana.* New York: Bonanza Books, 1995.

———. *The Official Record of a Court of Inquiry Convened at Chicago, Illinois, January 13, 1879, by the President of the United States upon the Request by Major Marcus A. Reno. . . .* Pacific Palisades, CA: W. A. Graham, 1951.

———. *The Story of the Little Big Horn: Custer's Last Fight.* Harrisburg, PA: Military Service Publishing Company, 1952.

Gray, John S. *Centennial Campaign: The Sioux War of 1876.* Fort Collins, CO: Old Army Press, 1976.

Greene, Jerome A., comp. and ed. *Lakota and Cheyenne Indian Views of the Great Sioux War, 1876–1877.* Norman: University of Oklahoma Press, 1994.

Grossman, James R., ed. *The Frontier and American Culture.* Berkeley: University of California Press, 1994.

Hanson, Patricia King, exec. ed. *The American Film Institute Catalog of Motion Pictures Produced in the United States: Feature Films, 1911–1920, Film Entries.* Berkeley: University of California Press, 1988.

Hardoff, Richard G. *Hokahey! A Good Day to Die!* Spokane: Arthur H. Clark, 1993.

———. *Lakota Recollections of the Custer Fight: New Sources on Indian-Military History.* Spokane: Arthur H. Clark, 1991.

Hardy, Phil. *The Western: The Complete Source Book.* New York: William Morrow and Company, 1983.

Hedren, Paul L. *First Scalp for Custer: The Skirmish at Warbonnet Creek, Nebraska, July 17, 1876.* Glendale, CA: Arthur H. Clark Co., 1980.

Heitman, Francis B. *Historical Register and Dictionary of the United States Army; From Its Organization, September 29, 1789, to March 2, 1903.* Washington, DC: Government Printing Office, 1903.

Heston, Charlton. *The Actor's Life: Journals 1956–1976.* New York: E. P. Dalton, 1976.

Heuman, William. *Custer, Man and Legend.* New York: Dodd, Mead & Company, 1968.

Hilger, Michael. *The American Indian in Films.* Metuchen, NJ: Scarecrow Press, 1986.

Hitt, Jim. *The American West from Fiction (1823–1976) into Film 1909–1986.* Jefferson, NC: McFarland & Company, 1990.

Hoig, Stan. *The Sand Creek Massacre.* Norman: University of Oklahoma Press, 1961.

Horn, W. Donald. *Portrait of a General: George Armstrong Custer and The Battle of Little Big Horn.* N.p.: Don Horn Productions, 1998.

Hunt, Frazier. *Custer: The Last of the Cavaliers.* New York: Cosmopolitan Book Corporation, 1928.

Hutton, Paul Andrew, ed. *The Custer Reader.* Lincoln: University of Nebraska Press, 1992.

———. *Phil Sheridan and His Army.* Lincoln: University of Nebraska Press, 1985.

Jackson, Donald. *Custer's Gold: The United States Cavalry Expedition of 1874.* New Haven: Yale University Press, 1966.

Katz, D. Mark. *Custer in Photographs.* New York: Bonanza Books, 1985.

Kent, Zachary. *George Armstrong Custer: Civil War and Western Legend.* Springfield, NJ: Enslow, 2000.

Kinnard, Roy. *Fifty Years of Serial Thrills.* Metuchen, NJ: Scarecrow Press, 1983.

Kinsley, D.A. *Favor the Bold.* Vol. 1, *Custer the Civil War Years. New York:* Holt, Rinehart and Winston, 1967.

———. *Favor the Bold.* Vol. 2, *Custer: The Indian Fighter.* New York: Holt, Rinehart and Winston, 1968.

Koestler, Arthur. *The Act as Creation.* New York: MacMillan, 1964.

Krause, Herman, and Gary D. Olsen, comps. *Prelude to Glory: A Newspaper Accounting of Custer's 1874 Expedition into the Black Hills.* Sioux Falls, SD: Brevet Press, 1974.

Kuhlman, Charles. *Custer and the Gall Saga.* Billings, MT: Privately published, 1940.

———. *The Custer Mystery: An Analytical Study of the Battle of the Little Big Horn.* Revised edition. Harrisburg, PA: Stackpole Company, 1952.

———. *Did Custer Disobey Orders?* Harrisburg, PA: Stackpole Company, 1957.

———. *Legend into History: The Custer Mystery.* Harrisburg, PA: Stackpole, 1952.

Lahue, Kalton C. *Continued Next Week: A History of the Moving Picture Serial.* Norman: University of Oklahoma Press, 1964.

Langman, Larry. *A Guide to Silent Westerns.* Westport, CT: Greenwood Press, 1992.

Lawrence, Elizabeth Atwood. *His Very Silence Speaks: Comanche—The Horse Who Survived Custer's Last Stand.* Detroit: Wayne State University, 1989.

Leckie, Shirley A. *Elizabeth Bacon Custer and the Making of a Myth.* Norman: University of Oklahoma Press, 1993.

Leighton, Margaret. *The Story of General Custer.* New York: Grossett & Dunlap, 1954.

Library of Congress Catalog of Motion Pictures and Film Strips, 1969. Washington, DC: Library of Congress, 1970.

Linenthal, Edward Tabor. *Sacred Ground: Americans and Their Battlefields.* Urbana: University of Illinois Press, 1991.

Luce, Edward S., and Evelyn Luce. *Custer Battlefield National Monument, Montana.* Washington, DC: National Park Service, 1952.

Luce, Edward S. *Keogh, Comanche and Custer.* St. Louis: N.p., 1939.

Lund, Karen C. *American Indians in Silent Film: Motion Pictures in the Library of Congress.* Washington, DC: Library of Congress, 1992.

Luther, Tal. *Custer High Spots.* Fort Collins, CO: Old Army Press, 1972.

MacGowan, Kenneth. *Behind the Screen: The History and Techniques of the Motion Picture.* New York: Dell Publishing Co., 1965.

Marschall, Rick. *History of Television.* New York: Gallery Books, 1986.

Mast, Gerald. *A Short History of the Movies.* New York: Pegasus, 1971.

McClellan, George B. *McClellan's Own Story.* New York: C. L. Webster & Co., 1887.

McVey, E. E. *The Crow Scout Who Killed Custer.* Billings, MT: E. E. McVey, 1952.

Merington, Marguerite, ed. *The Custer Story: The Life and Intimate Letters of George A. Custer and His Wife Elizabeth.* New York: Devin-Adair, 1950.

Miller, David Humphreys. *Custer's Fall: The Indian Side of the Story.* New York: Duell, Sloan and Pearce, 1957.

Mills, Charles K. *Harvest of Barren Regrets: The Army Career of Frederick William Benteen.* Glendale, CA: Arthur H. Clark Company, 1985.

Monaghan, Jay. *Custer: The Life of General George Armstrong Custer.* Lincoln: University of Nebraska Press, 1971.

Munden, Kenneth W., exec. ed. *The American Film Institute Catalog of Motion Pictures Produced in the United States: Feature Films, 1921–1930.* New York: R. R. Bowker, 1971.

Nash, Jay Robert, and Stanley Ralph Ross. *The Motion Picture Guide.* Vol 2. Chicago: Cinebooks, 1985.

Neihardt, John G. *Black Elk Speaks: The Life Story of a Holy Man of the Oglala Sioux, as Told to John G. Neihardt.* London: Barrie & Jenkins, 1972.

The New York Times Film Reviews, 1913–1968. 5 vols. New York: New York Times and Arno Press, 1970.

Nicolas, John H. *Tom Mix: Riding Up to Glory.* Oklahoma City: National Cowboy Hall of Fame, 1980.

O'Connor, John E. *The Hollywood Indian: Stereotypes of Native Americans in Film.* Trenton: New Jersey State Museum, 1980.

Paine, Lauran. *The General Custer Story: The True Story of the Battle of the Little Big Horn.* London: W. Foulsham & Co., 1960.

Parish, James Robert, and Michael R. Pitts. *The Great Western Pictures.* Vol. 2. Metuchen, NJ: Scarecrow Press, 1988.

Parker, Watson. *Gold in the Black Hills.* Lincoln: University of Nebraska Press, 1982.

Parsons, John E., and John S. duMont. *Firearms in the Custer Battle.* Harrisburg, PA: Stackpole Co., 1955.

Pascall, Jeremy. *50 Years of the Movies.* Middlesex, England: The Hamlyn Publishing Group, 1981.

Pearce, Roy Harvey. *Savagism and Civilization: A Study of the Indian and the American Mind.* Baltimore: Johns Hopkins Press, 1965.

Pinkleton, William T., and Don Graham, eds. *Western Movies.* Albuquerque: University of New Mexico Press, 1979.

Pitts, Michael R. *Hollywood and American History: A Filmography of Over 250 Motion Pictures.* Jefferson, NC: McFarland & Co. 1984.

———. *Western Movies: A TV and Video Guide to 4200 Genre Films.* Jefferson, NC: McFarland & Company, 1986.

Place, J. A. *The Western Films of John Ford.* Secaucus, NJ: Citadel Press, 1974.

Prucha, Francis Paul. *American Indian Treaties: The History of a Political Anomaly.* Berkeley: University of California Press, 1994.

Rankin, Charles E., ed. *Legacy: New Perspectives on the Battle of the Little Bighorn.* Helena: Montana Historical Society, 1996.

Reed, Joseph W. *American Scenarios: The Uses of Film Genre.* Middleton, CT: Wesleyan University Press, 1989.

Report of Committee on the Sale of Post Traderships. House Report no. 799, 44th Cong., 1st sess.

Reynolds, Quentin. *Custer's Last Stand.* New York: Random House, 1951.

Rickey, Don Jr. *History of Custer Battlefield.* Billings, MT: Custer Battlefield Historical and Museum Association, 1967.

Roe, Charles F. *Custer's Last Battle-March of the Montana Column.* New York: National Highways Association, 1927.

Ronsheim, Milton. *The Life of General Custer.* Cadiz, OH: Cadiz Republican, 1929.

Rosa, Joseph, and Robin May. *Buffalo Bill and His Wild West: A Pictorial Biography.* Lawrence: University of Kansas Press, 1989.

Rosenberg, Bruce. *Custer and the Epic of Defeat.* University Park: Pennsylvania State University Press, 1974.

Rotha, Paul. *The Film Till Now: A Survey of World Cinema.* London: Spring Books, 1967.

Russell, Don. *Custer's Last.* Fort Worth, TX: Amon Carter Museum of Western Art, 1968.

———. *Custer's List: A Checklist of Pictures Relating to the Battle of the Little Big Horn.* Fort Worth, TX: Amon Carter Museum, 1969.

———. *The Wild West; or, A History of the Wild West Shows.* Fort Worth, TX: Amon Carter Museum of Western Art, 1972.

Ryan, John D. *Custer Fell First.* San Antonio: The Naylor Co., 1966.

Scott, Douglas, and Richard Alan Fox, Jr. *Archaeological Insights into the Custer Battle.* Norman: University of Oklahoma Press, 1989.

Segal, Robert A. *Joseph Campbell: An Introduction.* New York: Garland Publishing, 1987.

Sell, Henry Blackman, and Victor Weybright. *Buffalo Bill and the Wild West.* Basin, WY: Big Horn Books, 1979.

Sinclair, Andrew. *John Ford.* New York: Dial Press, 1979.

Slotkin, Richard. *The Fatal Environment: The Myth of the Frontier in the Age of Industrialization, 1800–1890.* New York: Atheneum, 1985.

———. *Gunfighter Nation: The Myth of the Frontier in Twentieth-Century America.* New York: Atheneum, 1992.

———. *Regeneration Through Violence.* Middleton, CT: Wesleyan University Press, 1973.

Smith, Henry Nash. *Virgin Land: The American West as Symbol and Myth.* New York: Vintage Books, 1950.

Spigel, Lynn, and Michael Curtin. eds. *The Revolution That Wasn't: Sixties Television and Social Context.* New York: Routledge, 1996.

Steckmesser, Kent Ladd. *The Western Hero in History and Legend.* Norman: University of Oklahoma Press, 1965.

Stedman, Raymond William. *The Serials: Suspense and Drama by Installment.* Norman: University of Oklahoma Press, 1971.

———. *Shadows of the Indian in Film: Stereotypes in American Culture.* Norman: University of Oklahoma Press, 1982.

Stern, Seymour, comp. *An Index to the Creative Work of David Wark Griffith.* Part 1, *The Birth of an Art, 1908–1915.* Hollywood, CA: Sight and Sound Series, 1944.

Stevenson, Augusta. *George Custer: Boy of Action.* Indianapolis: Bobbs-Merrill Company, 1963.

Svaldi, David. *Sand Creek and the Rhetoric of Extermination: A Case Study in Indian-White Relations.* Lanham, MD: University of America, c. 1989.

Swinford, T. A. *Custeriana: A Field Guide to Custer Literature by T. A. Swinford and Tal Luther.* Tempe, AZ: Old Army Press, 1999.

Szabo, Joyce M. *Howling Wolf and the History of Ledger Art.* Albuquerque: University of New Mexico, 1994.

Tabor, Edward. *Changing Images of the Warrior Hero in America: A History of Popular Symbolism.* New York: Edwin Mellen Press, 1982.

Tenth Annual Report of the Bureau of Ethnology. Washington, DC: Government Printing Office, 1893.

Terrance, Vincent. *The Complete Encyclopedia of Television Programs, 1947–1976.* Vol. 1. New York: A. S. Barnes and Company, 1976.

Thomas, Tony. *The Films of Olivia de Havilland.* Secaucus, NJ: Citadel Press, 1983.

———. *The Films of Ronald Reagan.* Secaucus, NJ: Citadel Press, 1980.

———. *The West That Never Was.* Secaucus, NJ: Citadel Press, 1989.

Thomas, Tony, Rudy Behlmer, and Clifford McCarthy. *The Films of Errol Flynn.* New York: Citadel Press, 1969.

Thompson, Frank. *Lost Films: Important Movies That Disappeared.* New York: Citadel Press Book, 1996.

Thompson, Peter. *Narrative of the Little Bighorn Campaign.* Glendale, CA: Arthur Clark Co., 1974.

Tillet, Leslie, ed. and comp. *Wind on the Buffalo Grass: The Indians' Own Account of the Battle of Little Big Horn River, the Death of Their Life on the Plains.* New York: Thomas Y. Yoseloff, 1976.

Toplin, Robert Brent. *History by Hollywood: The Use and Abuse of the American Past.* Urbana: University of Illinois Press, 1996.

Trial of William Belknap in the Senate of the United States, 1876. Washington, DC: U.S. Government Printing Office, 1876.

Truettner, William H., ed. *The West as America: Reinterpreting Images of the Frontier, 1820–1920.* Washington, DC: Smithsonian Institution Press, 1991.

Turner, Victor W. *The Ritual Process: Structure and Anti-structure.* Chicago: Aldine Publishing Company, 1969.

Tuska, Jon. *The American West in Film: Critical Approaches to the Western.* Westport, CT: Greenwood Press, 1985.

———. *The Filming of the West.* Garden City, NY: Doubleday Company, 1976.

Upton, Richard, ed. and comp. *The Custer Adventure.* Fort Collins, CO: Old Army Press, 1975.

Urwin, Gregory J. W., and Roberta E. Fagan, eds. *Custer and His Times, Book Three.* A Publication of the Little Big Horn Associates. Conway: University of Central Arkansas Press, 1987.

———. *Custer Victorious: The Civil War Battles of George A. Custer.* East Brunswick, NJ: Associated University Press, 1983.

Utley, Robert M. *Cavalier in Buckskin: George Armstrong Custer and the Western Military Frontier.* Norman: University of Oklahoma Press, 1988.

———. *Custer and the Great Controversy.* Los Angeles: Western Lore Press, 1962.

———. *The Lance and the Shield: The Life and Times of Sitting Bull.* New York: Henry Holt and Company, 1993.

———, ed. *Life in Custer's Cavalry: Diaries and Letters of Albert and Jennie Barnitz, 1867–1868.* New Haven: Yale University Press, 1977.

Van de Water, Fredric. *Glory-Hunter: A Life of General Custer.* New York: Bobbs-Merrill Company, 1934.

Viola, Herman J. *Little Bighorn Remembered: The Untold Indian Story of Custer's Last Stand.* New York: Times Books, 1999.

Wheeler, Olin D. "The Custer Battlefield." *Wonderland: 1901.* St. Paul Northern Pacific Railroad, 1901.

Weiss, Ken, and Ed Goodgold. *To Be Continued. . . .* New York: Crown Publishers, 1972.

Weisser, Thomas. *Spaghetti Westerns—the Good, the Bad and the Violent: A Comprehensive, Illustrated Filmography of*

558 Eurowesterns and Their Personnel, 1966–1977. Jefferson, NC: McFarland & Company, 1992.

Welsh, James, with Paul Steckler. *Killing Custer.* New York: W. W. Norton and Company, 1994.

Wert, Jeffry D. *Custer: The Controversial Life of George Armstrong Custer.* New York: Simon & Schuster, 1996.

West, Richard. *Television Westerns: Major and Minor Series, 1946–1978.* Jefferson, NC: McFarland & Company, 1987.

West Point Alumni Foundation. *Register of Graduates and Former Cadets of the United States Military Academy.* Chicago: R. R. Donnelley & Sons Co., 1965.

Whittaker, Frederick. *The Complete Life of Gen. George A. Custer.* New York: Seldon & Company, 1876.

Woolley, Lynn, Robert W. Malsbary, and Robert G. Strange, Jr. *Warner Bros. Television.* Jefferson, NC: McFarland & Company, 1987.

Works Projects Administration in the City of New York. *The Film Index: A Bibliography.* Vol. 1, *Film as Art.* New York: The Museum of Modern Art Film Library and the H. W. Wilson Co., 1941.

Worster, Donald. *Under Western Skies: Nature and History in the American West.* Oxford: Oxford University Press, 1992.

Yoggy, Gary A. *Riding the Video Range: The Rise and Fall of the Western on Television.* Jefferson, NC: McFarland & Company, 1995.

Zicree, Marc Scott. *The Twilight Zone Companion.* New York: Bantam Books, 1989.

NEWSPAPERS, PERIODICALS, AND ARTICLES

"All-Time Box Office Champs." *Variety* (January 5, 1973).

The Army and Navy Journal (July 16, 1876).

Bailey, E. C. "Echoes from Custer's Last Fight." *Military Affairs* (1953): 170–73.

Berner, Robert L. "Review of *Killing Custer.*" *American Indian Culture and Research Journal* 19 (1995): 202–3.

"Big Rental Films of 1970." *Variety* (January 5, 1973).

"Big Year for General Custer." *The Hollywood Reporter* (March 30, 1965).

Blaisdell, George. "Vitagraph Shows Two Good Dramas." *The Moving Picture World* (January 15, 1916).

Boxoffice (June 2, 1951, and August 15, 1965).

Boxoffice Bookin' Guide (August 15, 1966).

Brininstool, E. A. "Replies to Custer Massacre." *Hunter-Trader-Trapper* (March 1926).

"*Bugles in the Afternoon* Is Valid Action Western." *Hollywood Reporter* (January 31, 1952).

Busch, Anita, and Michael Fleming. "Pitt to play Custer for New Line." *Daily Variety* (December 11, 1995).

Campbell, Russell. "Fort Apache." *The Velvet Light Trap* 2 (August 1971): 8–12.

Carroll, John M. "Son of the Morning Star." *Sight & Sound* (Winter 1990): 29.

Clepper, P. M. "He's Our George." *TV Guide* (September 23, 1967): 32–34.

"Checkup." *Motion Picture News* (December 11, 1926).

"Custer." *Variety* (October 13, 1967).

"Custer's Last Last Stand." *Newsweek* (March 11, 1974).

Dippie, Brian W. "Of Bullets, Blunders, and Custer Buffs." *Montana: The Magazine of Western History* 16, no. 1 (Winter 1991): 76–80.

———. "Review of 'Last Stand at Little Bighorn.'" *Public Historian* 15 (Fall 1993): 134–35.

Dippie, Brian W., and Edward T. LeBlanc. "Bibliography of Custer Dime Novels." *Dime Novel Roundup* 28, no. 7 (July 15, 1969): 66–70.

Dustin, Fred. "George Armstrong Custer." *Michigan History Magazine* (April–June 1946).

Eastman, Charles. "Rain-in-the-Face: A Story of a Sioux Warrior." *Outlook* (October 27, 1906).

Fife, Austin, and Alta Fife. "Ballads of the Little Big Horn." *American West* 4 (February 1967): 46–49; 86–89.

The Film Daily (January 24, 1968).

Film Index (November 6, 1909).

Film Review (January 31, 1952).

"Film Reviews." *Variety Weekly* (January 20, 1937).

Finley, Ned. "Stories of the Movies." *The Moving Picture World* (January 15, 1916).

"Fort Apache Brings Back Film Blood and Thunder." *The Hollywood Reporter* (March 10, 1948).

Gagliasso, Dan. "Custer's Last Stand on Celluloid." *Persimmon Hill* 10, no. 1 (Spring 1991): 4–12.

———. "Too Much History? A Review of the ABC-Television Movie *Son of the Morning Star.*" *Montana: The Magazine of Western History* 41, no. 1 (Winter 1991): 91.

Galaxy (September and December 1876).

Galloway, Stephen. "115 Years after Custer's Last Stand, Native Americans Are Back on the Warpath—over Hollywood's Portrayal of Them." *TV Guide* (February 2, 1991): 11–12.

Godfrey, Edward S. "Custer's Last Battle." *Century Illustrated Monthly Magazine* (January 1892).

"Grant The Murderer of Custer." *Atlanta Weekly Commonwealth* (July 18, 1876).

"Great Custer Massacre Graphically Repeated." *Billings Daily Gazette* (September 26, 1909).

Gruber, Frank. "The Ways to Plot a Western." *TV Guide* (August 30, 1958): 5–7.

Harrison, Louis Reeves. "The Final Battle of a Famous Indian Fighter in Two Reels by Bison." *The Moving Picture World* (June 22, 1912).

Heier, Vincent A., Jr. "Thomas Ince's *Custer's Last Fight*: Reflections on the Making of the Custer Legend in Film." [St. Louis Westerners] *Westward* 5 (May 1976): 21–26.

———. "Fiction Stranger than Truth: A 'Novel' Approach to Custer in Literature." 3rd Annual Symposium, Custer Battlefield Historical & Museum Assn., held at Hardin, Montana, on June 23, 1989.

"He Loses Last Stand on Gen. Custer Film." *Los Angeles Times* (March 18, 1969).

Hofling, Charles K., M.D. "George Armstrong Custer: A Psychoanalytic Approach." *Montana: The Magazine of Western History* 21, no, 2 (April 1971): 32–43.

The Hollywood Reporter (March 26, 1941; August 25, 1950; March 9, 1951; March 23, 1965; and June 9, 1965).

Hutton, Paul Andrew. "'Correct in Every Detail': General Custer in Hollywood." *Montana: The Magazine of Western History* 41, no. 1 (Winter 1991): 28–57.

———. "Custer Legend Rises Again in 'Son.'" *TV Guide* (February 2, 1991): 13.

———. "From Little Big Horn to Little Big Man: The Changing Image of a Western Hero in Popular Culture." *Western Historical Quarterly* 7, no. 1 (January 1976): 19–45.

———. "Hollywood's General Custer: The Changing Image of a Military Hero in Film." *Greasy Grass* 2 (May 1986): 15–21.

The Illustrated Police Gazette (July 13, 1876).

"Independent Film Stories." *Moving Picture World* (January 2, 1915).

"Injun Sal." *Newsweek* (January 5, 1959).

Jahant, Charles A. "Chicago: Center of Silent Film Industry." *Chicago History* 3, no. 4 (Spring–Summer 1974): 45–73.

Jennewein, Leonard. "Big Horn Battle Subject for Much Controversy." *Rapid City Journal* (January 20, 1957).

Kaufman, Dave. "Custer Rides Again: On TV." *Variety* (May 23, 1967).

King, Charles. "Custer's Last Battle." *Harper's Monthly* (August 1890).

King, Susan. "Dances With Custer." *TV Times* (February 3–9, 1991): 82.

Kinsey, Nora B. "Custer Memorial Highway." *American Review of Reviews* 64 (August 1921): 184–86.

Kronke, David. "The Warrior." *Entertainment Weekly* (February 1, 1991): 27.

"Little Big Horn." *Variety Weekly* (May 30, 1951).

"Little Big Man." *Motion Picture Exhibitor* (December 23, 1970).

"Miscellany and Advertiser." *Galaxy* (December 1876).

Moffitt, Jack. *Chief Crazy Horse* Okay Cavalry vs. Indian Yarn." *The Hollywood Reporter* (February 22, 1955).

Monthly Film Bulletin (May 1959).

Motion Picture Herald (January 31, 1968).

Motion Picture News (December 11, 1926).

The Moving Picture World (November 27, 1909; November 23, 1912; February 21, 1914; and January 2, 1915).

Newsweek (March 10, 1952, and August 7, 1967).

New York Daily Graphic (July 19, 1876).

New York Times (September 7, 1967).

"1954 Box Office Champs." *Variety* (January 5, 1954).

Oberbeck, S. K. "U.S. Can Go Home." *Newsweek* (August 26, 1970).

O'Connor, John J. "Custer, Call Your Spin Doctor." *New York Times Magazine* (February 3, 1991): 29.

O'Neil, Tom. "The Making of *They Died with Their Boots On.*" *Research Review: The Journal of the Little Big Horn Associates* 4, no. 2 (June 1990): 22–29.

Ornstein, Bill. "Four Companies Are After Fromkess' Custer Feature. *The Hollywood Reporter* (December 3, 1964).

"Overlong Cavalry-Indian Yarn, for Dual Situations." *Variety Weekly* (September 15, 1954).

Pearson, Roberta E. "Custer 'Still the Hero': Textual Stability and Transformation." *Journal of Film and Video* (Spring–Fall 1995): 82–92.

Photoplay (June 1926).

"The Plainsman." *Films and Filming* (April 1967).

Powers, James. "*Glory Guys*: Big Western with Spectacular Action." *The Hollywood Reporter* (June 9, 1965).

Reagan, Ronald W. "Looking Back at *Santa Fe Trail.*" *Greasy Grass* 4 (May 1990): 2–4.

Reedstrom, E. Lisle. "Custer's Paintings and Historical Accuracy." *Roundup Magazine* 2 (September–October 1994): 16–19.

Scharf, Wayne Michael. "Sabers and Tomahawks." *Custer/ Little Bighorn Battlefield Advocate* 2 (Spring 1995): 2.

Seals, David. "The New Custerism." *The Nation* (May 13, 1991).

"Selig Polyscope." *Film Index* (November 27, 1909).

Shlachter, Barry. "120 Years Later, Battles Rage On at Little Bighorn." *San Francisco Chronicle* (December 4, 1995).

"The Six Best Pictures of the Month." *Photoplay* (June 1926).

"*Sitting Bull* Comes Close to Having Last Stand Near Where Gen. Custer Had His." *Variety Daily* (September 2, 1954).

"Slicing 'Custer' Pie Thin." *Hollywood Reporter* (March 11, 1965).

Smith, Darr. Untitled. *Los Angeles Daily News* (October 13, 1950).

Steckler, Paul. "Custer and Crazy Horse Ride Again . . . and Again, and Again: Filmmaking and History at the Little Big Horn." *Montana: The Magazine of Western History* 42 (Autumn 1992): 63–72.

Steckmesser, Kent. "Custer in Fiction." *The American West* 1 (Fall 1964): 47–52, 63–64.

"'Susanna' Well Mounted Cavalry-Redskins Tale." *Hollywood Reporter* (March 9, 1951).

"Three Up, Three Down." *Time* (May 30, 1955).

"Title Change." *Hollywood Reporter* (August 25, 1950).

"Tonka." *Screen Stories* (February 1959).

"Touche Pas la Femme Blanche." *Variety* (January 30, 1974).

Tucker, Ken. "'Morning Star': The Review." *Entertainment Weekly* (February 1, 1991): 27.

Universal Weekly 23, nos. 1–20.

"U.S. Can Go Home." *Newsweek* (August 25, 1970).

Variety Daily (October 28, 1954).

Variety Weekly (January 29, 1937; May 29, 1941; May 30, 1951; February 6, 1952; September 22, 1965; September 7, 1967; October 13, 1967; and June 20, 1991).

Whittaker, Frederick. "General George A. Custer." *Galaxy* (September 1876).

"W. R. Frank on Warpath against Crix Who Scalped 'Sitting Bull.'" *Variety Daily* (October 28, 1954).

Zimmerman, Barbara. "Mo-nah-se-tah: Fact or Fiction." 4th Annual Symposium, Custer Battlefield Historical & Museum Assn., held at Hardin, Montana, on June 22, 1990.

FICTION

Alter, Judy. *Libbie, Novel of Elizabeth Bacon Custer.* New York: Bantam, 1994.

Anderson, Ian. *The Scarlet Riders #1: Corporal Cavannah.* New York: Kensington Publishing Group, 1985.

Appel, Allen. *Twice upon a Time.* New York: Dell, 1990.

Appel, David. *Comanche.* New York: World, 1951.

Barton, Del. *A Good Day to Die.* Garden City, NY: Doubleday, 1980.

Beede, A. McGaffery. *Sitting Bull and Custer.* Bismarck, ND: Bismarck Tribune Co., 1913.

Bellah, James Warner. "Massacre." *Saturday Evening Post* (February 22, 1947): 18–19, 140, 142, 144, 146.

Benchley, Nathaniel. *Only Earth and Sky Last Forever.* New York: Harper, 1972.

Bendell, Don. *Chief of Scouts.* New York: Penguin Books, 1993.

Benteen, John. *Dakota Territory.* New York: Leisure Books, 1972.

———. *Taps at Little Big Horn.* New York: Leisure Books, 1973.

Berger, Thomas. *Little Big Man.* New York: The Dial Press, 1964.

———. *The Return of Little Big Man: A Novel.* Boston: Little, Brown & Co., 1999.

Birney, Hoffman. *Dice of God.* New York: Henry Holt, 1956.

Bittner, Rosanne. *Savage Destiny.* New York: Kensington Publishing Corp., 1986.

———. *Song of the Wolf.* New York: Bantam Books, 1992.

Blackburn, Tom W. *A Good Day to Die.* New York: Leisure Books, 1995.

Blake, Michael. *Marching to Valhalla: The Last Testimony of George Armstrong Custer.* New York: Vallard, 1996.

Blake, Stephanie. *A Glorious Passion.* New York: Jove Publications, 1983.

Blevins, Will. *Stone Song: A Novel of the Life of Crazy Horse.* New York: Tom Doherty Associates, 1995.

Brady, Cyrus. *Britton of the Seventh: A Romance of Custer and the Great Northwest.* Chicago: A. C. McClurg, 1914.

Braun, Matthew. *The Second Coming of Lucas Brokaw.* New York: Dell, 1977.

Brierly, Barry. *Timeless Interlude at Wounded Knee.* Mesa, AZ: Blue Bird Publishing, 1995.

———. *Wasichu.* Fountain Hills, AZ: La Gare Publishers, 1993.

———. *Wasichu's Return.* Mesa, AZ: Bear Books Publishing, 1996.

Brinkley, Douglas. *The Magic Bus: An American Odyssey.* New York: Harcourt, Brace & Co., 1993.

Brooks, Elbridge. *The Master of the Strong Hearts.* New York: E. P. Dutton, 1898.

Burks, Brian. *Soldier Boy.* San Diego: Harcourt, Brace & Co. 1997.

Cain, Jackson. *Hellbreak Country.* New York: Warner Books, 1984.

Carney, Otis. *Frontiers: The Diary of Patrick Kelly, 1876–1944.* Los Angeles: General Publishing Group, 1995.

Chiventone, Frederick J. *A Road We Do Not Know: A Novel of Custer at the Little Bighorn.* NY: Simon & Schuster, 1996.

Clark, Bruce T. *The Custer Legacy.* LaGrange, GA: Four Winds Publishing, 1997.

Clark, Kathy. *Cody's Last Stand.* New York: Harlequin Books, 1992.

Coldsmith, Don. *South Wind.* New York: Bantam, 1998.

Combs, Harry. *The Scout.* New York: Delacorte Press, 1995.

Compton, Ralph. *The Deadwood Trail.* New York: St. Martin's Press, 1999.

———. *The Killing Season.* New York: Signet, 1996.

Cooper, Courtney Riley. *The Last Frontier.* Boston: Little, Brown, 1951.

Corder, E. M. *Won Ton Ton: The Dog Who Saved Hollywood.* New York: Pocket Books, 1976.

Cotton, Ralph W. *Trick of the Trade.* New York: Pocket Books, 1997.

Cunningham, Chet. *Pony Soldier: Battle Cry.* New York: Leisure Books, 1989.

———. *Pony Soldier #9.* New York: Dorchester Publishing Co., 1989.

Daly, Kathleen N. *Tonka.* New York: Pyramid Books, 1976.

Drury, Rebecca. *Savage Beauty.* Wayne, PA: Banbury Books, 1982.

Dugan, Bill. *Crazy Horse, War Chief.* New York: Harper Collins, 1992.

———. *Sitting Bull, War Chief.* New York: Harper Collins, 1994.

Eagle, Chief D. *Winter Count.* Denver: Golden Bell, 1960.

Ellison, Harlan. *Strange Wine: Fifteen Stories from the Nightside of the World.* New York: Harper & Row, 1978.

Estelman, Loren D. *This Old Bill.* New York: Pinnacle Books, 1984.

Fairman, Paula. *The Tender and the Savage.* Los Angeles: Pinnacle Books, 1980.

Farmer, Philip Jose, ed. *Quest to Riverworld.* New York: Warner Books, 1993.

Fergus, Charles. *Shadow Catcher.* New York: Soho Press, 1991.

Foreman, James. *Life and Death of Yellow Bird.* New York: Farrar, 1973.

Fraser, George MacDonald. *Flashman and the Redskins.* New York: Alfred A. Knopf, 1982.

Gentry, Georgina. *Nevada Dawn.* New York: Zebra Books, 1993.

Gibson, Walter B., adapter. *Rod Serling's Twilight Zone Revisited.* New York: Grossett & Dunlap, 1964.

Goble, Paul. *Red Hawk's Account of Custer's Last Battle.* New York: Pantheon Books, 1969.

Gould, Theodore Anthony. *Teat.* Bellingham, WA: World Promotions, 1986.

Gruber, Frank. *Broken Lance.* New York: Rinehart, 1949.

Hardin, J. D. *Raider: Black Hills Trackdown.* New York: Berkeley Books, 1989.

Harrington, Kathleen. *Warrior Dreams.* New York: Avon, 1992.

Harrison, Jim. *Legends of the Fall.* New York: Delta, 1994.

Hart, Catherine. *Summer Storm.* New York: Leisure Books, 1987.

Hawley, Zoe Grace. *A Boy Rides with Custer.* Boston: Little, Brown, 1938.

Hawkins, Paul. *The Vision of Benjamin One Feather.* New York: Signet, 1993.

Haycox, Ernest. *Bugles in the Afternoon.* Boston: Little, Brown, 1944.

Henry, Will. *The Bear Paw Horses.* New York: Leisure Books, 1996.

———. *No Survivors.* New York: Random House, 1950.

Hirt, Douglas. *Deadwood.* New York: Berkeley Books, 1998.

Hoyt, Edwin P. *The Last Stand: A Novel about George Armstrong Custer and the Indians of the Plains.* New York: Tom Doherty Associates, 1995.

Hunter, E. J. *White Squaw.* New York: Kensington Publishing Corp., 1985.

———. *White Squaw: Horn of Plenty.* New York: Zebra Books, 1985.

Irwin, Hadley. *Jim-Dandy.* N.p.: Troll Communications, 1994.

Jakes, John. *Heaven and Hell.* San Diego: Harcourt, Brace, Jovanovich, 1987.

Jakes, John, and Martin H. Greenberg, eds. *New Trails, 23 Short Stories of the West.* New York: Doubleday, 1994.

Jeffers, H. Paul. *Morgan.* New York: Kensington Publishing Corp., 1989.

Johnson, Dorothy. *All the Buffalo Returning.* Lincoln: University of Nebraska Press, 1996.

———. *Buffalo Woman.* New York: Dodd, Mead and Co., 1977.

Johnston, Terry C. *Ashes of Heaven.* New York: St. Martin's Press, 1998.

———. *Blood Song.* New York: St. Martin's Press, 1993.

———. *Cry of the Hawk.* New York: Bantam, 1992.

———. *Long Winter Gone.* New York: Bantam Books, 1990.

———. *Reap the Whirlwind: The Battle of Rosebud, June 1876.* New York: Bantam, 1994.

———. *Seize the Sky.* New York: Bantam Books, 1991.

———. *Sioux Dawn.* New York: St. Martin's Press, 1990.

———. *Trumpet on the Land: The Aftermath of Custer's Massacre.* New York: Bantam, 1995.

———. *Whisper of the Wolf.* New York: Bantam Books, 1991.

Johnstone, William W. *Scream of Eagles.* New York: Kensington Books, 1996.

Jones, Douglas. *Arrest Sitting Bull.* New York: Scribners, 1977.

———. *The Court-Martial of General George Armstrong Custer.* New York: Scribners, 1976.

Kammer, Robert. *Bloody Dakota Summer.* New York: Kensington Publishing Corp., 1989.

Kelly, Leo P. *Luke Sutton Indian Fighter.* Garden City, NY: Doubleday, 1982.

Kremer, Kevin. *Saved by Custer's Ghost.* Bismarck, ND: Sweetgrass Communications, 1997.

Kretzer-Malvehy, Terry. *Message to Little Bighorn.* Flagstaff, AZ: Rising Moon, 1999.

Lacy, Al. *Quiet Thunder.* Sisters, OR: Multnomah Books, 1996.

Lasky, Kathryn. *The Bone Wars.* New York: Morros Junior Books, 1988.

Launer, Charles A. *"Garry Owen."* New York: Vantage, 1995.

Logan, Jake. *Slocum's Run.* New York: Playboy Paperbacks, 1981.

Lott, Milton. *Dance Back the Buffalo.* New York: Pocket Books, 1968.

MacRae, Donald. *Conflict of Interest.* New York: Tom Doherty Associates, 1989.

Matheson, Richard. *The Memoirs of Wild Bill Hickok.* New York: Jove Books, 1996.

McCarthy, Gary. *The Legend of Lone Ranger.* New York: Ballantine Books, 1982.

McMurtry, Larry. *Buffalo Girls: A Novel.* New York: Simon and Schuster, 1990.

McElwain, Dean. *Preacher's Law: Trail of Death.* New York: Dorchester Publishing Co., 1990.

McSherry, Frank D., Jr., Charles G. Waugh, and Martin H. Greenberg. *Western Ghosts: Haunting, Spine-Chilling Stories from the American West.* Nashville: Rutledge Hill Press, 1990.

Medwar, Mardi Oakley. *People of the Whistling Waters.* New York: Affiliated Writers of America, 1993.

Miller, Jim. *That Damn Single Shot.* New York: Fawcett Books, 1988.

Mills, Charles K. *A Mighty Afternoon: A Novel of the Battle of Little Big Horn.* Garden City, NY: Doubleday, 1990.

Mitchell, Kirk. *Shadow in the Valley: A Civil War Thriller.* New York: St. Martin's Press, 1994.

Morris, Gilbert. *The Crossed Sabres.* Minneapolis: Bethany House Publishers, 1993.

Murray, Earl. *Flaming Sky.* New York: Tom Doherty Associates, 1996.

———. *Song of Wovoka.* New York: Tom Doherty Associates, 1992.

———. *Thunder in the Dawn.* New York: Tom Doherty Associates, 1993.

Myrick, Herbert. *Cache la Poudre: The Romance of a Tenderfoot in the Days of Custer.* New York: Orange Judd Co., 1905.

Oliver, Chad. *Broken Eagle.* New York: Bantam Books, 1989.

Parrish, Randall. *Bob Hampton of Placer.* Chicago: A. C. McClurg, 1906.

Patten, Lewis B. *Cheyenne Captives.* New York: Signet, 1979.

———. *Massacre Ridge.* New York: Signet, 1971.

Perry, Michalann. *Captive Surrender.* New York: Kensington Publishing Co., 1987.

Randle, Kevin, and Robert Cornett. *Remember the Little Bighorn!* New York: Charter Books, 1990.

Ritz, Deanna. *Yellow Bird: The Saga of George Armstrong Custer's Daughter.* Pittsburgh: Dorrance, 1997.

Ryan, Nan. *Savage Heat.* New York: Dell, 1989.

Sabin, Edwin. *On the Plains with Custer.* Philadelphia: J. B. Lippincott, 1913.

Sargent, Pamela. *Climb the Wind: A Novel of Another America.* New York: Harper Prism, 1999.

Scofield, Jonathan. *The Frontier War.* New York: Dell, 1981.

Sherman, Jory. *Red Tomahawk.* New York: Zebra Books, 1984.

Skimin, Robert. *The River and the Horsemen: A Novel of Little Bighorn.* New York: Herodias, 1999.

———. *Ulysses: A Novel.* New York: St. Martin's Press, 1994.

Slade, Michael. *Cut Throat.* New York: Penguin Books, 1992.

Steelman, Robert J. *Cheyenne Vengeance.* Garden City, NY: Doubleday, 1978.

———. *Surgeon to the Sioux.* Garden City, NY: Doubleday, 1979.

Straight, Michael Whitney. *Carrington: A Novel of the West.* New York: Alfred Knopf, 1960.

Stuart, Colin. *Walks Far Woman.* New York: Dial Press, 1976.

Summer, Mark. *Devil's Tower.* New York: Ballantine, 1996.

Swarthout, Glendon F. "A Horse for Mrs. Custer," In *New World Writings.* New York: The New American Library of World Literature, 1954.

Taylor, Janelle. *Savage Conquest.* New York: Zebra Books, 1985.

Travers, J. M. *Custer's Last Shot; or, the Boy Trailer of the Little Horn Boys of New York.* Vol. 2. *Wide Awake Library,* no. 1196, August–September 1876.

Turtledove, Harry, ed. *Alternate Generals.* Riverdale, NY: Bean Publishing, 1998.

———. *The Great War: American Front.* New York: Ballantine Publishing Group, 1998.

———. *How Few Remain.* New York: Ballantine Books, 1997.

Ulrich, Charles. *On the Little Big Horn: A Comedy-Drama of the West in Four Acts.* N.p.: T. S. Denison, Publisher, 1907.

Utley, Steven, and Howard Waldrop. "Custer's Last Jump." In *Universe 6,* edited by Terry Carr. Garden City, NY: Doubleday & Co., 1976.

Van de Water, Fredric. *Thunder Shield.* Indianapolis: Bobbs-Merrill, 1933.

Vaughan, Robert. *A Distant Bugle.* New York: Dell, 1984.

———. *Yesterday's Reveille.* New York: St. Martin's Press, 1996.

West, Charles. *Wind River.* New York: Signet, 1999.

Willard, Tom. *Buffalo Soldiers.* New York: Forge, 1996.

Wisler, G. Clifton. *Lakota.* New York: Evans, 1989.

———. *Massacre at Powder River.* New York: Berkeley Books, 1998.

———. *Under the Black Hills.* New York: Berkeley Books, 1999.

———. *The Weeping Moon.* New York: Jove Books, 1995.

Wright, Cynthia. *Fireblossom.* New York: Ballantine, 1992.

Index

CUSTER

144

Custer, George Armstrong. *See also* fictional representations (books)
artists' renderings, 2, 4
biographies, 13–16, 117n.12, 119n.37
Black Hills expedition (1874), 7–8
Civil War exploits, 2–4
command abilities, 4, 6–7
court-martial, 6
courtship of Elizabeth Bacon, 2–4, *3*
in Kansas, 5–6
mythologizing of, xi–xii, xiv, 6–7, 13–15, 16, 17, 88, 115n.36, 116n.32, 129nn.35, 39
in New York, 8
pseudonyms, 1, 115n.2
as self-serving militarist, 58
at West Point, 1, *2*
Custer, Tom (brother), 4, 85–86
Custer and the Gall Saga, 17
The Custer Myth, 16
Custer of the West, 67–69, *68*, 80, 92, 126n.37, 127n.11
Custerphilia, xii–xiii
Custerphobia, xii–xiii
The Custer Reader, 119n.64
"Custer's Last Battle," 15
"Custer's Last Charge," 11–13
Custer's Last Fight, 29–30, *30*, *34*, 89, 122n.35
Custer's Last Fight (painting), *22*, 22–23
"Custer's Last Jump," 19
Custer's Last Raid, 89
Custer's Last Scout, 31, 90
"Custer's Last Shot; or, the Boy Trailer of the Little Horn," 17–18
"Custer's Last Stand," 97
Custer's Last Stand (book), 119n.64
Custer's Last Stand (film), 27, 89, 90, 121n.25
Custer's Last Stand (serial film), 39–40, *40*, 90
"Circle of Death," 102
"Custer's Last Ride," 103
"Demons of Disaster," 102
"Fires of Vengeance," 101
"Firing Squad," 102
"Flaming Arrow," 102
"Ghost Dancers," 101–2
"Human Wolves," 102
"The Last Stand," 103
"Perils of the Plains," 101
"Red Panthers," 102
"Thundering Hoofs," 101
"Trapped," 102
"Warpath," 102
"White Treachery," 102
Custer's West, 92
Custer (television series), *79*, 80, 127nn.12, 13
"Dangerous Prey," 111

"Death Hunt," 110–11
"Desperate Mission," 109–10
"Massacre," 108–9
"Pursued," 112
"Sabers in the Sun," 107–8
"Spirit Woman," 111
"Under Fire," 110
Untitled: September 13, 1967, 108
Untitled: September 20, 1967, 108
Untitled: September 27, 1967, 108
Untitled: October 17, 1967, 109
Untitled: November 29, 1967, 111
Untitled: December 20, 1967, 111–12
"War Lance and Saber," 108–9
The Custer Tragedy: The Events Leading Up to and Following the Little Big Horn Campaign of 1876, 16

D
Dalton, Darren, 93
Danner, Blythe, 82
The Day Custer Fell, 64–67, *66*, 80, 127n.11
Death Valley Days
"The Great Lounsberry Scoop," 92
de Havilland, Olivia, 45
Dehner, John, 92
Dellenbaugh, Frederick, 13
Desmond, William, 90
The Dice of God. See The Glory Guys
Diehl, John, 94
dime novels, xiii, 11, 17–18, 113n.13
Dirty Dingus Magee, 92
"Discovery," 95
documentaries, 95–97, 129n.38
Don't Touch White Women. See Touche pas la femme blanche
Douglas, Warren, 90
Dr. Quinn, Medicine Woman, 83, *84*, 129n.30
"The Abduction," 93
"The Epidemic," 93
"For Better or Worse," 93
"The Prisoner," 93
"Washita," 93
"Dreams along the Little Big Horn," 95
Drury, Rebecca, 19
Dudley, Charles, *33*, 90
Due Sergenti del General Custer, 67, 92, 126n.33
Duggan, Andrew, *64*, 92
Dullea, Keir, 93
Dustin, Fred, 16, 118n.29

E
Edeson, Robert, 90
Elliot, Maj. Joel, 6
eyewitness reports, 20, 120n.76

F
Fairman, Paula, 19
Farnum, Dustin, *36*, 37, 90

fictional representations (books), 11, 17, 18–20, 119nn.38, 46
as basis for films, 123n.48
science fiction, 19, 119nn.62, 63
Fifield, Fanny, 2
films
popularity of, 1920s and 1930s, 37–39
Finley, Ned, 90
The Flaming Frontier, 34–37, *36*, 90
Flynn, Errol, 45, *49*, 90
Following the Guidon, 13
Fonda, Henry, 90
Ford, Francis, 89, 90, 122n.33
Ford, John, 51–53, 125nn.1, 2
Forepaugh, Adam, 25
Forepaugh's New and Greatest All-Feature Show, 25
Fort Apache, 51–53, *52*, *53*, 90, 125n.5, 128n.19
Fort Wallace, abandons, 5–6
Fraser, George MacDonald, 122n.34
F Troop
"Old Iron Pants," 80, 92

G
General Custer at Little Big Horn, 37, 90
George Armstrong Custer, 13
Gibson, Hoot, 34–35
The Glory Guys, 63–64, 92
Glory-Hunter: A Life of General Custer, 15, 18
Godfrey, Lt. Edward, 9, 15, 16, 117n.51, 118n.13
gold, discovered in Black Hills, 7, 8, 117n.42
The Golden Tide, 91
Goofs and Saddles, 42, 90
Graham, William A., 16–17, 118nn.28, 29, 119n.35
Grant, Ulysses S., 8, 115n.33
"Grant and Lee at Appomatox," 95, 128n.19
The Great Sioux Massacre, 62–63, *64*, 92
Green, Dorothy, 91
Griffith, David W., 30–31, 122nn.38, 39, 40
Gunsmoke
"Custer," 74–76, 91

H
Hancock, Winfield S., 5
"Haunted History: The Battle of Little Bighorn," 97
Have Gun Will Travel, 76, 91
Haycox, Ernest, 18, 57
Hays Office, 123n.71
Henry, Will, 18
Heroes of Fort Worth. See La Carica del 7 Cavalleggeri
Heroes of the Plains, 13
Heston, Charlton, 65